Beate Barbara Blaschczok → 193

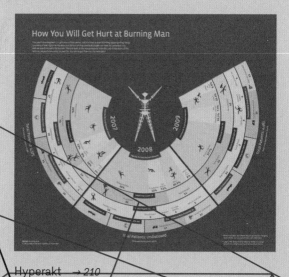

KircherBurkhardt GmbH → 81

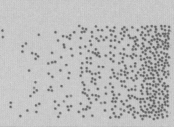

FOLLOWERS

Hyperakt → 210

Jana Lange, Kim Asendorf → 126

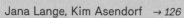

Alexandra Muresan → 109

David von Bassewitz → 100

ProjectProjects → 147

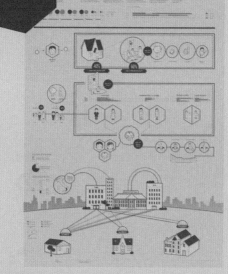

HunterGatherer → 199

DensityDesign → 17

OHHH | Esteve Padilla → 218

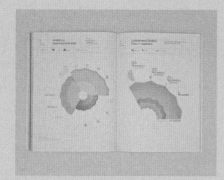

Les Graphiquants → 18

GR/DD → 122

Timo Arnall, Jørn Knutsen, Einar Sneve Martinussen → 116

Jan Hartwig → 96

VISUAL
STORYTELLING

Inspiring a New Visual Language

gestalten

Table of
CONTENTS

Introduction by
Andrew LOSOWSKY

The world provides us with a near-infinite level of input. Sights, sounds, smells, sensations are constant and unrelenting. According to many cognitive scientists, our first reactions to fresh external stimuli are determined not by our conscious minds, but by the parasympathetic nervous system, which provokes our bodies to produce immediate physical and chemical reactions, such as the production of tears, laughter or adrenalin. It's only a few milliseconds afterwards that the more evolved, computational processing parts of our brain get involved, adding logic and explanation to this instinctive emotional outpouring.

The essence of visual storytelling is this combination of emotional reaction and narrative information. The colors, typography, style, balance, format of an image will generate that first instinctive smile or frown, attracting or repelling the gaze for reasons we don't fully understand; only if the reader's instincts are sufficiently encouraged to continue focusing on the visual stimuli can the more complex, contextual information come into play. Like the soundtrack in a movie, the visuals create a barely perceptible emotional context to the telling of the main narrative.

There are many different ways to approach the challenge of visual storytelling. Sometimes, a designer will intentionally aim to maintain a sensation of continuity between the color scheme and the typography and the tone of the information itself. At other times, they might try to invoke contradictory emotions between a piece's visual language and the nature of its content, in order to shock or delight the viewer.

Though its theoretical basis may lie in measurable science, this is an imprecise art. It is dependent in part on the skill of the artist and also on the cultural background, personal experience and current state of mind of each individual viewer. As in every other aspect of design, there are many generally accepted guidelines, but no universally applicable rules. One person's serif is another person's sans—and such preferences are fickle, and change over time.

One thing is for sure, however: more than half our brains is dedicated to the processing of visual input, and so pure text and numbers simply cannot convey information in as memorable or digestible a form as that of successful visual-based storytelling.

This is not a new idea. Indeed, the existence of prehistoric cave paintings seems to suggest that abstracted recreations of reality predate written language by tens of thousands of years. Virtually every culture in recognized history has employed visuals as a way of communicating ideas and better understanding the world around it. Some of these methods have become so familiar in our own culture that we don't think of them anymore as visual sto-

Every field has some central tension it is trying to resolve. Visualization deals with the inhuman scale of the information and the need to present it at the very human scale of what the eye can see.

o Martin WATTENBERG,
   quoted in the *Economist* (2010)

SUPER FERTILE
o Kali Arulpragasam
1 CRA$H
→ 208

WILLIAM PLAYFAIR
2 The Commercial and
   Political Atlas
   William Playfair's book, *The Commercial and Political Atlas,* examines the imports and exports between Britain and other countries. To clarify these trade relationships, Playfair created line charts that showed the change in trade over time. In doing so, he invented the first line chart.
   Year: 1786

1

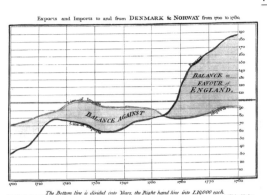

Exports and Imports to and from DENMARK & NORWAY from 1700 to 1780

BALANCE in FAVOUR of ENGLAND.

BALANCE AGAINST

The Bottom line is divided into Years, the Right hand line into L.10,000 each.

2

rytelling. These include religious sculptures, weather vanes, signs of the zodiac, playing cards, maps, musical scores, road signs, thermometers, barometers, seismographs, dashboards, analog clocks, flags, chalk outlines at a murder scene, sets of scales, measuring jugs. Visual abstraction is a human instinct, and a societal necessity.

Though the inventors of most of these abstractions are lost to history, the canon of visual storytelling does have its share of pioneers. Perhaps the most curious, and ultimately influential, character in the field was William Playfair [fig.2]. A Scotsman who, it seems, rarely lived up to his name, he was variously an engineer, a silversmith, a journalist, a real-estate salesman, a fraudster, a liar, and a blackmailer.

One of his money-making schemes involved writing books on economics and trade. To accompany his wordy explanations, Playfair decided to employ what he called "lineal arithmetic." His books were published between 1786 and 1801, and included what are considered by many to be the very first instances of the pie chart, the circle graph, the bar chart, and line graphs.

His innovations gained some attention, especially in France, but did not meet with much initial enthusiasm. In 1805, the writer Jacques Peuchet wrote that "No one will ever believe that such methods can serve any useful purpose in the study of statistics. They are but plays of the imagination as foreign to this science as the details of natural history or of topography with which some writers unfortunately wish to embellish it."

In Germany, the economist Karl Knies wrote that the increased

It would be ridiculous to try to express by curved lines moral ideas, the prosperity of peoples, or the decadence of their literature. But anything that has to do with extent or quantity can be represented geometrically. Statistical projections which speak to the senses without fatiguing the mind, possess the advantage of fixing the attention on a great number of important facts.

○ Alexander von HUMBOLDT, *Political Essay on the Kingdom of New Spain (1811)*

In recent years there has been a tremendous increase in the use of visual materials for the presentation of ideas and facts. Nowhere is this trend better illustrated than in the field of statistics, where there has developed a widespread use of graphs so extensive, in fact, that one might say that the graphic method is rapidly becoming a universal language.

○ H. Gray FUNKHOUSER, Historical Development of the Graphical Representation of Statistical Data (1937)

use of this lineal arithmetic in economic circles was frivolous at best. "Outside of its use as a pedagogic means," he said, "it is only a plaything without importance."

And yet, mostly after Playfair's death, the popularity of graphs as mathematical visualizations grew to the point where they not only entered the canon but became the default way of succinctly displaying changes in numbers over time.

As mentioned earlier, virtually every human culture has represented the world according to its particular needs and values. Today, in the field of visual storytelling, there are many names, both past and present, who are regarded as exemplars of the art and the science of such a challenge.

They include Charles Joseph Minard (best known for his 1861 diagram showing the retreat of Napoleon's troops from Russia), Florence Nightingale (for her 1858 visualization of war casualties), John Venn (inventor of the Venn diagram in 1880), Winsor McCay (pioneering early animator), Otl Aicher (creator of the now-iconic stick figures for the 1972 Olympics), Harry Beck (designer of the London Underground map), Peter Sullivan (the designer who introduced infographics into the *Sunday Times* of London in the 1970s), Nigel Holmes (infographer at Time magazine for 16 years), Richard Saul Wurman (designer and inventor of the phrase "information architect"), Edward Tufte (prominent visual designer and author), Ben Fry (new media visualization expert), David Small (creator of interactive visualizations), Chris Ware (remarkable illustrator and storyteller), Nicholas Felton (champion of personal data-led infographic design) and Jamie Serra (major visual innovator in the Spanish media).

There are just a few of those whose work has pushed the area of visual storytelling in new directions and among disciplines. There are many more. It should also be noted that all bar Nightingale are white men; the field, like so much of design, remains painfully lacking in diversity. We can only hope that this will change as it spreads and grows, encouraging also a wider range of narrative themes.

Each piece of work by these famous names must also be viewed in the context of the technological and cultural conditions under which it appeared. Until the 1930s, for example, the economics of printing technology remained the greatest barrier to the widespread use of visuals in print. Over the following 70 years, technological developments, spurred on and paid for in part by the growing demands of advertising, changed everything. Offset printing made large print runs affordable. The desktop computer allowed text to be typeset quickly and efficiently, and graphs to be plotted automatically, based on numbers crunched at inhuman speeds. Image manipulation software introduced a box of tricks far beyond the capacity of the darkroom. New terms, such as vector graphics and Bézier curves, described the movement from page to screen.

The introduction of the internet and mobile technology has brought with it further visualization challenges and opportunities. Publishing frequency has shifted from daily to minute by minute. Huge amounts of data are now available, much of which can be shared, stolen, reproduced, slipped illegally onto a thumb drive in a matter of moments. While the media struggles to deal with the quantities of data that emerge from leaks and Freedom of Information requests to government, so we too strain not to become overwhelmed by the near-constant information flow.

We had the Encyclopaedia Britannica at home. When I was a small boy, [my father] used to sit me on his lap and read to me from the Britannica. We would be reading, say, about dinosaurs. It would be talking about the Tyrannosaurus Rex, and it would say something like "This dinosaur is twenty-five feet high and its head is six feet across."

My father would stop reading and say "Now let's see what that means. That would mean that if he stood in our front yard, he would be tall enough to put his head through our window up here... But his head would be too wide to fit in the window." Everything he read to me he would translate as best he could into some reality.

○ Richard P FEYNMAN, as told to Ralph Leighton, *What Do You Care What Other People Think?* (1988)

Infographics are neither illustrations nor "art". Infographics are visual journalism and must be governed by the same ethical standards that apply to other areas of the profession.

○ Juan Antonio GINER and Alberto CAIRO, Checklist for Infographics, Nieman Watchdog website (2011)

In reaction to this, over the past decade, the use of visual storytelling by the mass media has increased enormously. From editorial illustrations to detailed maps, from data visualizations to process outlines, placed within art installations and company reports, content is being re-contextualised through increasingly sophisticated visual forms.

Compelling abstractions don't now merely accompany a story, but are often the principle manner in which it is told. Combining beauty and truth, they are, at their best, inspiring, fascinating, visually interesting and easy to read, while conveying complex levels of information in an impactful way. We are now in an age of show and tell.

In order to visualize effectively this influx of data, there are three stages of response: first, track down and then verify the quality and truth of the data. Second, structure the data and try to establish a clear narrative from within it. And third, come up with an appropriate, succinct and visually engaging method of representation.

In order to tackle such a huge task, we are seeing the emergence a new kind of visual journalist or graphic editor, one more likely to have a background in statistics or systems programming than politics or literature, a person who has to have a capacity both to process and visualize large quantities of anything from balance sheets to satellite photography, for journalistic ends.

As the genre has grown and matured, embracing both professional and hobbyist storytellers alike, so have arisen a number of visual-based controversies. The most elegant visual solution imaginable can't salvage imprecise or incorrect data. A series of inaccurate infographics about the death of Osama Bin Laden led to the creation of a six-point Statement Against Fictional Infographics in May 2011, written by Juan Antonio Giner, a Britain-based president of a media consultantancy, and Alberto Cairo, infographic director of the

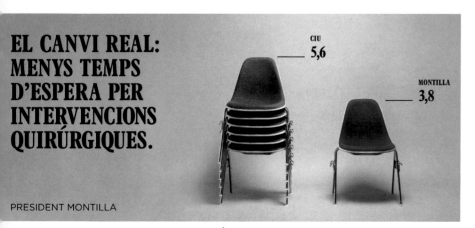

EL CANVI REAL: MENYS TEMPS D'ESPERA PER INTERVENCIONS QUIRÚRGIQUES.

CIU
5,6

MONTILLA
3,8

PRESIDENT MONTILLA

1

SARAH ILLENBERGER
1   Campaign for PSC, Socialist Party
     of Catalonia (Kampagne für PSC,
     Sozialistische Partei Katalonien)
     → 76 – 77

Brazilian newsweekly *Epoca*. It includes the demand that every infographic state its sources, and makes very clear that infographics are not art.

The question of the artistic value of such carefully crafted pieces of graphic design is a complicated one. Every publication wants their stories to be visually attractive—indeed, the graphic design aspect of visual storytelling is much of the reason for its popularity. Yet the visuals have to serve the data as well as the audience.

At the time of writing, visualizations have reached the point where most audiences understand their journalistic value, whether online, on television or in print; this level of cultural recognition has encouraged the development of data-based art, being visuals whose aesthetics are often more important than a need to convey information in a clear and immediate fashion. If visualisation is a language, then new dialects are being created all the time, often with grammatical rules all their own.

By narrative we take the best stock we can of the world and our predicament in it. What we see and recreate is seldom the blinding literal truth. Instead, we perceive and respond to our surroundings in narrow ways that most benefit our organismic selves. The narrative genius of Homo sapiens is an accommodation to the inherent inability of the three pounds of our sensory system and brain to process more than a minute fraction of the information the environment pours into them. In order to keep the organism alive, that fraction must be intensely and accurately selective. The stories we tell ourselves and others are our survival manuals.

○ Edward O WILSON, Introduction to *The Best American Science and Nature Writing* (2001)

News, Science, Geography, The Modern World, and Sports. We felt that these topics allowed us to feature an incredibly varied selection of voices and visuals, whose styles and methods range from experimental to conventionally journalistic, while also showing a common thread between them all. This is not a how-to manual, though we hope visual storytellers will find it helpful and inspiring. This is a book of stories.

We also spoke to some of the leading practitioners, from photographers to computer-led designers, to reveal their very different approaches to converting information into attractive and informative visuals.

Where the industry goes from here is, as ever, as exciting as it is uncertain. In the hands of skilled visual storytellers, we are starting to see a combination of disciplines being applied to tell different aspects of a narrative. Text, photography, computer-generated and hand-drawn illustration are all being applied at various times by individual designers and publications. Visualizations are also being used as online tools for dynamic reporting, rather than snapshots of a particular moment, with some interactive infographics allowing users to zoom in on the area of data that is most relevant to them.

A glut of recent, relatively meaningless data visualizations has led to a call from many for visual storytellers to refocus their efforts on the need for a clear narrative. An interactive web interface in itself is not a story; a series of changing graphs does not explain anything on its own. In order to be successful, a narrative has to be central to the communication form.

This is why we have called this book Visual Storytelling. A successful visualisation is the same as any successful story, regardless of medium, or even whether it is fiction or fact: it informs, it makes the reader think about the world around them, and about our own lives. It stirs emotions, it encourages action, it equips us, it inspires us. It enriches our world in tiny ways that we may never understand.

Inside these pages, you will find a wide variety of visual solutions that do just that, divided into five narrative themes:

The brain finds it easier to process information if it is presented as an image rather than as words or numbers. The right hemisphere recognizes shapes and colours. The left side of the brain processes information in an analytical and sequential way and is more active when people read text or look at a spreadsheet. Looking through a numerical table takes a lot of mental effort, but information presented visually can be grasped in a few seconds. The brain identifies patterns, proportions and relationships to make instant subliminal comparisons.

○ The *Economist,* The Data Deluge (2010)

There is no doubt that our narratives across all media are only going to be more visual. The data that we increasingly generate and surround ourselves with demands explanation, context, comparison. As we seek to read, understand, and then move on to so many other distractions with increasing efficiency, those who truly inform us will be those who convey information in an attractive, elegant and easily comprehensible form.

Visual storytelling is increasingly becoming the most effective way of finding order among the chaos. It gives us the tools to process, to look and to learn. Only then can we try to understand.

Part

A

Visual

STORYTELLER

Carl Kleiner, *The Big Blur,* 2010

DensityDesign

DensityDesign is a research lab in the Design Department (INDACO) of the Politecnico di Milano in Italy, headed by Paolo Ciuccarelli. It focuses on the visual representation of complex social, organizational and urban phenomena. It is open to collaborations with private institutions, NGOs, other universities and private companies.

o *www.densitydesign.org*

How did you create the Greenpeace infographic? → 14

In late November 2010, Greenpeace UK commissioned DensityDesign to make this infographic as part of their "Oceans" campaign. The brief was fairly ordinary but we decided to embrace it as a chance to formulate and test a new design process, one which could enhance our ability to transform data and stories into a visual narrative.

The brief was 10 pages long, and we had just two weeks to complete it. We decided to divide the brief into different parts, and then sketched separately—or, as we like to say, "visually rephrased"—the elements of the story. All those visual concepts were then combined into a single schematic. Then we sent the illustration to Greenpeace and asked them to participate in a sort of game, performing three actions:

- Rate the different parts of the drawing from one to five stars, ranking the importance they wanted to give to each piece of information in the final infographic;
- Put the different sections in sequence, numbering each one
- Finally, the most important contribution: annotate, delete, add details, cut details, rewrite, move, underline, enlarge, select, shrink, write down everything that occurred to them from looking at that first draft.

When they sent back the schematic, we were able to look at their changes, and then formulate the final structure of the story and its subplots.

As for the visuals themselves, after some geo-referenced sketches, we choose a bird-eye view on a fictional landscape in which we could depict the journey of fish from the sea to the supermarket. We drew the schematics and sketches by hand, scanned them, printed and then sketched and scanned again before finally moving onto computer software (Adobe Photoshop and Illustrator) to achieve the final look.

How do you decide what data to include?

It really depends on the specific needs of the client. In some cases the data are all there. In other cases, we could propose and integrate other data, even if it was not in the original plans of the client. We are intrinsically curious (as any designer should be), and so we always question the content we receive; we always verify the sources, or at least try to have our own idea about the story behind the data, and surprisingly often clients appreciate this kind of proactive behavior.

The visual storyteller is fully responsible for the visualization, not for the data and its accuracy. In representing any phenomena, especially social ones, a visual storyteller shouldn't see himself as a holder of any truth. Phenomena are often complex and fuzzy, show many different dimensions, and can be perceived from many different points of view. That's why there are lots of different—in some cases opposite—truths.

Even if the phenomenon is described by accurate data (and statisticians could say a lot here about the existence of accuracy in gathering, organizing, and communicating data), a visual narration rarely can be scientifically accurate, because, as with every type of narration, it deals with causality of events, and causes are often fuzzy.

How important is the hierarchy of narrative in your work?

If the order of events is fundamental to understand of the phenomenon we're describing then we highlight the starting point and make the flow of reading very visible. These techniques derive from graphic design basics: left-right reading orientation, sizing, coloring, common symbols such as arrows, techniques borrowed from comics.

When the main narrative doesn't hinge upon strict sequences, we often conceive our visual stories like a panorama, where the eye is free to wander. There are no starting or end points. It's the viewer's choice which part of the story to follow, which arguments to combine.

How do you balance precision and aesthetics?

The surface of a visualization cannot be seen as an epiphenomenon (a secondary effect that arises from, but does not influence, a process) but has to be considered to be an essential part of the discourse itself. That can be a controversial idea because appearance can be illusory, vague, superfluous.

But the same illusion of easy knowledge can be induced by reducing things to their primordial structures: the depth obtained by robbing things of their qualities can be as much illusive as the superficiality of their image. As the artist David Hockney once said: "Surface is illusion—but so is depth."

Have you ever made a mistake in an infographic?

Well, it wasn't really so embarrassing, but it can be considered a mistake: in 2009, *Wired UK* asked us to create something for their "Information" section. We decided to create a visualization to show how people in the 27 EU countries perceive the impact of the internet and mobile phones on their lives—and then contrast this with the real penetration of those technologies in each country; a new map of Europe.

The result was a bit too complex for the target of the magazine, and it was never published. That happens sometimes: as we are a research lab, we try to use any opportunity to test an idea, and it doesn't always match the needs of our clients. Especially big publishers!

How does being within an academic environment affect your work?

The benefits are the possibility (and the need) of working at the frontier; the ability to chose the projects we want to tackle; the ability to collaborate with many other disciplines within the Politecnico di Milano (engineering, computer sciences etc.) or within other universities.

The downsides are the need to work only on reasonably big projects, with a certain perspective in terms of time and resources; we don't have a great deal of flexibility or speed: we're not an agency, we can't (and we don't want) to accept small projects that need to be done tomorrow. But we are entirely self-funded, through grants and projects.

What are your ambitions for the future of the laboratory?

We would love to merge our visual storytelling with the potential of interactivity. To be able to combine animation, interaction and visual narrative would be a huge leap forward towards our goals of engagement, inclusiveness and meaning making.

Are we in a golden age of infography? Why?

We're at a point where data and information are more and more widely available, and the visual language of data and information is becoming more popular, thanks to mass media and designers sharing their work on the web. The web itself is also increasingly based on the visual communication of data. So there is a huge potential, but the transformation of this into a golden age is not at all obvious. We first have to avoid the risk of producing too many ineffective visualizations, and adopt a consistent visual language, and create a stronger visualization literacy based on research into its effectiveness.

But no single discipline alone, visual storytelling included, can cope with the complexity of the issues and the phenomena we have to face in this world.

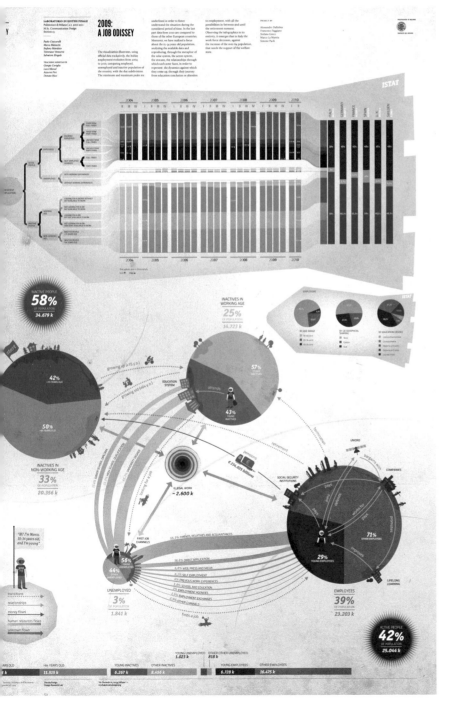

2009 A Job Odissey

Using official data from 2004 to 2010, this infographic shows the evolution of employment in Italy. The employed, unemployed, and inactive population are compared with minimum and maximum peaks highlighted in order to emphasize the situation during particular periods of time. Data from 2010 is compared to that of the other European countries. When viewed in its entirety, the infographic reveals that as the workforce in Italy decreases due to the aging population, support of the welfare state will be needed.

Year: 2011—Client: University Project—DensityDesign - Final Synthesis Design Studio A.Y. 2010–2011 M.Sc. Communication Design Faculty of Design Politecnico di Milano—Students: Alessandro Dallafina, Francesco Faggiano, Stefano Greco, Marco La Mantia, Simone Paoli

Visual Storyteller

DENSITYDESIGN

1 Feeding the Planet, Energy for Life. Expo Themes Visualization

A graphic commissioned by Expo to communicate the complex theme of food. DensityDesign worked with Expo's scientific committee to develop a better understanding of this theme by investigating the relationships of its sub-themes. Food is much more than simply a means of feeding man; it has influenced history, the environment, industrial, economic, and social development.

3 How Do You Feel, Italy?

Italy's national health care system aims to improve the health and lives of citizens through care activities, education, and prevention. Using data from the National Institute of Statistics, a path has been mapped that shows the investments, infrastructure, and guaranteed benefits of this system. It focuses on the perception of the health care service as well as the most common types of diseases, discovering the causes, connections, and complexities

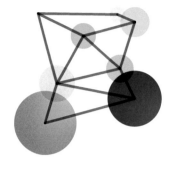

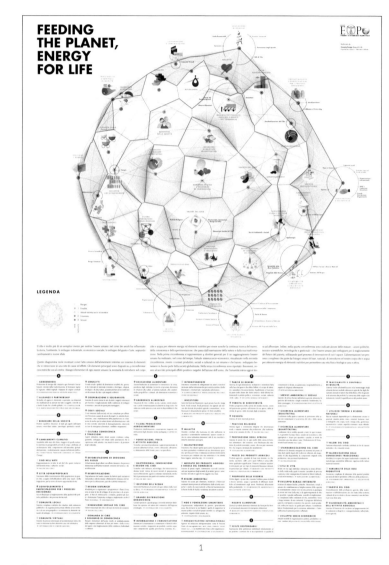

1

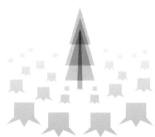

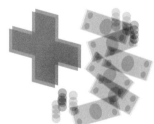

2 Feeding the Planet, Energy for Life. Expo Themes Pictograms.

Pictograms developed to describe the themes and subtheme of the Expo visualization.

Year: 2010—Client: Expo 2015 S.p.A.—DensityDesign Research Lab INDACO Department Politecnico di Milano Scientific—Coordinator Prof. Paolo Ciuccarelli—Project Leader: Michele Mauri—Team: Luca Masud, Mario Porpora, Lorenzo Fernandez, Giorgio Caviglia

that surround them. The resulting data reveals the presence of multiple health care systems with deep territorial differences at regional and provincial levels. The overall picture of the system is that it is structurally complex and fragmented—and not always clear in its communications with the citizens it serves.

Year: 2011—Client: University Project—DensityDesign - Final Synthesis Design Studio A.Y. 2010 – 2011 M.Sc. Communication Design Faculty of Design Politecnico di Milano—Students: Felipe Alejandro, Ospina Borras, Stefano Cotzia, Jacopo Marcolini, Davide Martinotti, Xuan Wu

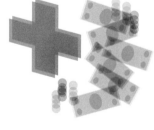

2

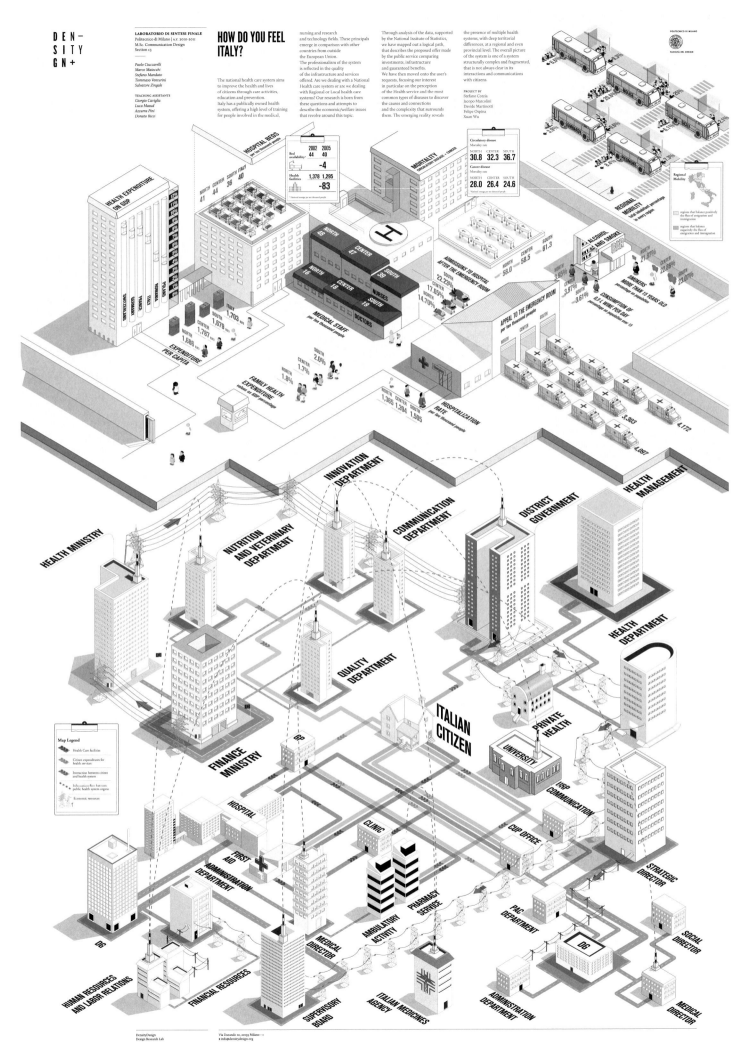

1 — Greenpeace "Oceans" Campaign — How's My Fishing?

Greenpeace "Oceans" Campaign — How's My Fishing?
Greenpeace UK commissioned this infographic as part of their "Oceans" campaign. It shows the devastating effects of FADs (fish aggregation devices), which are used by industrial fishing fleets to catch tuna.
Year: 2011 — Developed by: DensityDesign — Research Lab: INDACO Department Politecnico di Milano — Scientific Coordinator: Prof. Paolo Ciuccarelli — Project Leader: Donato Ricci — Researcher: Michele Graffieti — Team Luca Masud, Mario Porpora

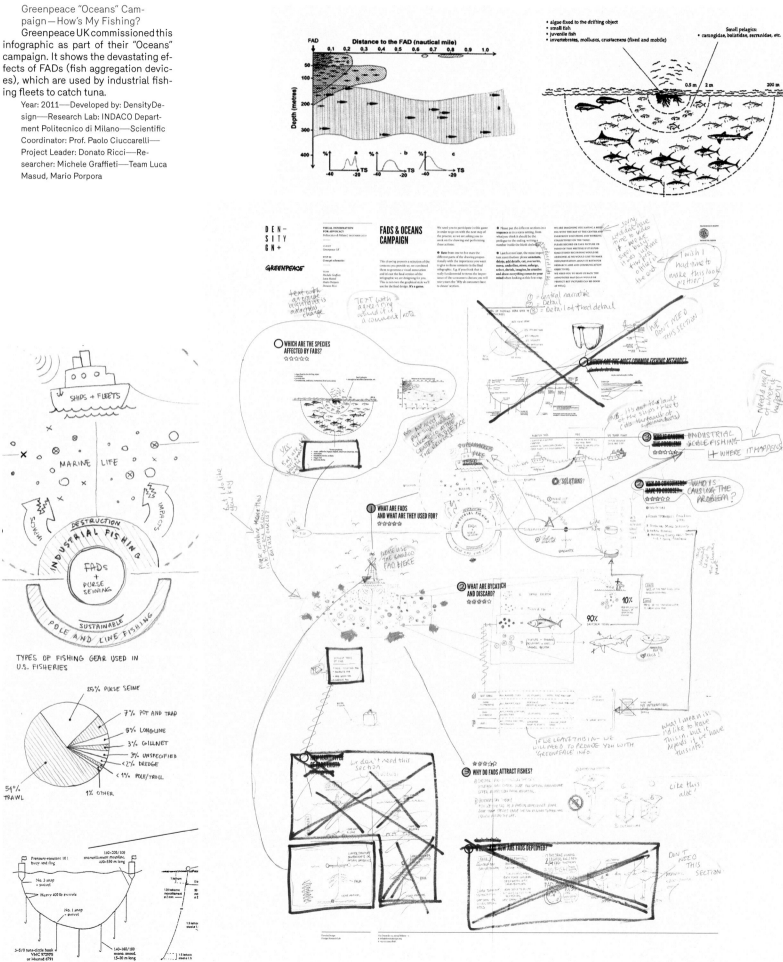

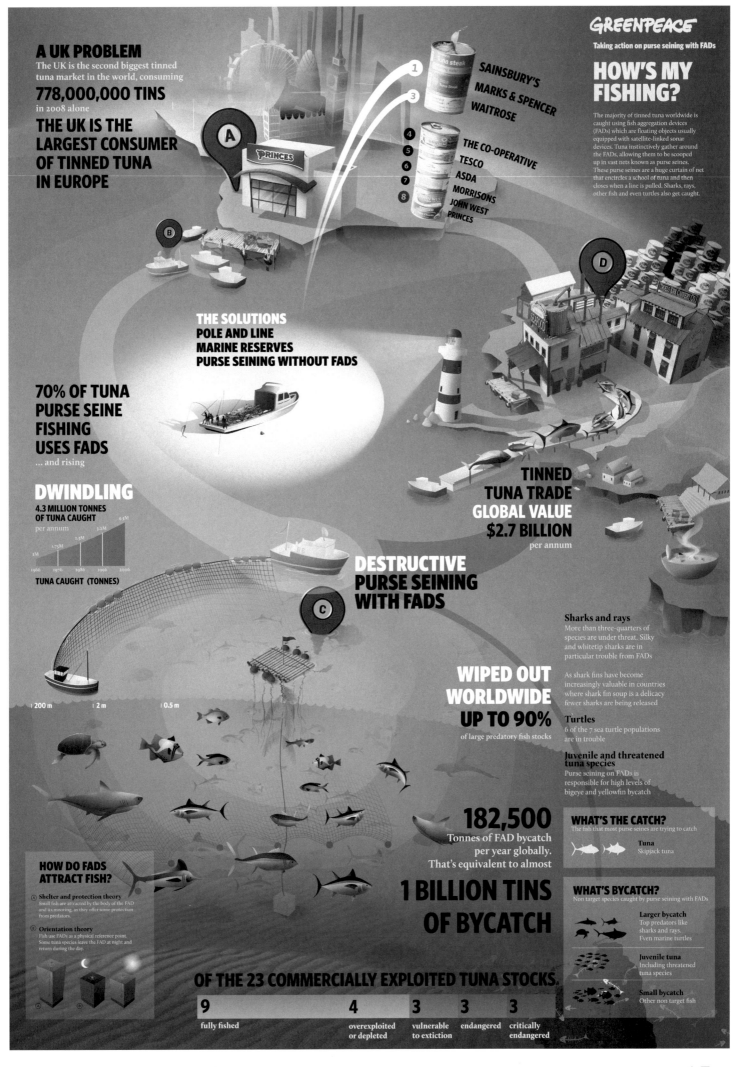

A UK PROBLEM
The UK is the second biggest tinned tuna market in the world, consuming
778,000,000 TINS
in 2008 alone
THE UK IS THE LARGEST CONSUMER OF TINNED TUNA IN EUROPE

A

PRINCES

B

1 — SAINSBURY'S
3 — MARKS & SPENCER
— WAITROSE

4 — THE CO-OPERATIVE
5 — TESCO
6 — ASDA
7 — MORRISONS
8 — JOHN WEST
— PRINCES

HOW'S MY FISHING?
The majority of tinned tuna worldwide is caught using fish aggregation devices (FADs) which are floating objects usually equipped with satellite-linked sonar devices. Tuna instinctively gather around the FADs, allowing them to be scooped up in vast nets known as purse seines. These purse seines are a huge curtain of net that encircles a school of tuna and then closes when a line is pulled. Sharks, rays, other fish and even turtles also get caught.

D

THE SOLUTIONS
POLE AND LINE
MARINE RESERVES
PURSE SEINING WITHOUT FADS

70% OF TUNA PURSE SEINE FISHING USES FADS
... and rising

DWINDLING
4.3 MILLION TONNES OF TUNA CAUGHT
per annum

1M | 1.75M | 2.3M | 3.2M | 4.3M
1966 | 1976 | 1986 | 1996 | 2006

TUNA CAUGHT (TONNES)

TINNED TUNA TRADE GLOBAL VALUE $2.7 BILLION
per annum

DESTRUCTIVE PURSE SEINING WITH FADS

C

200 m | 2 m | 0.5 m

Sharks and rays
More than three-quarters of species are under threat. Silky and whitetip sharks are in particular trouble from FADs

As shark fins have become increasingly valuable in countries where shark fin soup is a delicacy fewer sharks are being released

Turtles
6 of the 7 sea turtle populations are in trouble

Juvenile and threatened tuna species
Purse seining on FADs is responsible for high levels of bigeye and yellowfin bycatch

WIPED OUT WORLDWIDE UP TO 90%
of large predatory fish stocks

182,500
Tonnes of FAD bycatch per year globally. That's equivalent to almost

1 BILLION TINS OF BYCATCH

HOW DO FADS ATTRACT FISH?
A **Shelter and protection theory**
Small fish are attracted by the body of the FAD and its mooring, as they offer some protection from predators.

B **Orientation theory**
Fish use FADs as a physical reference point. Some tuna species leave the FAD at night and return during the day.

WHAT'S THE CATCH?
The fish that most purse seines are trying to catch
Tuna
Skipjack tuna

WHAT'S BYCATCH?
Non target species caught by purse seining with FADs
Larger bycatch
Top predators like sharks and rays. Even marine turtles

Juvenile tuna
Including threatened tuna species

Small bycatch
Other non target fish

OF THE 23 COMMERCIALLY EXPLOITED TUNA STOCKS.

9	4	3	3	3
fully fished	overexploited or depleted	vulnerable to extinction	endangered	critically endangered

1

2

3

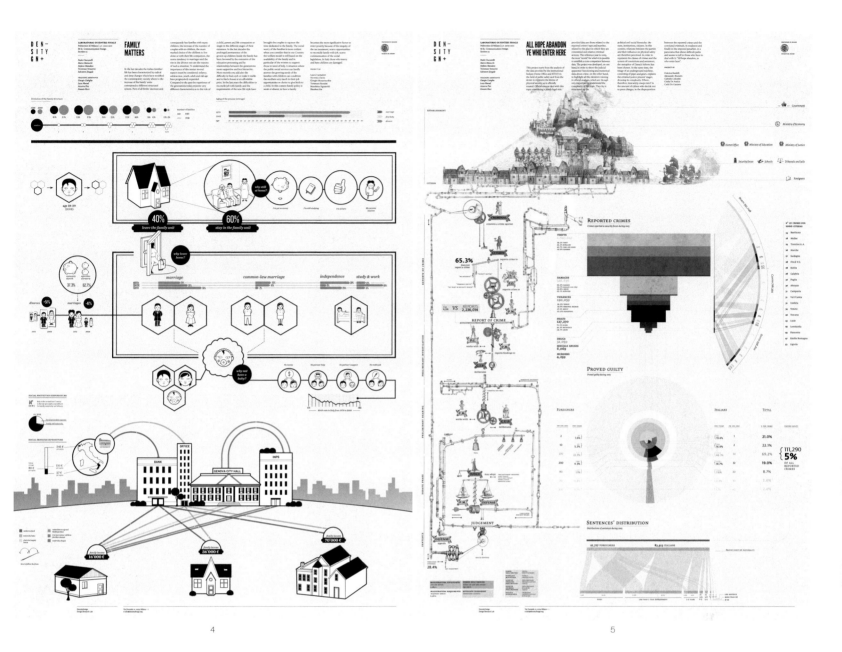

1   Brain Houses:
    Three Intérieur Stories
    Brain Houses was commissioned to accompany an article written by the architect Italo Rota about three interior designs "derived from the mind and not from the hand." It is the visualization of an intricate story of three intériéurs and their three auteurs: Sigmund Freud's study in Vienna which is defined as "the house of the mind"; Ludwig Wittgenstein's sister's house in Vienna, "the number house"; and Pierre Chareau's "glass house."
    Year: 2010—Client: *Domus* magazine Scientific Coordinator: Prof. Paolo Ciuccarelli—Project Leader and Creative Direction: Michele Graffieti

2   The Map of the Future
    This map, based on scenarios developed by the Institute for the Future in Palo Alto, California, is intended to help the reader navigate the ideas and hypothesis built by 7,000 influencers from all over the world.
    Year: 2009—Client: *WIRED Italia*—

Credits: DensityDesign—Research Lab: INDACO Department Politecnico di Milano—Scientific Coordinator: Prof. Paolo Ciuccarelli—Project Leader: Donato Ricci—Concept development, Gaia Scagnetti—Designer: Luca Masud—Illustrator: Mario Porpora—Artist: Michele Graffieti

3   Net@Work
    Project developed for *WIRED Italia* based on Kevin Kelly's May 2009 article in *WIRED US* about a new form of socialism: the internet. The image, which was styled after Russian posters from the 1930s and 1940s, is a landscape in which every robot represents one of the 300 websites selected to represent this new form of socialism. The shape of the robots' bodies was based on Chernoff's faces concept: trunk width is the economic value of a website; head size is the amount of users; saturation is the age of the website (the oldest are less saturated); overall height is the worldwide ranking position.
    Year: 2010—Client: *WIRED Italia*

4   Family Matters
    In recent decades, Italian family life has experienced deep and radical changes that have modified contemporary society: births have decreased, resulting in fewer large families; the number of couples with no children has increased; and more children choose to live alone or with their partner. The decrease in marriages and the rise in the divorce rate have also contributed to this situation. In Italy, those who marry and have children are often at a disadvantage.
    Year: 2011—Client: University Project DensityDesign - Final Synthesis Design Studio A.Y. 2010 – 2011 M.Sc. Communication Design Faculty of Design Politecnico di Milano—Students: Laura Cantadori, Veronica Clarin, Giorgio Mozzorecchia, Tommaso Renzini, Benedetta Signaroldi, Shuzhen Xia

5   All Hope Abandon
    Ye Who Enter Here
    This project, which is based on 2005 public safety data provided by Home Oce and The National Institute of Statistics, represents how physical security in Italy is dealt with. It was developed to show numerical data about crime and what is missing in the social analysis of it. The metaphor of *Dante's Inferno* was chosen to represent the classes of crimes and the system of convictions and sentences. The image of an underground machine, consisting of pipes and gears, explains the complex stages of the criminal justice process.
    Year: 2011—Client: DensityDesign—DensityDesign - Final Synthesis Design Studio A.Y. 2010 – 2011 M.Sc. Communication Design Faculty of Design Politecnico di Milano —Students: Federica Bardelli, Alessandro Marino, Giuseppe Brunetti, Gabriele Colombo, Giulia De Amicis, Carlo Alessandro, Morgan De Gaetano

Les Graphiquants

Les Graphiquants is a design studio based in Paris. They create posters, signage, identities, visualizations and artwork. Their work has been exhibited around the world, and received several major design awards.

○ *www.les-graphiquants.fr*

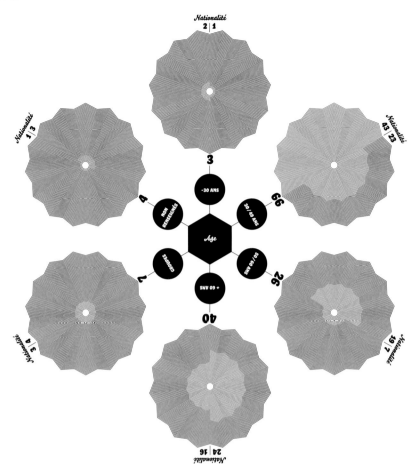

Rapport D'activité 2009

The boundary between understanding the data and rich and ornamental patterns was questioned in this report for the Centre National des Arts Plastiques (CNAP). A simple, graphic vocabulary was decided upon: solid colors illustrate the budget; gradients represent artists and frames for the works; straight lines refer to photography; dotted lines for visual arts; wavy lines for the decorative arts. The combination of these six elements defines a graphic system that summarizes all the activities of the CNAP.

Year: 2010—Client: Centre National des Arts Plastiques—In collaboration with Caroline Fabès

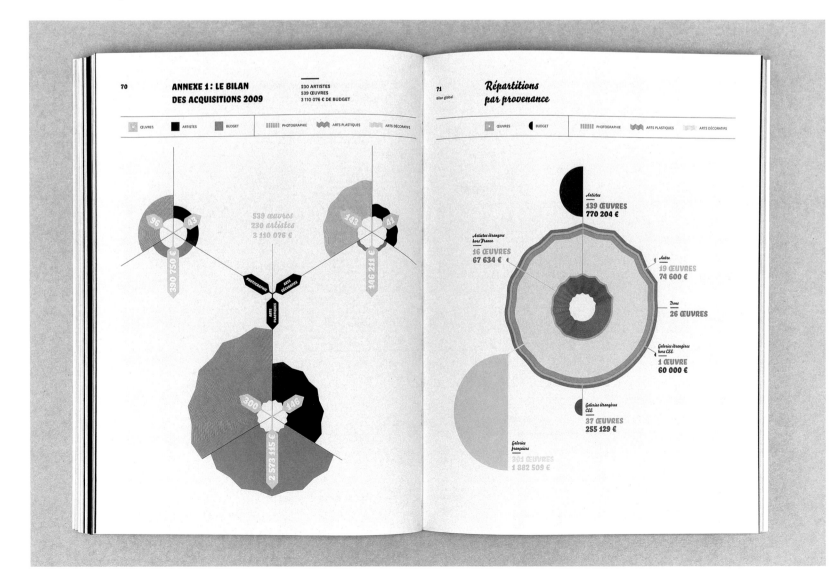

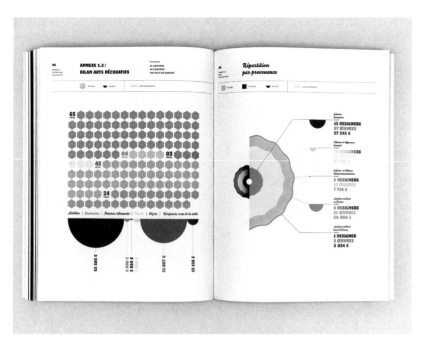

How would you describe your approach?

We approach all stages of creation—concept, project management, design and production—with the same care. Whatever the project or whoever the client, we impose our graphic look onto the work, within the constraints we are given.

How did the visuals for the CNAP annual report come about? [20]

The CNAP is the National Centre of Art and Design in Paris. They have a very keen interest in design and art experimentation.

As a studio, we were offered an almost-unlimited field of play. We began our work in a conventional manner, but in the early phases of our collaboration, the CNAP pushed us to adopt a more experimental approach. We worked on research for the piece over three weeks, and conceptualized the entire idea just with paper, a pencil and a calculator.

Our visual interpretations of data are most often guided by a search for an immediate impact, and providing a quick and efficient read. These diagrams were developed more as abstract landscapes within which the eye could wander and get lost.

The rules that we set on this piece were very strict: a consistent form of representation, using a vocabulary of three forms and three types of colorisation, containing an accumulation of broken lines, solid colors or gradients.

All of these combined to create a complex visual world, but once the caption was added, the reader could easily understand the overall scheme.

How different to your other work are the data visualization projects?

For our signage and poster work, each piece is designed, composed and controlled from conception to production. For data visualizations, as soon as we have decided upon a system of representation, the final shape of the work is entirely determined by the data.

How important is the hierarchy of narrative?

We try to simplify as much as possible the levels of information, forms, color and typography. It doesn't matter if people are first attracted to the work by a shape, color or piece of typography. The eye is completely free to move from the foreground to the background, from one detail to another. It is only by embracing all of the elements in an image that we can get a reasonable understanding of its content.

What are the major issues facing visual storytelling today?

There is right now an unlimited amount of accumulated electronic data. There are, for example, one billion tweets posted every week. However, there is no possible single system for manipulating all of this data, and representing it all in an intelligible way.

We do however have some new flexible, fun and useful systems of representation to help us, such as animation, 3D and interactivity. But the principle challenge for a visual storyteller today is trying to avoid dizziness.

Which visual storytellers do you admire?

Past: Otto Neurath, the creator of the International System of Typographic Picture Education. Present: Caroline Fabès, a brilliant new designer.

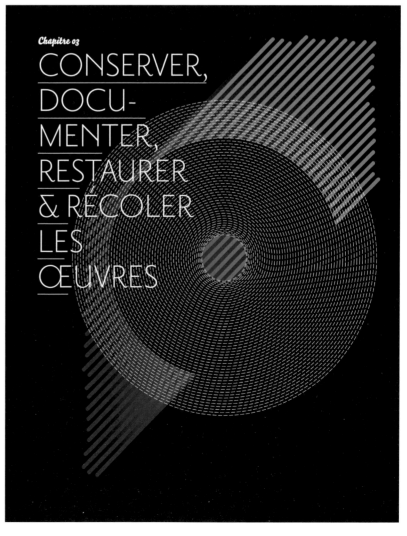

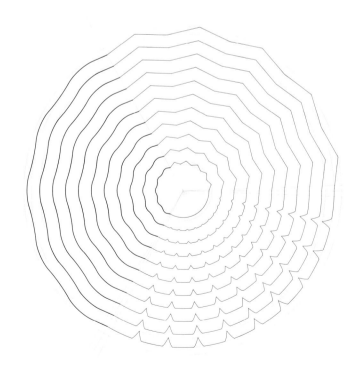

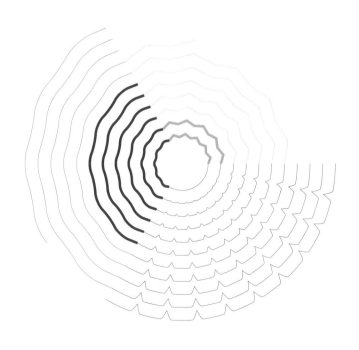

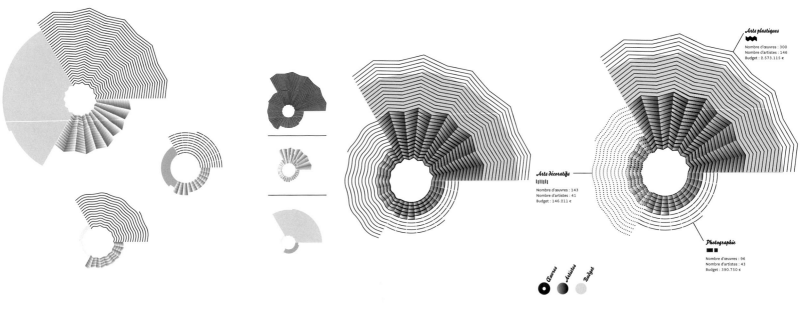

Arts plastiques

Nombre d'œuvres : 300
Nombre d'artistes : 146
Budget : 2.573.115 €

Arts décoratifs

Nombre d'œuvres : 143
Nombre d'artistes : 41
Budget : 146.211 €

Photographie

Nombre d'œuvres : 96
Nombre d'artistes : 43
Budget : 390.750 €

Œuvres   Artistes   Budget

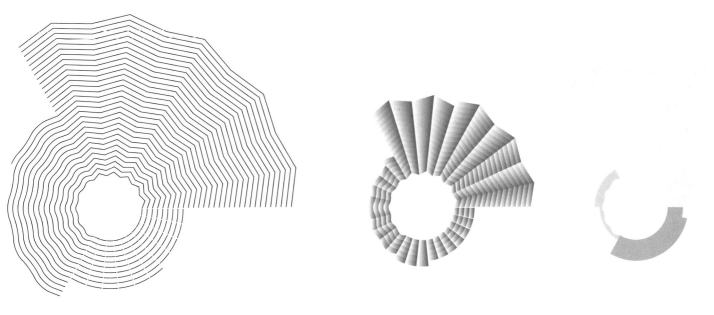

78

Répartion par âge et nationalité

**SUR 146 ARTISTES :
92 SONT FRANÇAIS
54 SONT ÉTRANGERS**

● FRANÇAIS   ● ÉTRANGERS | 〰〰 ARTS PLASTIQUES

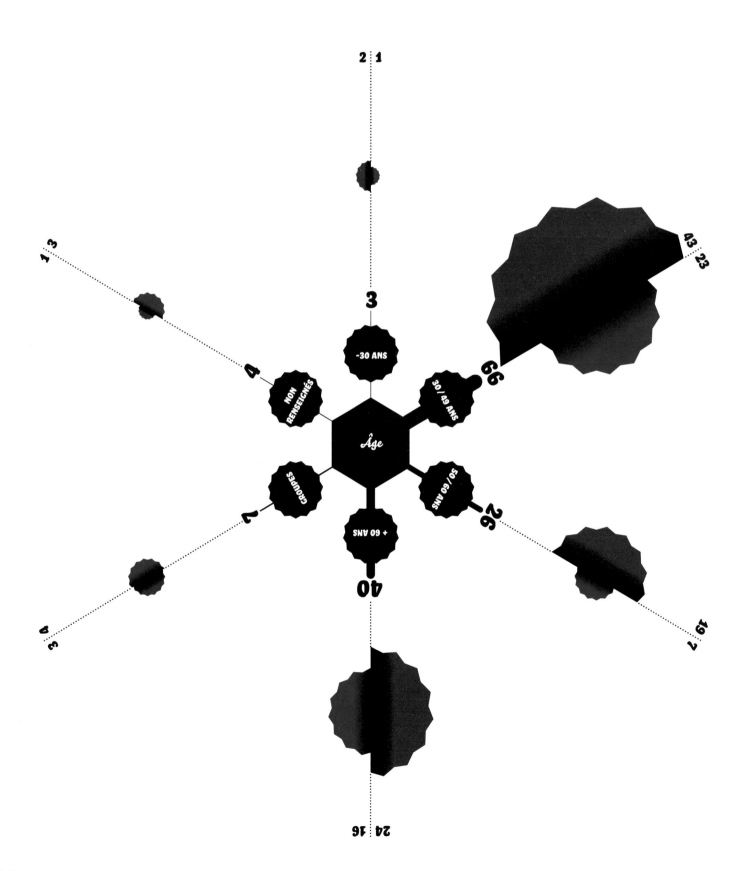

Familistère de Guise

An exercise in which the research for each topic had to represent scientific and historical data in spreadsheets and statistical diagrams. Each illustration is the result of this balance between complexity and clarity within the dense and miscellaneous world of the utopia Godin.

Year: 2010—Client: Familistère de Guise—Collaboration with Sabine Rosant

LA RÉPARTITION DES BÉNÉFICES DANS L'ASSOCIATION COOPÉRATIVE
entre le Capital, le Travail et le Talent

Distribution of the profits of the Association Coopérative between capital, work and talent

CHIFFRE D'AFFAIRES INDUSTRIEL ET COMMERCIAL

FRAIS GÉNÉRAUX DE LA SOCIÉTÉ

SALAIRES

BÉNÉFICES BRUTS

CHARGES SOCIALES

BÉNÉFICES NETS

PART DU TALENT: 25% des bénéfices nets

PART DU CAPITAL: 25% des bénéfices nets

PART DU TRAVAIL: 50% des bénéfices nets

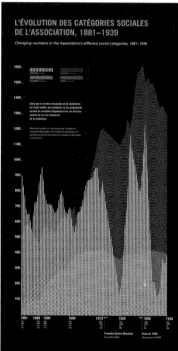

L'ÉVOLUTION DES CATÉGORIES SOCIALES DE L'ASSOCIATION, 1881–1939

Changing numbers in the Association's different social categories, 1881–1939

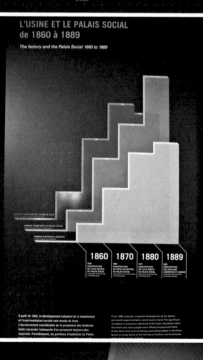

L'USINE ET LE PALAIS SOCIAL
de 1860 à 1889

The factory and the Palais Social 1860 to 1889

| 1860 | 1870 | 1880 | 1889 |

L'APPROPRIATION DU CAPITAL DE LA SOCIÉTÉ DU FAMILISTÈRE
par les employés de l'Association, 1881–1893

Transfer of the Société du Familistère capital to Association employees, 1881–1893

La fondation en 1880 de l'Association coopérative du Capital et du Travail est l'accomplissement du projet du Familistère. La répartition des bénéfices fonctionne comme un processus d'appropriation par les salariés du capital social apporté par Jean-Baptiste André Godin. Par leur travail, les membres de l'Association deviennent capitalistes. Évalué à 4 600 000 francs, ce capital comporte le Palais Social et ses dépendances, les usines de Guise et de Laeken avec les matières premières, le matériel, les modèles et les brevets industriels. En 1889, au lendemain de la mort du fondateur et suivant les volontés exprimées dans son testament, l'Association reçoit la moitié des biens composant sa succession, soit 2 500 000 francs. En 1893, la totalité du capital est passée entre les mains des travailleurs-habitants du Familistère : ils sont collectivement propriétaires de leur outil de travail et de leur lieu de vie.

The foundation in 1880 of the Association coopérative du Capital et du Travail was the fulfilment of the Familistère project. Profit sharing was the process by which employees gradually took over the issued capital invested by Jean-Baptiste André Godin. Through their labour, members of the Association became capitalists in their turn. Valued at 4,600,000 francs, this capital comprised the Palais Social and its outbuildings, the factories at Guise and Laeken, along with raw materials, product lines and patents.
In 1889, on the day after Godin's death and according to the instructions in his will, the Association received half of the value of his estate, some 2,500,000 francs.
In 1893, the entire capital was handed over to the worker residents of the Familistère who thus entered into collective ownership of their work tools and their housing.

Steve Duenes

Steve Duenes has been graphics director of the *New York Times* since 2004,
and currently oversees 28 visual journalists. They are the most highly lauded
infographics team in the world.

○ *www.nytimes.com/pages/multimedia*

How do you split your time between print and online?
Each medium takes up about half of our time and resources.

What software do you use?
For print, we mostly use off-the-shelf or open-source
software, such as Illustrator or R, to create graphics. For
the Web, we mostly write our own HTML/CSS/javascript,
but we also use open-source javascript libraries, such as
jQuery. Obviously, there's a range of complexity when we
talk about coding. Some in the department are doing fairly simple things with HTML/CSS/javascript. Others have
generated entire software packages for interactive maps
or back-end databases that allow us to update text and images quickly.

**How has the rise of data visualizations changed the
way that the *New York Times* reports the news?**
There are now real opportunities for those who can man-
age data, and the sheer volume of data that requires interpretation has definitely changed how the *New York Times*
approaches certain stories. Now, when reporting teams
are assembled in the newsroom, they might include one or
two journalists who can sort data efficiently and identify
different kinds of patterns. But this kind of reporting team
is more of an outlier than the norm.

**How often do you send a visual journalist "into the
field"?**
It's generally better to be physically close to a story, either to locate sources or to witness events firsthand. This
year, with major news breaking in the Middle East and Japan, we haven't managed to send people. Even though our
graphics have been pretty strong, I'm sure we could have
made improvements if we had been able to get people to
the scene.
  One significant hurdle is the expense. Obviously, it
costs a lot to send graphics people to Japan and Cairo,
which is part of the reason why the practice is uncommon
in the industry. But it's not the only reason. At many news
outlets, even here, there's still some shortsightedness
when it comes to the role that visual journalists can and
should play.

**Does your team spend much time doing due diligence
on the data you receive?**
The due diligence starts before we receive any data. All
of our visualizations are made up of data that we pursue
ourselves, so the diligence is really just basic journalistic
practice.
  Just like reporters, we try to learn as much as we can
about data sources before we ask them for information or
download a spreadsheet. Once we have the data, we try
to understand the methodology behind it—how it was assembled or calculated.
  I can't think of too many cases when we've been burned
with bad data, although I do remember making graphics
that summarized then secretary of state Colin Powell's
speech before the United Nations back in 2003.

**Has the growth of graphics redefined the function of
the words and pictures in the newspaper and online?**
Not really. For the most part, the words, graphics, and
pictures come alongside each other but remain separate.
If you look at the article-level template for almost every
news organization, you'll see a large column of text with
pictures and graphics embedded on the side. This is mostly because the staffs at news organizations contain people
who report and write words, or people who shoot still pictures and video, or people who make charts and maps. And
most news organizations are structured so these groups
are clustered into departments that focus only on a single
discipline.

You probably won't see a real redefinition of words and pictures until you have more editors who are also designers or photographers. To combine words, pictures, and graphics into stories that can be generated as quickly as traditional stories with picture and graphic accompaniments requires more sophisticated design than has been implemented at any major publication I've seen.

Is there a particular visualization you or your team were excited about but couldn't do because either the data, the amount of time, or the skills weren't available?
Of course. You rarely have all the information or resources you need to make the ideal visualization when it's appropriate. Most news graphics are compromises based on the best information that can be gathered at the time.

Would you say that the ability actually to see the relationships in a data set for themselves helps increase people's trust in the reporting?
Highlighting the relationships in a data set is not new. That's what good information have always done.

Readers now have more access to the raw data, so they can peer into it themselves and see how the relationships were pulled out. Providing the raw data isn't always practical, but I suppose it increases reader trust in some ways.

But providing readers with just the raw data is a disservice. It is essential that you also explain what the data shows and why it is important. Only a very small portion of our readers have the time to dissect a dataset and draw conclusions.

to possess all these skills, so we need a lot of people (or resources, in corporate speak), and we'll never have all the people we really want, so we need to be almost perfectly organised. We need to work together really smoothly, and sometimes we do, but not always. It can be a challenge.

Which visual storytellers do you admire?
In most of these responses, I'm trying to speak for the graphics team at the *Times,* but here it's impossible, so my personal list includes people such as Errol Morris, Paul Thomas Anderson, Henri Cartier-Bresson, and Massimo Vignelli.

In the world of graphics, I have to say that I really admire many of the people I work with. Folks like Archie Tse, Matt Ericson, Shan Carter, Amanda Cox and others in and out of the graphics department at the *Times* are frequently able to do things that inspire real awe.

Outside the building, I admire the illustrators and cartographers at *National Geographic* magazine, and works by people such as Aaron Koblin and Martin Wattenberg.

Are we in a golden age of infography? Why?
I don't really know, but I think the answer is no. Obviously, there are plenty of terrific infographics out there, but there are also so many bad ones. Right now, there's a lot of noise. The only reason that I'd say we might be in a "golden age" is because of the amount of experimentation I see. With so many people trying so many things, something good is likely to result, but a golden age should really be defined by lots and lots of quality.

2

Which are the most complicated infographics to create?
It varies, but good linear pieces that require 3-D modeling, animation, and synchronization with audio consistently take more time than we anticipate.

What is the definition of a successful infographic?
It should be clear and compelling. It should encourage thought.

What are the major issues facing visual storytelling today?
The issues facing visual storytelling as our group practices it at the *New York Times* are skills, resources and organisation. The things we want to do require fairly deep skills in a lot of areas. It's nearly impossible for individuals

1   Behind the Hunt For Bin Laden
    An infographic accompanying a *New York Times* article about the search for and assassination of Osama bin Laden. The compound he was living in is shown and described in detail as is its location within the Pakistani city of Abbottabad.
        Year: 2011—Client: The *New York Times*—www.nytimes.com/interactive/2010/11/03/us/politics/election-results-house-shift.html

o   Alan McLean, Kevin Quealy, Matthew Ericson, and Archie Tse. Before/after slider by Jason Alvich
2   Satellite Photos of Japan, Before and After the Quake and Tsunami
    A series of before and after satellite images reveals the extent of the devastation following the 2011 earthquake and tsunami in Japan. Each corresponding pair of images is superimposed over one another with a line down the middle, which the viewer can adjust. Moving the line back and forth lets the viewer see either the full before/after image or a combination of the two, allowing them to compare and contrast the images.
        Year: 2011—Client: The *New York Times*—www.nytimes.com/interactive/2011/03/13/world/asia/satellite-photos-ja pan-before-and-after-tsunami.html—Source: Satellite images by GeoEye/EyeQ

1 — Mariano Rivera Pitching

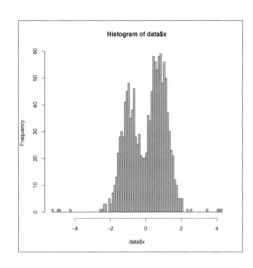

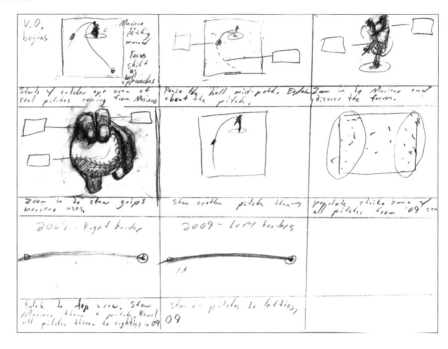

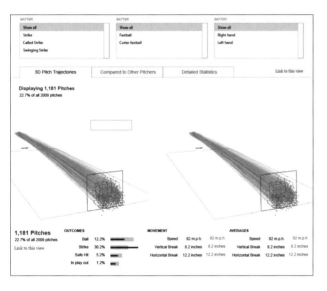

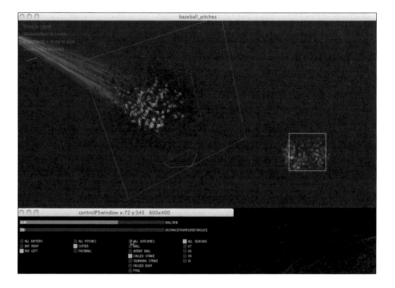

o   Graham Roberts, Shan Carter,
    and Joe Ward
    Mariano Rivera Pitching
    Instead of using interactive means
to explain the cutter (the puzzling sig-
nature pitch of Yankee's pitcher Maria-
no Rivera) to its readers, the *New York
Times* created a series of graphics for a
video that shows all of Rivera's pitches
from 2009. Each pitch is stopped and
suspended at a certain point in the air.
This method helps viewers understand
how difficult it is for the batter to determine whether the pitch is being thrown
as a cutter or as a fastball.
    Year: 2010—Client: The *New York
Times*—Graham Roberts, Shan Carter,
and Joe Ward | Send Feedback—Sourc-
es: Major League Baseball; New York
University Movement Lab; Complete
Game Consulting—www.nytimes.com/
interactive/2010/06/29/magazine/
rivera-pitches.html

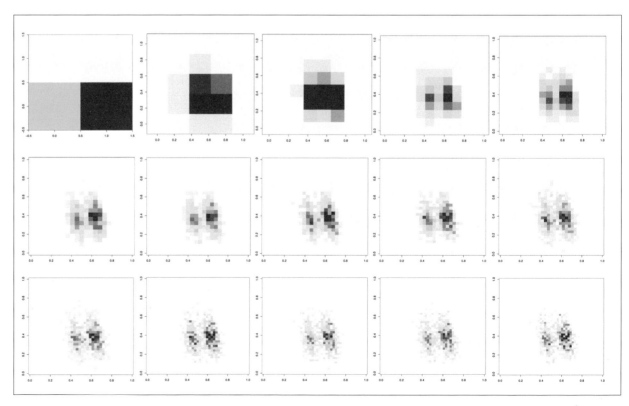

Visual Storyteller

STEVE DUENES

o Shan Carter, Amanda Cox, Xaquín G. V., Kevin Quealy, and Amy Schoenfeld

1 A Historic Shift

A special interactive feature for the *New York Times* comparing the 2010 midterm elections in the United States with previous midterm elections. In contrast to the previous congressional election, for example, nearly all congressional districts voted Republican in 2010. The results, which showed both changes and similarities to past years, were analyzed according to data such as demographics and current issues.

Year: 2010—Client: The *New York Times*—www.nytimes.com/interactive/2010/11/03/us/politics/election-results-house-shift.html

2 Districts Across the Country Shift to the Right

In 2010, just two years after the US presidential election in which Democrats saw large wins, the country shifted back to the right. Starting in 2002, this graphic illustrates shifts from previous two-year election cycles.

Year: 2010—Client: The *New York Times*

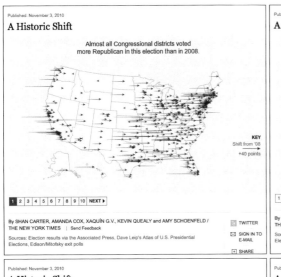

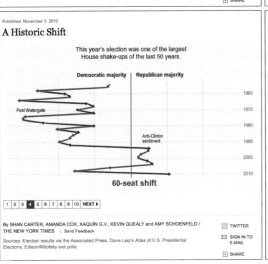

After the Vote

The New York Times

Districts Across the Country Shift to the Right

In a sign of discontent with the party in power, 9 of every 10 House districts voted more Republican than they did in 2008.

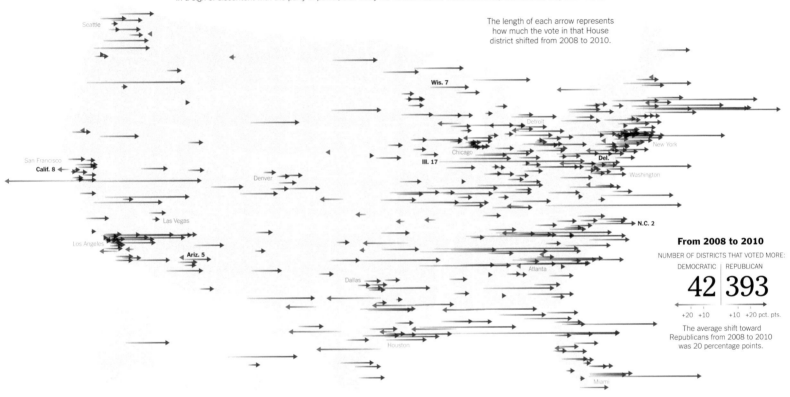

The length of each arrow represents how much the vote in that House district shifted from 2008 to 2010.

From 2008 to 2010

NUMBER OF DISTRICTS THAT VOTED MORE:

DEMOCRATIC | REPUBLICAN

42 | 393

+20 +10 | +10 +20 pct. pts.

The average shift toward Republicans from 2008 to 2010 was 20 percentage points.

While Republicans increased their share of the vote in **California 8**, Nancy Pelosi's lead still increased in the absence of a strong third-party candidate.

Arizona 5 shifted right about 20 points — enough to switch the seat to Republicans. David Schweikert defeated the Democrat he lost to in 2008.

The shift in **Wisconsin 7** was about average for an open race. Here, Sean P. Duffy, a Republican district attorney, won by 8 percentage points.

One of the largest shifts was in **Illinois 17**, where Republican Bobby Schilling, a pizza business owner, beat Phil Hare, a two-term Democratic incumbent.

Only a few districts voted more Democratic. In **Delaware**, the shift helped John Carney defeat Glen Urquhart for the seat held by Michael N. Castle since 1993.

Renee Ellmers delivered one of the Republican Party's narrowest gains in **North Carolina 2**, a district that Democrats won by 36 percentage points in 2008.

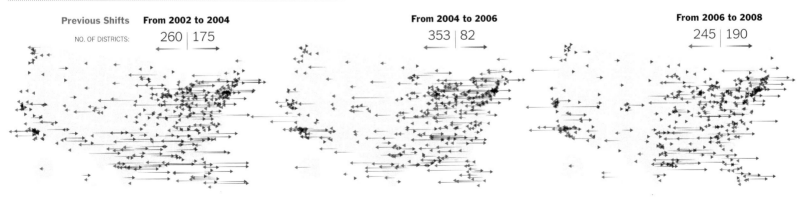

Previous Shifts | **From 2002 to 2004**

NO. OF DISTRICTS: 260 | 175

With President George W. Bush up for his second term in a close race against John Kerry, most districts voted more Democratic.

From 2004 to 2006

353 | 82

Discontent with President Bush, the war in Iraq and the handling of Hurricane Katrina helped the Democrats take control of the House and Senate.

From 2006 to 2008

245 | 190

A majority of districts, riding the wave of Barack Obama's campaign, moved toward the Democrats, but the shift was less widespread than in 2006.

Sources: 2010 vote data is as of 7 p.m. Wednesday and is from The Associated Press; 2002-8 vote data from Dave Leip's Atlas of U.S. Presidential Elections

AMANDA COX, KEVIN QUEALY, AMY SCHOENFELD AND ARCHIE TSE/THE NEW YORK TIMES

2

1   For Much of the Country, A Sizeable Shift

Published directly after the 2008 presidential elections in the United States, this graphic examines the voting trend as compared to the 2004 election. Red and blue in gradation from light to dark illustrates which party got the vote and at what percentage. Analysis along the bottom looks at trends in the 2008 shifts including geography, urban areas, and demographics.

Year: 2008—Client: The *New York Times*—By Graphics Staff

2   Where the Donors Are

The addresses of donors who contributed to the 2004 presidential campaigns were charted on a map, revealing areas of Republicans and Democrats in Manhattan, Los Angeles, and Washington DC.

Year: 2004—Client: The *New York Times*—Source: Federal Election Committee

---

□NY   P1

After the Vote

THURSDAY, NOVEMBER 6, 2008

The New York Times

For Much of the Country, a Sizeable Shift

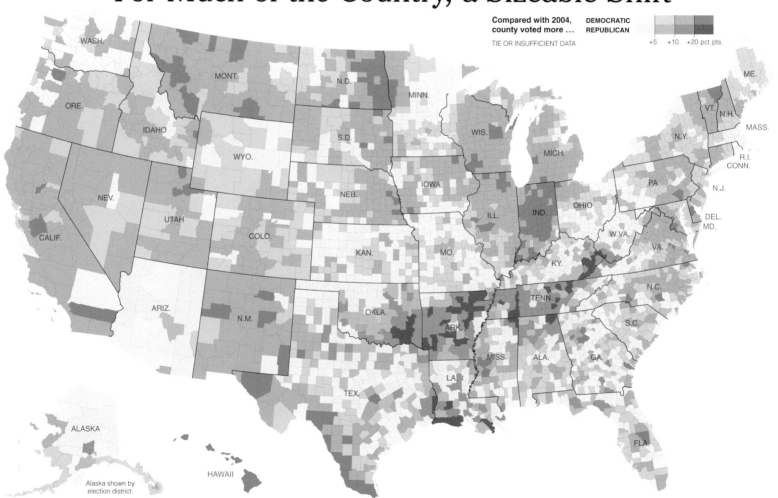

Compared with 2004, county voted more ...   DEMOCRATIC   REPUBLICAN

TIE OR INSUFFICIENT DATA   +5   +10   +20 pct. pts.

Alaska shown by election district.

The Republican West
Even strongly Republican states like **Idaho** and **Utah** took large steps toward the Democratic side. John McCain won Salt Lake County, Utah, but by just 2,000 votes. President Bush had carried it by 80,000 votes.

Northern High Plains
Barack Obama was familiar to voters in **North Dakota** and **Montana** after the primaries. He held 11 events in Montana and had a large field operation from the primary that was retained for the general election.

Rural and Urban Texas
Big cities moved in large numbers to Mr. Obama, providing a sharp contrast here between urban and rural voters. Mr. Obama won Dallas County, a place that Mr. Bush won in 2004 by 125,000 votes.

Rio Grande Valley
Hispanics in the southern tip of **Texas**, who had shown affinity for Mr. Bush in past elections, shifted to the Democratic side. Mr. Obama gained votes from Hispanics who favored Hillary Rodham Clinton in the primaries.

Indiana
Much of the state shifted away from Republicans, but the move was most noticeable in rural counties that had kept the state reliably red in previous elections.

White Southern Counties
Rural white counties from **Kentucky** to **Texas** took a different tack from the rest of the country, moving strongly toward Mr. McCain. Turnout in 90-percent-white counties in **Tennessee** and **Arkansas** was barely changed from 2004.

Blacks in the South
Black voters flooded to the polls in rural counties from **Virginia** to **Mississippi**. In **Alabama**, a safely Republican redoubt, turnout in majority-black counties was up 15 percent.

Source: Historical election data from Dave Leip's Atlas of U.S. Presidential Elections; 2008 results from the Associated Press

THE NEW YORK TIMES

1

CAMPAIGN FINANCE

For a Presidential Politician Looking for Funds, Here Are Two Useful Addresses

Continued From Page A1

an adviser to California's Republican governor, Arnold Schwarzenegger. He has collected at least $100,000 for Mr. Bush, attaining the fund-raising status of "Pioneer." Along with his wife, Kelly P. Day, he has contributed at least as much from his work address to the Republican National Committee since last year, records show.

Marc I. Stern, the company's president, is a "Ranger" — a Bush fundraiser who has collected at least $200,000. With his wife, Eva S. Stern, he gave at least $100,000 to the party from the T.C.W address, according to records. Mr. Stern and Mr. Day declined requests for interviews.

Across the country in Manhattan, the San Remo is a more impressive and better-known Depression-era

Ann Johansson for The New York Times
President Bush has supporters in the building above; John Kerry has his share in the one below.

John Marshall Mantel for The New York Times

In Los Angeles, they gave at the office; in New York, at home.

building with two towers where Mr. Kerry and the Democratic National Committee received the biggest trove of contributions. As of the end of April, a collection of lawyers, bankers and investors who live at 146 Central Park West had provided Mr. Kerry and the committee with almost $192,000. (For whatever reason, the residents of the second tower, at No. 145, have given less.)

"Everybody who is anybody is in these two buildings," said Julian Schlossberg, a Democratic donor and theatrical producer who lives there. "But the people in the building do not want you to know they are in the building."

Many residents did not return phone calls asking to talk about their donations, but one who did, a recording industry executive, asked not to be named because he said identifying where he lived would draw

droves of musicians to his doorstep to audition.

"I'd have to move," he said.

Indeed, some San Remo residents say it is impolitic to talk politics, even among themselves in the hallways.

"If you give someone more than a nod in New York, they start to get nervous," Mr. Schlossberg said.

Andrew Tobias, the well-known financial adviser whose name has adorned the popular do-it-yourself tax software, is a notable exception. He has worked as treasurer for the Democratic National Committee for the last five years.

Mr. Tobias and his partner, Charles Nolan, a fashion designer, contributed at least $77,000 to Mr. Kerry and the party from their New York apartment in this year's election (and $27,000 more counting their contributions from a home in Miami). Mr. Tobias said he had also done his part to carry the party line to his neighbors in the decades he has lived in the building.

"Some of them run away when they see me coming," he joked. "They take the next elevator."

The Times's analysis counted only contributions directly to the candidates, who can accept $2,000 from a single donor, and the national political parties, which can accept $25,000 a year.

This left out many of the country's largest contributors, who because of the new McCain-Feingold campaign finance law banning unlimited donations to the national political parties direct their money to independent organizations if they want to give six- and seven-figure donations. When those kinds of donations are considered, the real top address may be whatever George Soros, the philanthropist and financier who has given more than $15 million to Democratic-leaning organizations, lists when he writes his largest check.

Meanwhile, the campaigns and the parties make their relentless push for money, shifting the financial geography somewhat as they work, even if the top-giving metropolitan areas tend to remain the same as they have in the past: New York, Washington, Chicago and Los Angeles.

In this year's contest, Houston and Boston also made the list. New York ranks as Mr. Kerry's top metropolitan area and Mr. Bush's second largest, in fund-raising figures through April. Manhattan's 10021 ZIP code provided more money than any other in the country, leading the list for both campaigns.

While Republican support is clustered on the Upper East Side, Democrats generally have done better on the Upper West Side and throughout much of the rest of Manhattan.

Still, Mr. Kerry has made inroads on the East Side. His second-most-lucrative address is 770 Park Avenue, where bankers, real estate agents, financial experts and lawyers gave $151,000 to him or his party.

A little to the north, the residents of 830 Park Avenue gave $134,000, to rank the building as Mr. Kerry's third-most lucrative. Candidates and party regulars are familiar with that address because it is the home of Susan and Alan Patricof, two of New York's larger Democratic donors and fund-raisers. The Patricofs have entertained Bill and Hillary Rodham Clinton, Senator Tom Daschle of South Dakota and Senator Charles E. Schumer of New York over the years. More recently, they backed Gen. Wesley K. Clark before throwing their support behind Mr. Kerry.

"We are all trying to work really hard," Ms. Patricof said. "People are super-concerned right now and looking for ways to be helpful."

On the Republican list, other big-money addresses include 1100 Main Street in Lady Lake, Fla., southwest of Daytona Beach. There, five development executives and their families gave about $260,000 to the president and his party, records show.

In Mr. Bush's home state, Texas, supporters at 300 Crescent Court in Dallas gave $213,000, ranking the address third on the list, records show. Occupants of that address include Charles and Sam Wyly, two Texas businessmen and supporters of Mr. Bush who gained notoriety in the 2000 primaries when they financed advertisements attacking Senator John McCain's campaign.

And in Los Angeles, there are the occupants of 11100 Santa Monica Boulevard, an innocuous white high-rise near the San Diego Freeway entrance that provided about $170,000 to Mr. Bush and the party, records show. Inside, at the offices of the investment firm Freeman Spogli & Company, is Bradford Freeman, a longtime friend of the president's and a major Bush fund-raiser. His business partner, Ron Spogli, was a Harvard Business School classmate of Mr. Bush's.

The two men gave more than $100,000 from that address and have raised many times that over the years. Mr. Freeman was not surprised to see his building on the list.

"I'd be disappointed if we weren't," he said.

In Presidential Politics, Where the Donors Are

By plotting the addresses of donors to presidential campaigns and the national party committees on a map, patterns of giving emerge. Data from the Federal Election Commission show apartment buildings, offices and other addresses where the occupants have given tens or hundreds of thousands of dollars to support the candidates. *MATTHEW ERICSON*

JOHN KERRY
and the Democratic National Committee

Contributions to each candidate and his party's national committee

GEORGE W. BUSH
and the Republican National Committee

Manhattan

For both sides, the top ZIP code in the nation for contributions was 10021 on the Upper East Side. Mr. Kerry's appeal, however, was greater throughout much of the rest of Manhattan, bringing in more money than Mr. Bush and the R.N.C. in areas like the Upper West Side, Greenwich Village and SoHo.

Los Angeles Area

Mr. Bush and the R.N.C. led not only in traditionally Republican areas like Orange County, but also in Los Angeles itself.

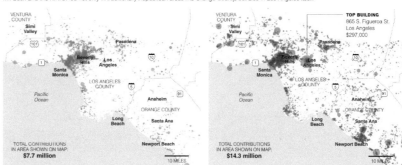

Washington, D.C. Area

While Mr. Kerry and the D.N.C. raised more money in Washington, suburbs like McLean, Arlington and Alexandria, Va., were more Republican in giving.

ABOUT THE DATA The maps are based on the addresses of donors as reported by the campaigns to the Federal Election Commission. The F.E.C. requires that an address be listed for each donor; it does not specify whether the address be a home address or work address, so the types of addresses shown on the map vary. The maps do not include the 15 percent of contributions that were missing addresses, had addresses that could not be found or listed post office boxes rather than street addresses. Data include itemized contributions of $200 or more by individuals from Jan. 1, 2003, through April 30, 2004, to the presidential campaigns and national party committees.

Sources: Federal Election Commission; Queens College Department of Sociology

The New York Times

Antoine Corbineau

Antoine Corbineau works as a free-lance illustrator and designer. He works on a variety of personal and profession-al projects. His clients include Nokia, Alfa Romeo, the airports of Paris and Southern Comfort. He lives in Paris, and his work has been exhibited around the world.

○ *www.antoinecorbineau.com*

How do you approach a commission?

I tend to approach each commission case by case, try-ing to find an answer that best fits the client's brief—while also trying to avoid repeating ideas.

Over the last few years, I have received more and more commissions with large amounts of information to visual-ize, so I have learned to be methodical in the process of researching, collecting the elements and coming up with ways to unify them all in a coherent and original composi-tion.

Once I have the ingredients ready, I start sketching out a really quick general idea, then a rough of each element. That gives me a better sense of the amount of work it will take, and also gives me ideas on how I could connect them together.

Next step is a detailed black-and-white sketch that I will then scan and start working on the final colorized file.

How do you describe your illustration style?

It's a colorful and dense combination of logically in-terconnected hand-drawn elements, typography and tex-tures—but that sounds a bit cold! I just draw how I can, and my colorful, hand-drawn style is not only inviting but also an interesting way to communicate more complex sub-jects.

It might appear childish or naive for some people at first glance, but if the subject is serious, it can be a less aggres-sive way to talk to people. Probably a bit in the same spirit as the hand-painted healthcare prevention campaigns in some countries in Africa, my work can have a very naive look but also be serious and very informative.

I don't like the weight of a visual education to be too visible, maybe because it reminds me too much of the dark side of propaganda, and its visual tricks being used to fool the uneducated.

Your colors are always very distinctive and joyful. How do you choose each one?

I'm a painter as well as an illustrator, and I used to use color spontaneously, without limit or preselection. But I am now trying to restrict myself to a limited and specific range of color that I wouldn't select that way. Color choice is very important, especially in my work. It gives the first overall mood and vibration, the ones that makes the viewer want to come look closer.

1

Do you see your work as fitting the term infographics?

I have never really liked the word infographics (or may-be the way it is used in France) but that is probably what I do. I represent information graphically.

But pleasing aesthetics are as important to me as con-veying information. The infographics that really get into your head, the ones you remember, are the ones that look good, the ones where your imagination is stimulated, where words and numbers are more than just words and numbers.

That is why many people here buy old hand-illustrated school maps of France and its agriculture in the 1950s or Air France posters from the 1960s—not only for the infor-mation, but because they look great, with their imperfec-tions and fantasies: they demand your attention. Not that I don't like some of the works by the army of Swiss minimal-ism, but I am more part of the "more is better" gang.

What are the major issues facing visual storytelling today?

Time! Visual storytelling entails a huge amount of work (which also means a higher cost) but the deadlines are often very short, and briefs often arrive very late, so it is not always possible to have enough time to experiment and to create a proper and well-thought piece of visual storytelling.

What visual storytellers do you admire?

I have always admired Bosch and Bruegel, and more recent artists Jean-Michel Basquiat, Paul Noble, and Raymond Pettibon. I don't have a very large knowledge of illustration and graphic design history but I really admire classic figures such as Saul Steinberg and Pierre Bernard. Milton Glaser too, he raises the bar very high. I read interviews with him each time I have any doubts about my career choices.

Within my generation, I have a strong admiration for the visual stories created by Emmanuel Romeuf, Adam Simpson, and Christopher Hittinger. But writers are probably the best visual storytellers for me, books such as Ravage and Barjavel and One Hundred Years of Solitude are pure visual stories that stimulate my imagination.

What story/information data set would you like to illustrate one day? Why?

I have just finished a large illustrated map of Italy and its wines, and that made me look forward to doing more maps. A very large and detailed map of a city like Paris or a country like the USA, or even the world, would be very exciting. Any kind of project that is designed to last, that could be used for years and have real utility for the community.

1   Mardi Gras Melodie
    The Southern Comfort Creative Exchange asked participants to create an image inspired by the theme "big city carnival" during the Berlin and New Orleans 2011 Mardi Gras carnival.
    Year: 2010—Client: Southern Comfort

2   Melbourne
    A poster for the Melbourne Public Restaurant. The graphics represent the city of Melbourne and the area that surrounds the restaurant.
    Year: 2009—Client: Projects fo Imagination

3   Aéroport de Paris—
    Orly Illustrated Murals
    Large illustrated mural in Paris-Orly Airport.
    Year: 2010—Client: Aéroport de Paris / W&Cie—Additional credits: www.wcie.fr

1 — The Grange School World

Large poster illustration that represents all of the school's activities including academics, extracurricular activities, and preparation for the future. Used on walls, brochures, and advertising.

Year: 2011—Client: DesignForce /
The Grange School—Additional credit:
www.designforce.co.uk

The design and strategy agency OPS2 wanted a illustrated poster that clients could hang on their walls for the entire year. The artwork references the four seasons, elements about the agency and its clients, and the idea of project production through time and space, from brief to finalization, from Paris to Nice.

Year: 2011—Client: OPS2—
Additional credit: www.ops2.com

2 — OPS2 Greetings Poster

3 \ 4

5

BEST WISHES
2011
ANTOINE
CORBINEAU

2

1   Plastic World
    Artwork and poster for eco-friend-
ly shopping bags that are printed on
with eco-friendly inks.
    Year: 2008—Client: Iamgreen
Amsterdam

2   2011 Greetings
    Self-promotional campaign repre-
senting the fact that each year, humans
face new adventures, complexities, and
challenges—and try to make their way
through them. The jellyfish that the
character is throwing into the world attempts to bring a lighter touch to a me-
chanical and violent environment.
    Year: 2011—Self-promotion

Carl Kleiner

Carl Kleiner is a Swedish photographer based in Stockholm. His distinctive images have been published in fashion magazines, and on billboards around the world.

○ *www.carlkleiner.com*

How do you come up with your ideas?

I always carry a custom bag for two rolls of film and my sketchbook. When I am bored or have a spare moment, I usually sketch—I have a lot of sketchbooks on the shelf filled with good and bad ideas. Both ideas and the line of action tend to be born in the shower or on my morning walk.

You shot a very unique and eye-catching series of photographs for IKEA's cookbook. What was your process? → 40

I worked on this project together with Evelina Bratell, who is a stylist and my fiancee. Evelina made a lot of paper cutouts in shapes similar to the ingredients we later used. Since the ingredients were pretty greasy and hard to move around, it was important to have a clear idea of how everything would be placed.

With the cutouts, we tested different compositions and planned the execution of each image in advance. It took a couple of weeks before we started shooting. During the actual production, we made an average of four images per day.

The biggest challenge before we started was to make the boring ingredients, such as flour and sugar, interesting. Once we'd begun, the ingredients that we expected would be easiest to work with, such as strawberries, proved to be the most difficult.

What message do you think it conveys?

The concept was developed by advertising agency Forsman & Bodenfors. I think the very organized grids and compositions, in combination with the organic materials

1

on the colourful backgrounds, was the key to its success. When raw materials are shot in this way, as consistent and clean, you see the textures and shapes in a whole new way. The concept really fits IKEA, as they deliver their products in sections and pieces, with accompanying instructions.

Have you ever tried to a create narrative through one of your images that didn't work as you hoped?

This happened recently. I made a series I call *Zootany,* a mix of zoology and botany. I used both photography and drawing, and felt very happy with the results. When I showed it to the client, he didn't understand the bigger story. I was disappointed at first, but realized pretty quickly that there was some material missing from the piece, that prevented it from being a coherent whole. I will continue working on the project. It will be great eventually.

Do you prefer to photograph objects to people?

Objects are much easier than living creatures to work with. They never complain that they are tired (except wilting flowers and melting ice).

You can twist and turn an object however much you want, without insulting it. I also find it easy to give personalities to dead things. That said, I don't dislike photographing people. I do so much still life probably because my portfolio contains a lot of still lifes, and so I get more still-life commissions.

Do objects have a life of their own?

Before I started photographing professionally, I often shot things around me that I thought looked alive: cabinets, drainpipes, houses. The first time I went to New York, I came home with hardly a picture of a skyscraper but with a lot of pictures of happy telegraph poles and sad manhole covers.

I have a friend who is an abstract painter. He hates to show me his paintings because I always see something figurative in them. My brain is always looking for life in inanimate objects and abstractions.

That way of looking affects the way I work. Consciously or subconsciously, I set the light, and place the objects in a way that gives them some kind of life.

What are the broader themes of your work?

Emotion, harmony, experiments of different kinds, unexpected meetings.

How important is it that the viewer understands the story you have created?

The stories of my images are probably more often subconscious and intuitive. When I was younger, I struggled a lot with being clever and complicated in my photographs, but that often led to poor results. Over time, I have learned to trust my imagination and intuition, and to not worry so much if all my pictures should have clear messages. Some pictures just have good energy. I'm happy with that.

What are the major issues facing visual storytelling today?

I believe that, in our world of perfect surfaces and strange ideals, authenticity is important. That sounds very political, but that might be demonstrated purely through the imperfect surface of an object. I think the survival of photography depends – at least in part – on the authenticity of the scene that the photograph captures, a scene that cannot be recreated digitally with the same quality and spontaneity.

I also believe in simplicity. Everyday, we get hundreds of messages that are screaming for our attention. When I see something quiet that doesn't require an immediate response, it invites me to take a closer look.

Which visual storytellers do you admire?

Past: Irving Penn. Salvador Dali. Rene Magritte. Frida Kahlo.

Present: David Lynch, Sophie Calle, Tim Walker, David Simon, Bryan Ferry

What narrative would you like to photograph one day?

I'm very interested showing in science and natural science, in an imaginative way. I would like to visualize fantastic and impossible inventions in a very realistic way. I also have an entire exhibition about weather in my head, which is technically impossible to implement—for me, at least.

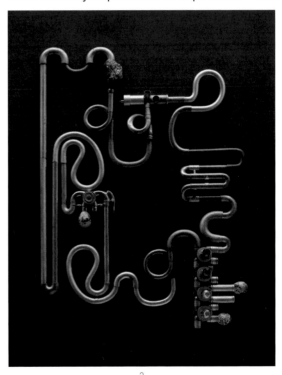

2

○ Carl Kleiner with
Forsman & Bodenfors
1 Homemade Is Best — Mandelkubb
A baking book that contains 30 classic Swedish baking recipes. The ingredients for each recipe—everything from small biscuits to large cakes—are laid out on various colored backgrounds and styled to highlight their colors and textures.
Year: 2010—Client: Ikea—Stylist: Evelina Bratell—Retouch: F&B Factory

○ Collaboration with Evelina Bratell
2 X / Y
The packaging for the two-disc album *X / Y,* by the Swedish trumpet player Goran Kajfes, takes the form of an art book. Each page is dedicated to a track from the album and contains a visual interpretation by a different Swedish artist. The *Y* disc feels like a science fiction dream; Kleiner's image for the book is taken from the *Star Wars* series.
Year: 2010—Client: Goran Kajfes

39

1 — Homemade is Best

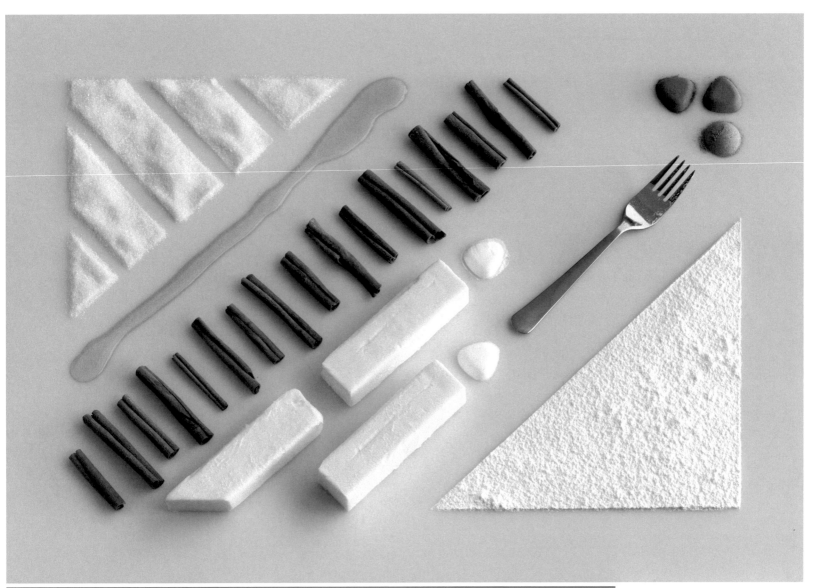

o   Carl Kleiner with
    Forsman & Bodenfors
1   Sketches Evelina Bratell and Carl
    Kleiner Made Before the Ikea
    Shoot
2   Homemade Is Best — Pepparkaka
3   Homemade Is Best — Princess
    Cake
    Year: 2010—Client: Ikea—Stylist:
    Evelina Bratell—Retouch: F&B Factory

Visual Storyteller CARL KLEINER

1   Everyday Geometry
    A series working with the concept
of everyday geometry and the things
we need but take for granted.
    Year: 2009—Personal work—Paper bag,
    different papers

2   The Big Blur
    Year: 2010—Client: *BLEND* Magazine

3   Under the Umberella
    From a story about umbrellas for
the Swedish design magazine *Form*.
    Year: 2008—Client: *Form* magazine

4   Green City
    The population of the earth stands
at 6,890,000,000. This image is part
of a series that represents different
themes that affect the world's population. They were created for *Green City*,
a book about environmentally friendly
construction, written by the construction company Skanska.
    Year: 2009—Agency: Brindfors—Client:
    Skanska—Paper collage

5   Kaleido
    A continuation of *Everyday Geom-
etry* series.
    Year: 2008—Personal project—Ruler,
    different papers, mirrors
6   Year: 2010—Personal project—Post-it,
    different papers, mirrors

2

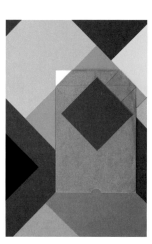

1

3

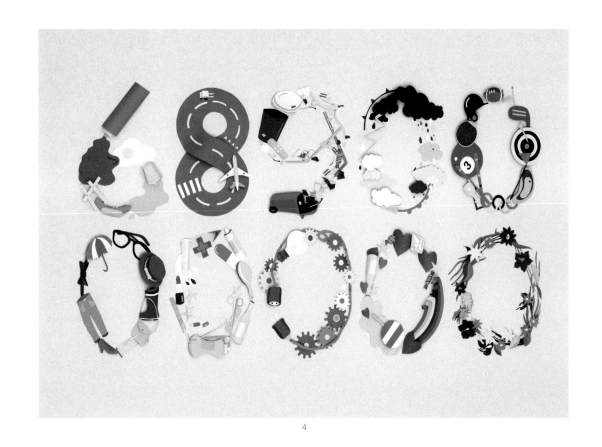

4

5

6

Peter Grundy

Peter Grundy has been working in information design since 1980. He is a British-based designer and illustrator, and has created work for the World Bank, the United Nations, Shell, the *Guardian* and *Wired* magazine.

○ *www.grundini.com*

How did you develop your distinctive style?

When I started working with Tilly Northedge as Grundy & Northedge (Tilly retired five years ago), we intended to work as designers, having ideas and commissioning others to produce the craft. However, budgets decreed that we needed to find a way of producing the imagery ourselves.

Neither of us ever considered ourselves illustrators, so we developed a way of drawing that was within our limited skills. This became our style. It's important to emphasise that, in any piece of my work, it's the idea that is most important. I recognize the reader sees the style above everything, but the idea is king.

Can you talk us through the process of creating the *Price on Your Head* **infographic?** → 46

The client wanted me to propose an idea, which I discussed with them on the phone. I told them I wanted to create a character for whom all the body parts were laid out like an army display. That was stage one. Stage two was the finished piece.

I don't tend to do roughs for clients, though I do often scribble for myself. Following the initial sketches, there were various color changess and design tweaks that you can see. The artwork was done on Creative Suite 4. It took me two weeks.

Do you keep a library of elements from previous illustrations to reuse?

I do, I reuse a lot of icons in my work. I see my drawing as a sort of collage made from elements I've been building over the years.

What do you think are the benefits to the viewer of your illustration style?

I aim to simplify and to entertain. I also aim to show an opinion on the informational messages conveyed through my work.

Are there any kinds of information for which you feel your style would not be suitable?

No.

How do you know when a piece has succeeded?

I feel, after all these years, that I can tell when something is working—but ultimately, it's the reader's call.

What are the major issues facing visual storytelling today?

The internet requires an international language. Visual storytelling offers that.

What infographic would you like to create one day?

I still seek a brave, public mural on energy. Though the recent Shell International "New Energy Future" campaign came close.

What is the essence of a good infographic?

It tells an interesting story in a visual way. I think that information designers and illustrators should put good ideas above all other factors when creating a good piece of work. They need not to be scared to voice their own opinions and personality within their visual solutions.

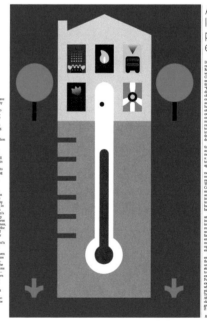

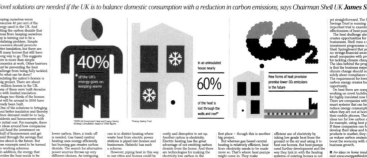

2

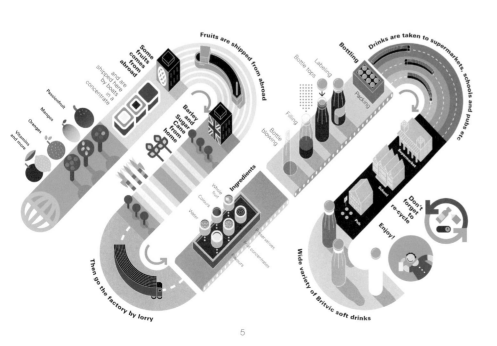

3

1 Age of energy spreads for Shell
Monthly illustrations for a feature story about energy in the *Telegraph* newspaper
Year: 2011—Client: *Telegraph*

2 Arm Frieze
A series of spreads for the Arm annual report, showing that Arm chips appear in everything.
Year: 2010—Client: Luminous Design

3 Interoute Poster
A graphic that illustrates all of the voice and data products offered by Interoute.
Year: 2009—Client: Interoute

4 Sex Spread
Infographic of sex facts based on surveys of men and women.
Year: 2008—Client: *Maxim* magazine

5 Britvic Process Diagram
A diagram that appeared in the annual report for the British soft drink company, Britvic, showing its production process from beginning to end.
Year: 2007—Client: Luminous Design

6 Hampton Court Diagram
An illustration of the food consumed in the court of Henry VIII. The animals, vegetables, fruit, drinks, bread, and fish are contained in a structure that is a combination of a castle building and the head of the king.
Year: 2005—Client: Hampton Court

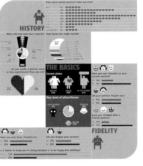

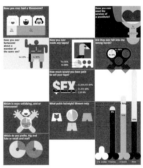

4

5

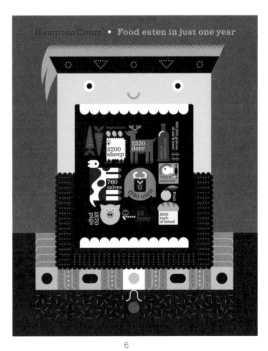

6

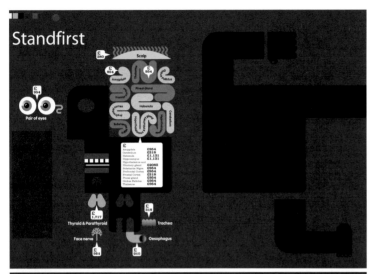

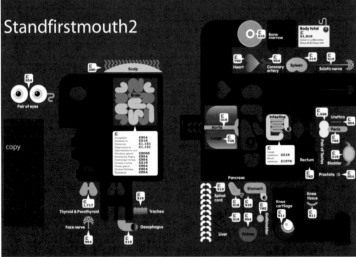

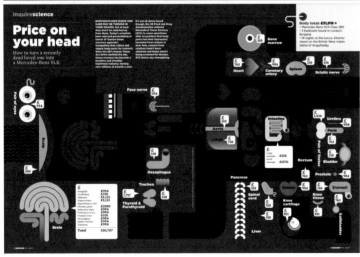

1 — Bodyparts/Price On Your Head

Bodyparts Spread and Sketches
An infographic accompanying an article in *Esquire* magazine about companies that pay high prices for body parts to be used in research. Each body part has an individual price tag attached to it as well as the total sum for an entire body and what that would equal when buying a house or a car.
Year: 2007—Client: *Esquire* Magazine

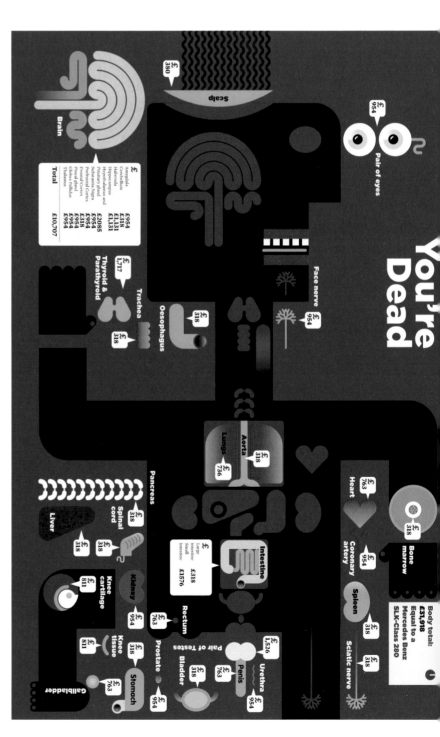

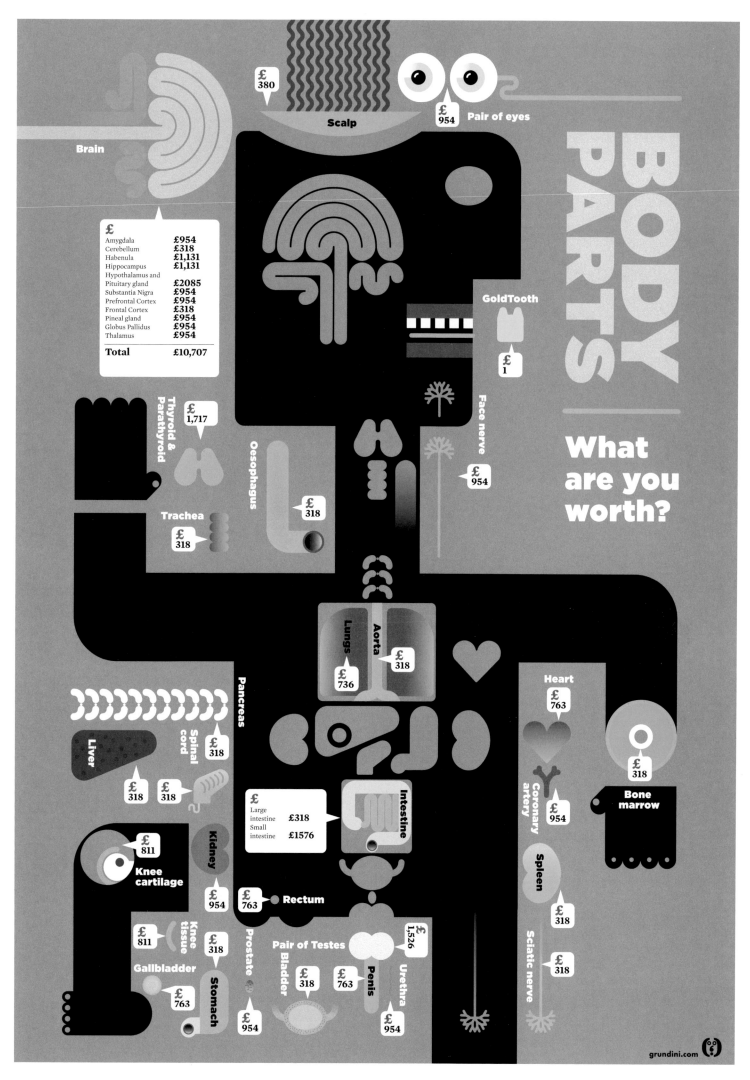

BODY PARTS

What are you worth?

Brain

Scalp

£380

£954 Pair of eyes

GoldTooth

£1

Face nerve

£954

£	
Amygdala	£954
Cerebellum	£318
Habenula	£1,131
Hippocampus	£1,131
Hypothalamus and Pituitary gland	£2085
Substantia Nigra	£954
Prefrontal Cortex	£954
Frontal Cortex	£318
Pineal gland	£954
Globus Pallidus	£954
Thalamus	£954
Total	**£10,707**

Thyroid & Parathyroid £1,717

Oesophagus £318

Trachea £318

Lungs £736

Aorta £318

Heart £763

Bone marrow £318

Coronary artery £954

Spleen £318

Sciatic nerve £318

Pancreas

Spinal cord £318

Liver £318 £318

Large intestine £318
Small intestine £1576

Intestine £1,526

Knee cartilage £811

Kidney £954

Rectum £763

Knee tissue £811

£318

Prostate

Pair of Testes £318

Penis £763

Bladder

Urethra £954

Gallbladder

Stomach £763

£954

grundini.com

47

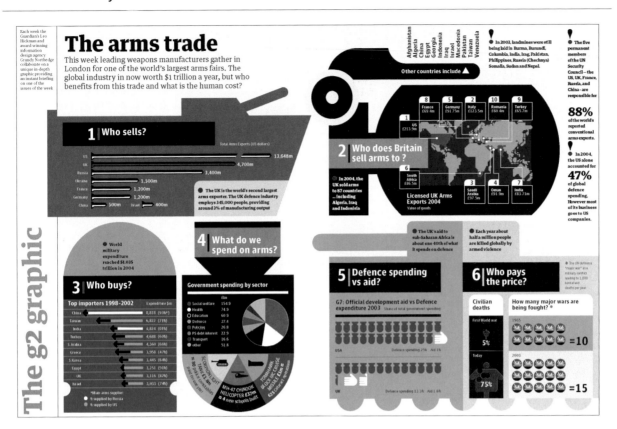

1 G2 Spreads
The G2 spreads appeared as a weekly collaboration with the *Guardian's* Leo Hickman. Each week they created a graphic that analyzed one of the week's most important topics.
Year: 2006/7—Client: The *Guardian*

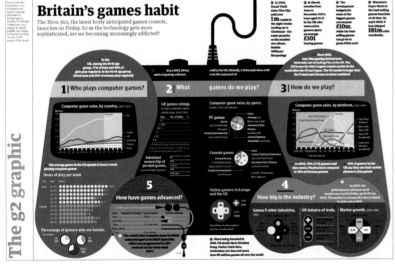

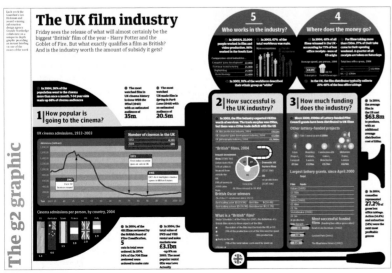

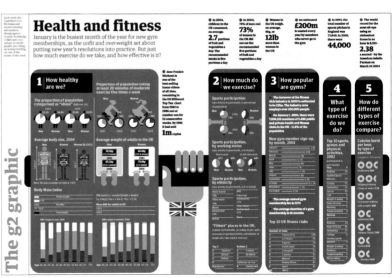

48

The Los Angeles Magazine Pet Survey

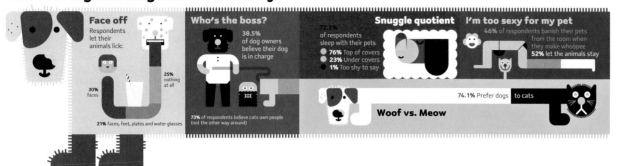

Face off
Respondents let their animals lick:

30% faces

25% nothing at all

21% faces, feet, plates and water glasses

Who's the boss?

38.5% of dog owners believe their dog is in charge

73% of respondents believe cats own people (not the other way around)

72.3% of respondents sleep with their pets
- 76% Top of covers
- 23% Under covers
- 1% Too shy to say

Snuggle quotient

I'm too sexy for my pet
46% of respondents banish their pets from the room when they make whoopee
52% let the animals stay

74.1% Prefer dogs to cats

Woof vs. Meow

2   Pets Spread
An illustration containing facts about pets and the people who live with them. The data was taken from a survey of readers of the Los Angeles Magazine.
Year: 2010—Client: *LA* magazine

3   F1 Spread
An infographic showing all of the details that go into a Formula 1 event including traveling furniture, bottles of vodka, and spare engines.
Year: 2008—Client: *Red Bull* magazine

Hello Kitty
Cat owners report the following breakages:

9% Heart

27% Broken vase

3% Computer

13% All of these

Begging pays off
68.5% of respondents feed animals human food

R.I.P
- 45% of respondents prefer to cremate their fallen pets *
- 31% prefer burial
- 24% couldn't deal with the question

Let's play dress up
38% of respondents said they own clothes for their pet

Secret admirer

6% like their pets more than their mates

40% like their pets more than their bosses

You look Mahvelous
58% of respondents believe that the longer a dog and person live together the more they look alike

38% of respondents said their pet was better looking than their friends' pets
6% said their pet was better looking than their friends.

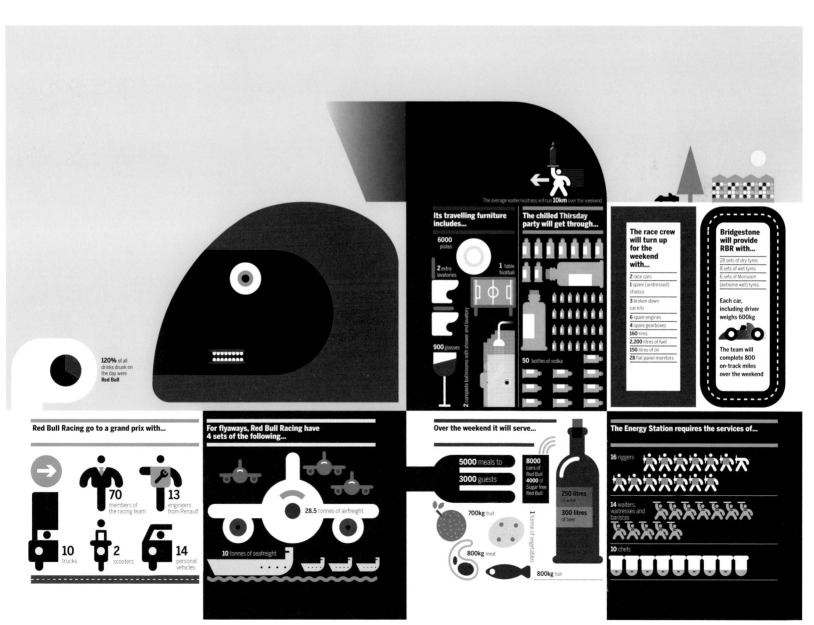

The average waiter/waitress will run 10km over the weekend.

120% of all drinks drunk on the day were **Red Bull**

Its travelling furniture includes...

6000 plates

2 extra lavatories

1 table football

900 glasses

2 complete bathrooms with shower and lavatory

The chilled Thirsday party will get through...

50 bottles of vodka

The race crew will turn up for the weekend with...

2 race cars

1 spare (undressed) chassis

3 broken down car kits

6 spare engines

4 spare gearboxes

160 rims

2,200 litres of fuel

150 litres of oil

28 flat panel monitors

Bridgestone will provide RBR with...

28 sets of dry tyres
8 sets of wet tyres
6 sets of Monsoon (extreme wet) tyres

Each car, including driver weighs 600kg

The team will complete 800 on-track miles over the weekend

Red Bull Racing go to a grand prix with...

70 members of the racing team

13 engineers from Renault

10 trucks

2 scooters

14 personal vehicles

For flyaways, Red Bull Racing have 4 sets of the following...

28.5 tonnes of airfreight

10 tonnes of seafreight

Over the weekend it will serve...

5000 meals to

3000 guests

8000 cans of Red Bull
4000 of Sugar free Red Bull

250 litres of wine

300 litres of beer

700kg fruit

800kg meat

1 tonne of vegetables

800kg fish

The Energy Station requires the services of...

16 riggers

14 waiters, waitresses and baristas

10 chefs

Jan Schwochow

Jan Schochow runs Golden Section Graphics, an infographics studio based in Berlin. Their clients include print media, television, major brands and organizations. They also make their own magazine containing only visualizations, called *IN GRAPHICS*.

o *www.golden-section-graphics.com*

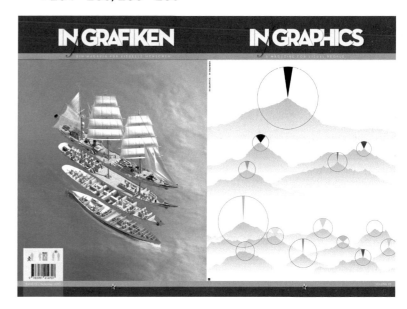

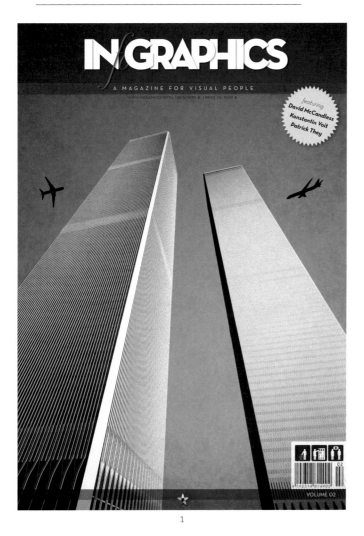

1

2\3

1   Cover—IN GRAPHICS Vol. 02
The Twin Towers were chosen for the cover of the second issue of *IN GRAPHICS,* whose main story dealt with the ten-year anniversary of the September 11, 2001 attacks.
Year: 2011—Client: *IN GRAPHICS* magazine by Golden Section Graphics GmbH

2   Cover—IN GRAPHICS Vol. 01
The first issue of *IN GRAPHICS* featured a double page cover with the English title on the front and the German title on the back. Each covered used graphics taken from the inside of the magazine.
Year: 2010/2011—Client: *IN GRAPHICS*

magazine by Golden Section Graphics GmbH

3   Germany's Big Six-0
Starting with the year 1949, these graphics detail the development of demographic and economic factors in Germany.
Year: 2010/2011—Client: *IN GRAPHICS* magazine by Golden Section Graphics GmbH—Design: Katharina Schwochow, Jan Schwochow

How did you create the infographic of Museum Island? → 52

It was a request by the Corporate Publishing Agency of *Lufthansa Magazin,* who wanted to make a page about the Museum Island with the new planned Humboldt Forum. Our agency is only a few hundred meters away from the Museum Island, so I could go and have a look at all the buildings, to get a better vision of what there is to explain.

We then had a meeting with employees from the managing company, who gave us all the blueprints for the new building. The plans of the existing buildings we found in old books—books are still a great resource!

We had a few of the buildings already rendered in 3d from jobs we have done before, so we reused them. The next step was to build up a rough scene in the 3d program Cinema 4D. This is a good way to find a perspective and to put all needed objects in place. It was important to keep in mind the centre of the page that would be hidden later in print, and to leave enough space for callouts and headlines.

When the client had approved the layout, we could continue with details. We had a few 3D artists working on the project, each concentrating on one building or the surrounding scene.

The graphic took about one and a half months. Since then, we have updated it several times—we are lucky to have been able to keep the rights, and so it is an ongoing project. We can now sell this exclusive graphic to other media, so in the end all the work we invested will be profitable.

How many versions do you make of each graphic?

A lot. It depends on the complexity of the graphic and the responses of the client. But I can reduce it to three steps: First the sketch, then a rough graphic and then the final version.

You have to work from the rough to the details. Many designers make the mistake of working first on the details, and then they have no idea how all works together.

Do you reuse elements of your infographics in other works?

Yes, of course. You have to be careful of the rights of use, but when you have a 3D object, you can render it in another perspective and the graphic is new. A good example are maps. You can't change borders but you can change the style of the elements. It's a good idea to build up a big archive of maps, signs and 3D objects.

How important is the hierarchy of narrative in your work? Do you plan where the viewer's eye will look first, then where it goes next? If you do, what techniques do you use to encourage this?—How do you choose the color palette and the typography? How important are they as infographic elements?

In our culture, it is normal to start in the upper left on a page. Here you will often find a headline. If you have a good emotional headline, the reader will be interested in looking at the whole graphic.

It is also important to have one big element on the page, the eye-catcher. All the other elements will be in the background, and may have a simple style. You can lead the reader's eye by using a series of numbers or letters, such as 1,2, 3 or A, B, C, in an eyecatching color.

Color and typography are also very important. You highlight the important things by using red and a bold typeface. The reader can then navigate very quickly through the graphic and the story.

But the story should not be linear like a text. The reader should also be able to start with the parts he is interested in.

How large is your team?

We are a team of five people plus some freelancers and interns. Everybody is good with Illustrator, Photoshop, InDesign, and Excel. We also have employees who are good with Flash, After Effects, Cinema 4D, and one person uses Processing and ActionScript.

What are the most difficult infographics to tackle?

The ones where you don't have the right data or not enough information or you have a difficult client who is unable to say what they want. It's not unusual for me to say, "There is no story, there is no information, so we cannot make a graphic."

Have you ever made an embarrassing mistake in an infographic?

I once had a misunderstanding over the use of abbreviations. In a graphic about the economy for a big German daily newspaper, we said there were billions of unemployed people in Germany, instead of millions.

What is the definition of a successful infographic?

The reader must learn something or understand something better after looking at the graphic.

Why did you decide to make the magazine *IN GRAPHICS*?

It was always a big dream of mine to tell stories in my own magazine. I can decide which stories are worth telling.

Are animated infographics much more complicated than print infographics?

Animated graphics provide another dimension. You need to know more software such as Flash or After Effects. And you don't have to draw one sketch at the beginning - you have to draw a storyboard. But it also allows you to go deeper into a subject.

What are the major issues facing visual storytelling today?

We have to distinguish between pure journalism, communication between companies and end customers (BtoC), and communication between companies (BtoB). Every sector needs a form of infographic communication, but we have to be clear on where the borders are between telling the truth and manipulating people.

What visual storytellers do you admire?

I'm a big fan of TinTin. A good infographic is sometimes like a comic—it tells a story frame by frame.

Is there a particular infographic you would like to tackle one day?

I would like to make an historic exhibition for a museum, designing everything inside, from the orientation system right down to the visitor's book.

Are we in a golden age of infography?

We are in a golden age of information and knowledge. The role of infographics is to help us understand it.

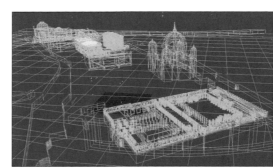
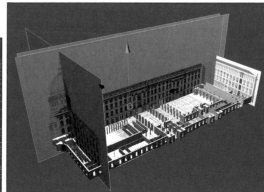

1 — Museum Island

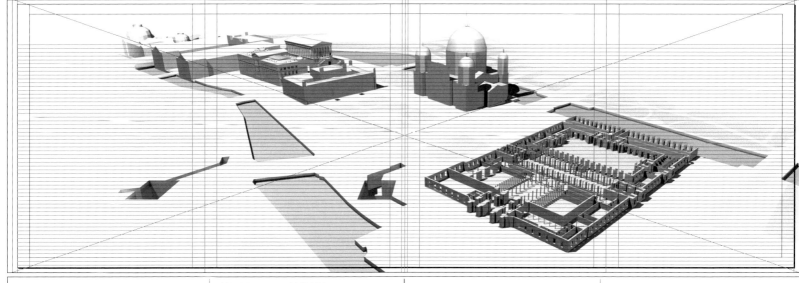

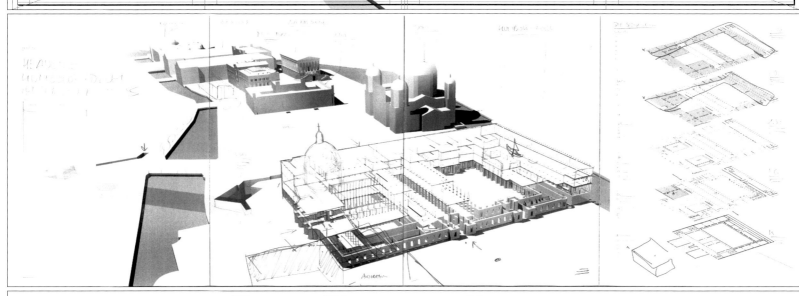

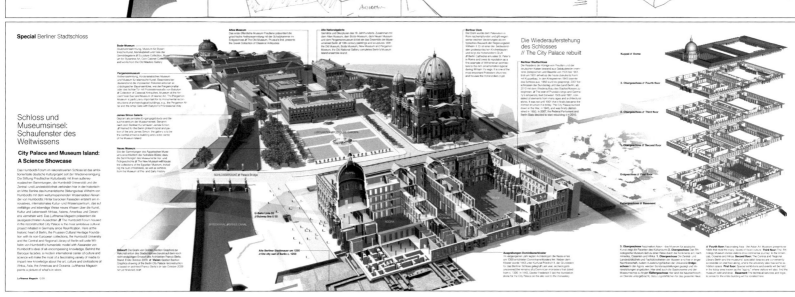

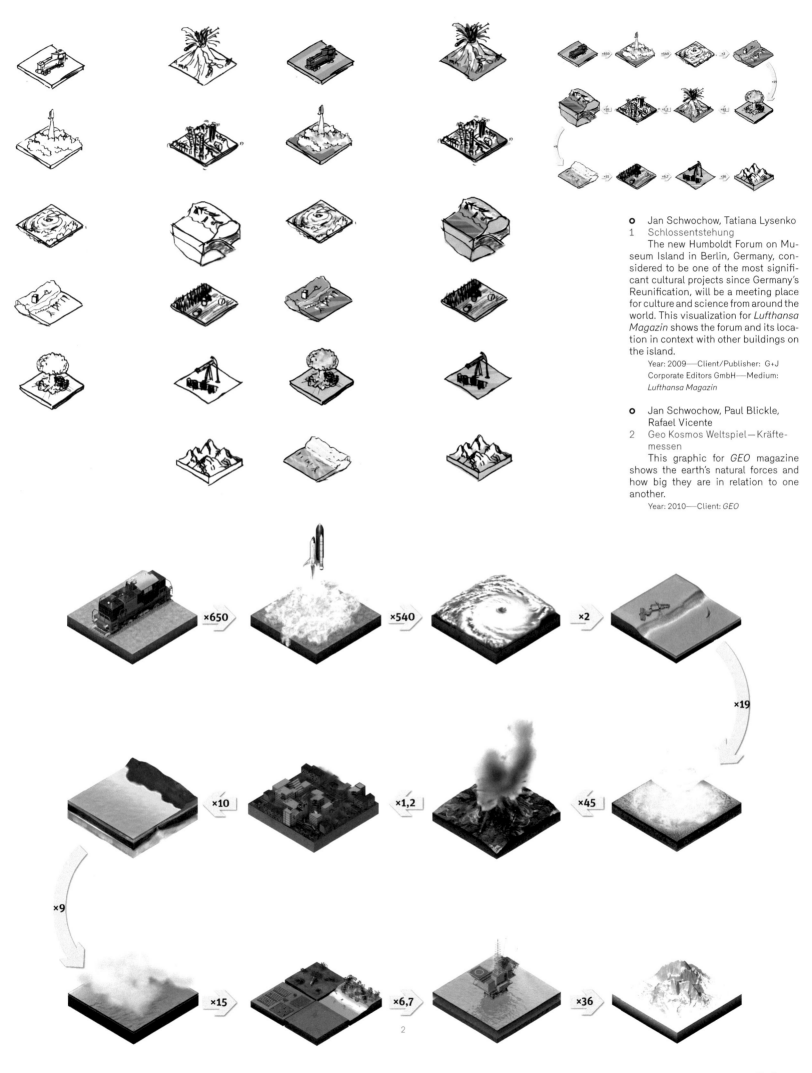

o   Jan Schwochow, Tatiana Lysenko
1   Schlossentstehung
    The new Humboldt Forum on Mu-
seum Island in Berlin, Germany, considered to be one of the most significant cultural projects since Germany's
Reunification, will be a meeting place
for culture and science from around the
world. This visualization for *Lufthansa
Magazin* shows the forum and its location in context with other buildings on
the island.
    Year: 2009—Client/Publisher: G+J
    Corporate Editors GmbH—Medium:
    Lufthansa Magazin

o   Jan Schwochow, Paul Blickle,
    Rafael Vicente
2   Geo Kosmos Weltspiel—Kräfte-
    messen
    This graphic for *GEO* magazine
shows the earth's natural forces and
how big they are in relation to one
another.
    Year: 2010—Client: *GEO*

AUTOBAHN
SPEED LIMITS IN A SELECTION OF COUNTRIES
// TEMPOLIMITS AUSGEWÄHLTER LÄNDER

traffic deaths per 100 000 inhabitants (2008) ▶
// Verkehrstote pro 100 000 Einwohner (2008)

term in native language ▶
// Bezeichnung in Landessprache

GERMAN TRAFFIC SIGNS
// DEUTSCHE VERKEHRSZEICHEN

speedlimit within towns
// Tempolimit innerorts

speedlimit outside built up areas
// Tempolimit auf Landstraßen

speedlimit highways
// Tempolimit auf Schnellstraßen

minimum speed on motorways
// Mindestgeschwindigkeit auf Autobahnen

maximum speed on motorways
// Höchstgeschwindigkeit auf Autobahnen

speed limits in km/h ▶
// Tempolimits in km/h

country // Land ▶

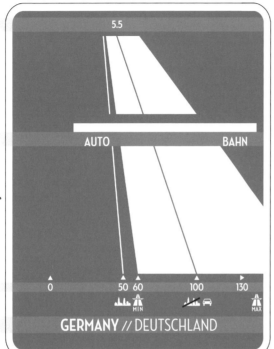

GERMANY // DEUTSCHLAND

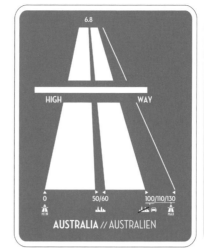

AUSTRALIA // AUSTRALIEN

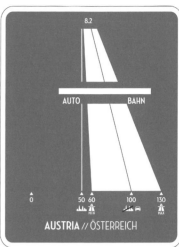

AUSTRIA // ÖSTERREICH

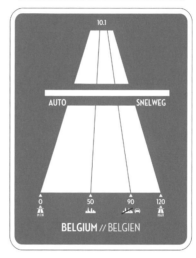

BELGIUM // BELGIEN

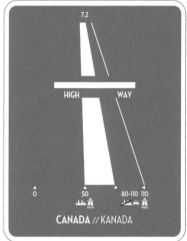

CANADA // KANADA

CZECH REPUBLIC // TSCHECHIEN

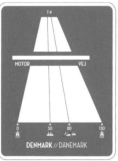

DENMARK // DANEMARK

FINLAND // FINNLAND

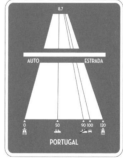

PORTUGAL

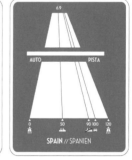

SPAIN // SPANIEN

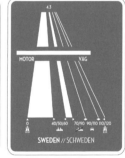

SWEDEN // SCHWEDEN

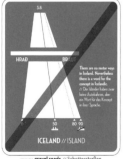

There are no motorways in Iceland. Nevertheless there is a word for the concept in Icelandic.
// Die Isländer haben zwar keine Autobahnen, aber ein Wort für das Konzept in ihrer Sprache.

ICELAND // ISLAND

gravel roads // Schotterstraßen

IRELAND // IRLAND

ISRAEL

SWITZERLAND // SCHWEIZ

LUXEMBOURG // LUXEMBURG

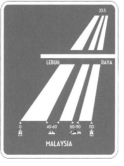

MALAYSIA

THE NETHERLANDS // NIEDERLANDE

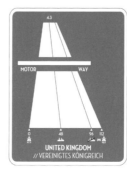

UNITED KINGDOM
// VEREINIGTES KÖNIGREICH

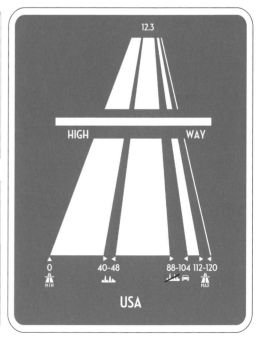

USA

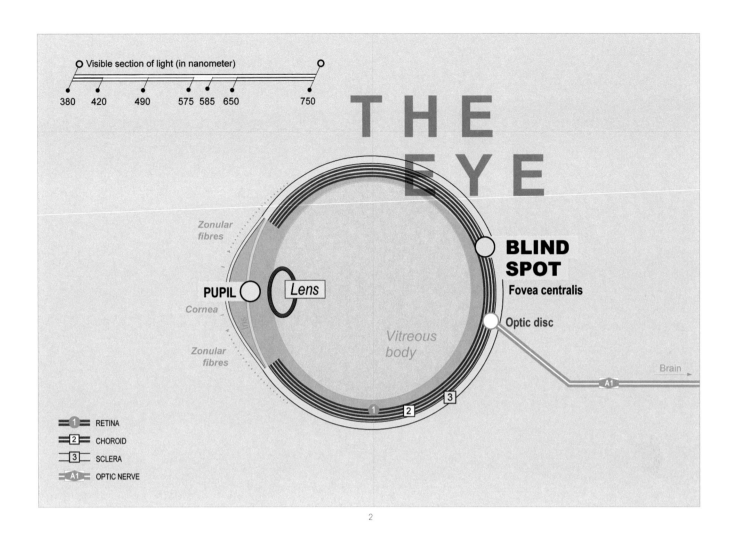

THE EYE

Visible section of light (in nanometer)

380 420 490 575 585 650 750

BLIND SPOT

Fovea centralis

Optic disc

PUPIL

Lens

Cornea

Iris

Zonular fibres

Zonular fibres

Vitreous body

Brain

|1| RETINA
|2| CHOROID
|3| SCLERA
|A1| OPTIC NERVE

2

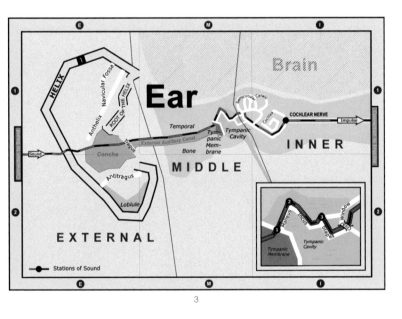

3

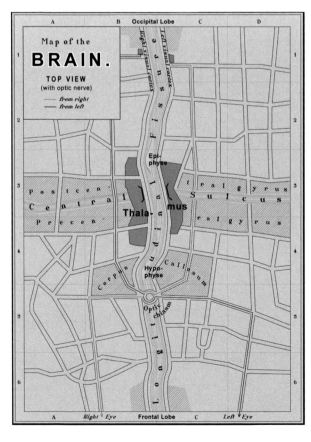

Map of the BRAIN.

TOP VIEW
(with optic nerve)

from right
from left

Occipital Lobe

Right Eye   Frontal Lobe   Left Eye

○ Jan Schwochow, Katharina Stipp,
  David Weinberg
1   Autobahn
    A graphic comparing highway
speed limits in countries across the
world including Germany, Canada,
Australia, Israel, and Malaysia. The
data also shows how many traffic
deaths per 100,000 inhabitants each
country has.
    Year: 2010—Client: *IN GRAPHICS* maga-
zine by Golden Section Graphics GmbH

○ Katja Günther
  Cartographic
2   Road Map of The Eye
3   Map of The Inner Ear
4   Map of The Brain (from 1930)
    Cartographic is a project that fo-
cuses on the visualization of information by mapping relevant elements.
These maps illustrate parts of the human anatomy and its micro- and macro
surroundings.

Visual Storyteller

JAN SCHWOCHOW

○ Jan Schwochow,
Lukas Engelhardt
1 Visual Music
   Visualization of chord progressions and lyrics in music.
   Year: 2011—Client: *IN GRAPHICS* Vol. 02 magazine by Golden Section Graphics GmbH

○ Jan Schwochow, Katharina Stipp
2 Terror in Numbers
   The World Trade Center was first attacked in 1993. This graphic show the number of terrorism victims since that year as well as soldier fatalities from subsequent wars.
   Year: 2011—Client: *IN GRAPHICS* Vol. 02 magazine by Golden Section Graphics GmbH

○ Jan Schwochow, Lukas Engelhardt, Katja Günther, Bernd Riedel
3 The Average Anthem/Landowncountryhomegod
   The national anthems from 32 different countries were averaged based on key and rhythm; from this average, a new "average anthem" was composed. The lyrics of each anthem were then analyzed for common themes, resulting in the title *Landowncountryhomegod*, which lists the most common themes in order of frequency.
   Year: 2010/2011—Client: *IN GRAPHICS* Vol. 01 magazine by Golden Section Graphics GmbH

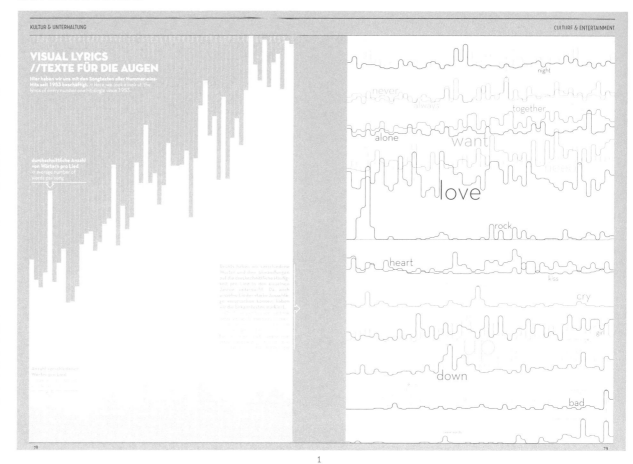

1

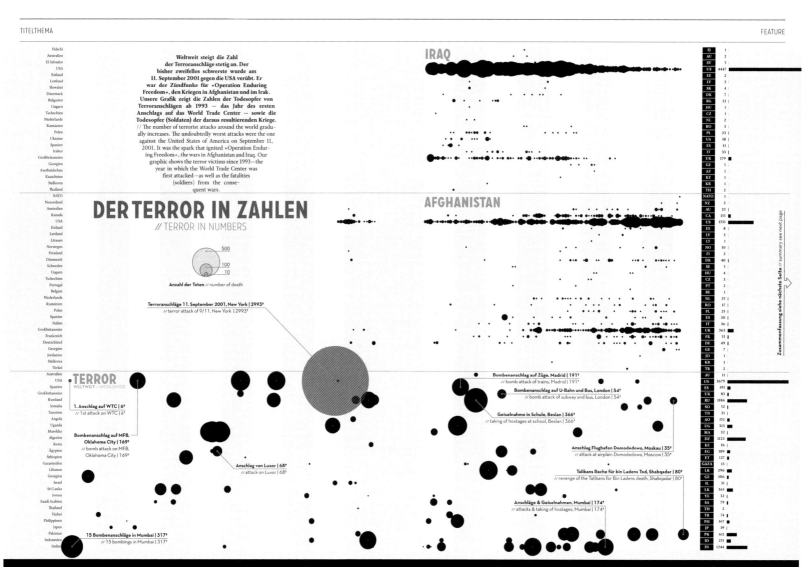

2

LANDOWNCOUNTRYHOMEGOD

generated by the national anthems of // ermittelt durch die Nationalhymnen von
**USA, CAN, GRL, ISL, NOR, SWE, FIN, RUS, GBR, BEL, GER, NED, AUT, SUI, HUN, FRA, ITA,
TUR, POR, NZL, AFG, IRQ, EGY, RSA, ARG, BRA, PAR, URU, BOL, PER, CUB, MEX**

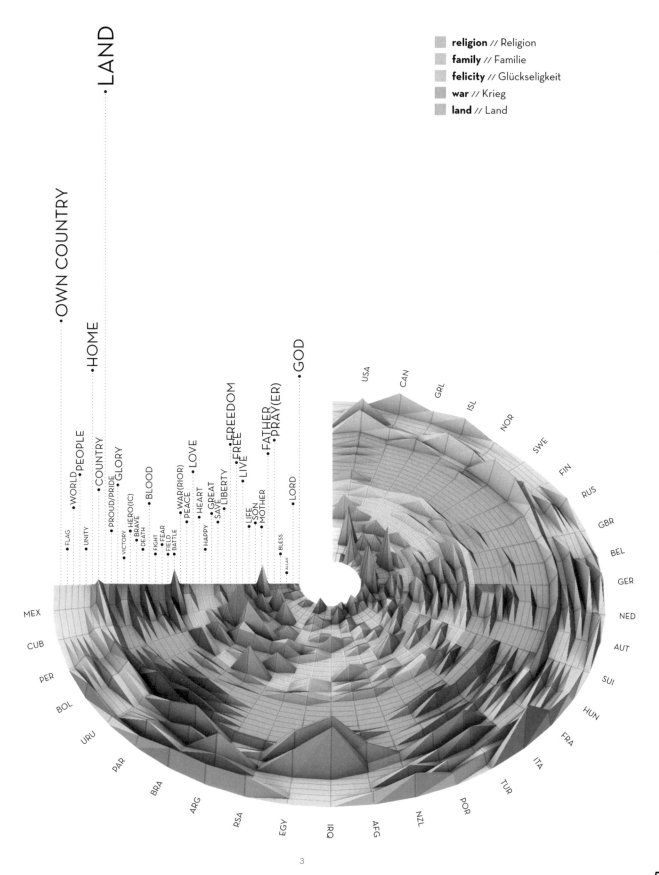

religion // Religion
family // Familie
felicity // Glückseligkeit
war // Krieg
land // Land

Francesco Franchi

Francesco Franchi is the art director of *IL – Intelligence in Lifestyle,* the monthly news magazine of the Italian finance newspaper *Il Sole 24 ORE.*

⊙ *www.francescofranchi.com*

Why did you decide to include infographics in the magazine?

It's simple. I believe in infographics. Firstly because, in contemporary society, the technology of communication is undergoing a huge change, embracing multiple visual and written styles. The biggest challenge right now is how to combine all of these, in order to increase understanding.

Secondly, because infographics are a good tool for a magazine, as they are both informative and entertaining. Aesthetics have become an increasingly important consideration when conveying messages.

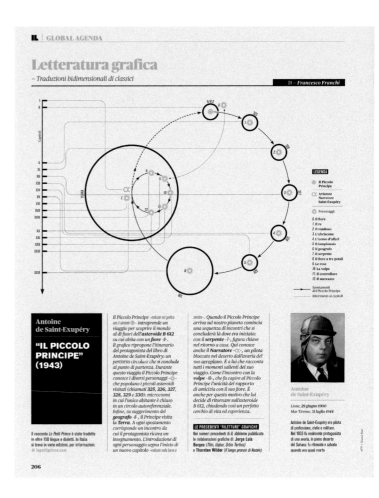

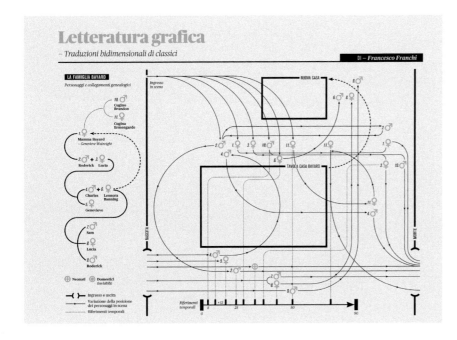

Letteratura Grafica

The column *Letteratura Grafica,* published in the journal *IL – Intelligence in Lifestyle,* is an attempt to translate some works of classical literature into a nonlinear format using two dimensional graphics and maps. The goal is to produce synoptic maps, which allow the relationships between the elements of literary narrative to be easily seen, revealing the complex relationships in a clear format.

Year: 2008–2009—Publisher: *IL – Intelligence in Lifestyle*

How do you choose the themes?

The idea behind each image is that we talk about soft news as if it was hard news, in a serious, journalistic style that aims to be both informative and elegant. We prioritize lifestyle themes, because *IL* is dedicated to contemporary trends and consumer interests, and so we often use current events as a way of interpreting lifestyle changes. However, we have also created infographic spreads about foreign affairs, including an economic and political report on Iran. Sometimes, we also do pages with a more technical and scientific approach or graphics related to the environment and sustainability.

How do you make the infographics?

We soon realized that the perfect team for these pages is made up of an information designer, an editor and an illustrator. Each of them works on a specific stage of the process. They must filter the information, establish relationships, discern patterns and represent all of this in a way that allows the consumer of that information to process and digest knowledge in a meaningful way.

We always start with a journalistic idea. Once the abstract is fixed, we research all the data and then we sort them according to a storyboard. The amount of information we are trying to convey forces us to be careful about how we organize the space on the page.

Each graphic is made up of a flow of individual elements that we label, integrate and prioritize. If we feel that a particular illustration could be a key element that will help explain the data, we will ask the illustrator to work on a specific portion of the page, to help us contextualize the rest of the piece, and to make the page more appealing. The final result should be an enjoyable, accessible and appropriate experience for our readers while also being aesthetically appealing.

Does the color of the paper in *IL* affect the designs?

Yes, a lot. The background color of our pages is printed on, and this is a great advantage because this means that we can use white as well. A white background sometimes makes the page more flat, while working with a color in the background helps to create more dynamism in the image.

How have the infographics been received by your readers?

In Italy, is not so common to see infographic spreads inside a magazine. For this reason, it was quite easy to make our product seem different by placing the emphasis on the informational design aspect of the piece. We try to merge design, content, and visual thinking. It seems to work.

How would you describe your infographic style?

Simplicity, above all, is the key to an effective infographic. The best way to achieve simplicity is through the intelligent reduction of the elements and objects that distract from the key message.

I usually try to create dense and structured pages. I'm accustomed to working with type and a grid, as well as with a limited color palette, to create distinctive layouts that the reader can recognize.

I always try to create different layers of reading. The main visual impact of the page is important, but we have to give the reader the opportunity to go deeper into the page, in order to discover curious details that we include —such as when we used the page number itself as an infographic tool.

How do you balance the graphic needs of the page with the information being portrayed?

I see visual language as a spectrum. On one side you have illustration; on the other side you have information. Personally, I think that works that are too close to either end of the spectrum (too arty or too utilitarian) are rarely interesting.

While you can say that infographics are a product of the imagination of the designer, they should not be works of art. Applying a graphic style to the information is not nearly as important as giving a graphic form to the content, with a clear understanding of how that content will then be perceived and processed by an audience.

What makes a successful infographic?

The best solutions are those that are both aesthetically appealing and easily understood. First comes the journalistic idea behind it, and then the balance of the design between simplicity and complexity. However, design is not just about making things simple, it's also about innovation, stimulation and creating a satisfying and provocative solution.

By allowing data to shape their vision, designers have to reach a level of complexity that allows just the right amount of contrast to drive profile, focus, and definition. What that level is depends on the visual literacy of the intended audience.

However, the latest software offers a dazzling amount of tools to give shape and meaning to massive amounts of data. We have to be careful that a tool does not become the message, and that we still allow the possibility of serendipity to point us to new ways of thinking.

What makes a good designer?

A good designer has to work with editors to create the best-possible end product. Form and content have to co-exist and work cohesively together to deliver a result that is enjoyable, useful and informative. Design does not necessarily mean something beautiful. Beauty in design is evoked when a harmonious creation emerges directly from the logic, function and usefulness of the object.

Editorial design, because it is a form of journalistic expression, acts as a vivid cultural snapshot of the era in which it is produced. Magazines printed in the 1960s, for example, not only evoked the visual vibrancy of the decade, but also captured the spirit of an age that celebrated experimentation, innovation, and new directions.

At its very best, designing for editorial content is an exciting and constantly evolving launching pad for stylistic innovation. In this particular editorial moment, a good designer must continue to learn, experiment, and be willing to embrace new experiences with an open mind.

What visual storytellers do you admire?

Above all, I admire the work done by Otto Neurath and Gerd Arntz, more commonly known as Isotype, between 1925 and 1934. Neurath developed the notion of transformation to describe the process of analyzing, selecting, ordering, and then making information, data, ideas and implications into visual objects.

Today, my main reference points are the infographic departments of the *New York Times,* because Steve Duenes and his team of editors are always raising the level and the quality of work all over the world; and Nicholas Felton, because of his infographic explorations that redefine the borders of our personal and our public personae, shaping our habits and attitudes, desires and needs, and our values.

1   La Babele Delle Birre
Consumption, prices, taxation, and restrictions; a status report about the world of beer.
Year: 2010—Client: *IL—Intelligence in lifestyle*—Illustrator: Laura Cattaneo—Editor: Alessandro Giberti

2   Ladri di Lamette
How much are the world's retailers losing to retail crime? This infographic seeks to answer that question as well as who is doing the stealing, which products are most at risk of being stolen, and how much money is spent on preventing theft each year (answer: 26.8 billion dollars). It turns out that accessories and children's wear are the most often stolen in the apparel sector, while meats do the most of the disappearing in grocery stores. Retailers in India, Morocco, and Brazil need to keep the tightest eye on the security of their products; shopkeepers in Austria, Hong Kong, and Taiwan can rest a little easier.
Year: 2011—Client: *IL—Intelligence in lifestyle*—Illustrator: Francesco Muzzi—Editor: Elena Montobbio

3   Fai le Fusa, Persiano
A world status report about Iran.
Year: 2010—Client: *IL—Intelligence in lifestyle*—Illustrator: Laura Cattaneo \\\ Editor: Alessandro Giberti

4   Altro Che Disarmo
A world status report about military spending and armaments.
Year: 2010—Client: *IL—Intelligence in lifestyle*—Illustrator: Laura Cattaneo \\\ Editor: Sara Deganello

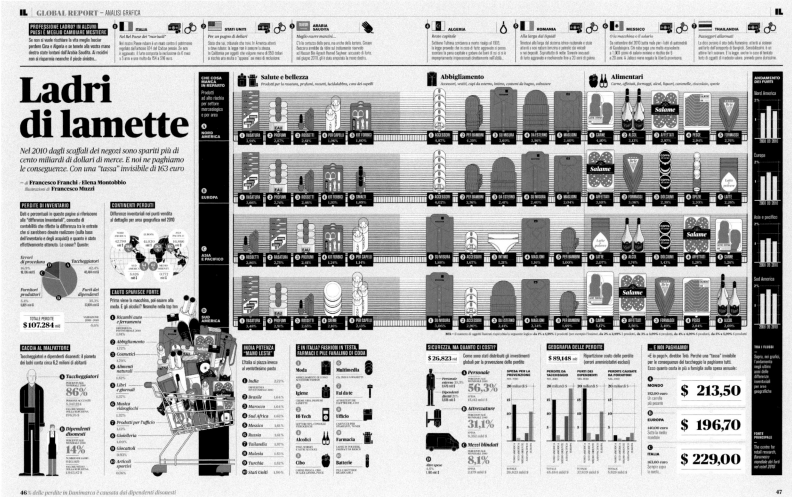

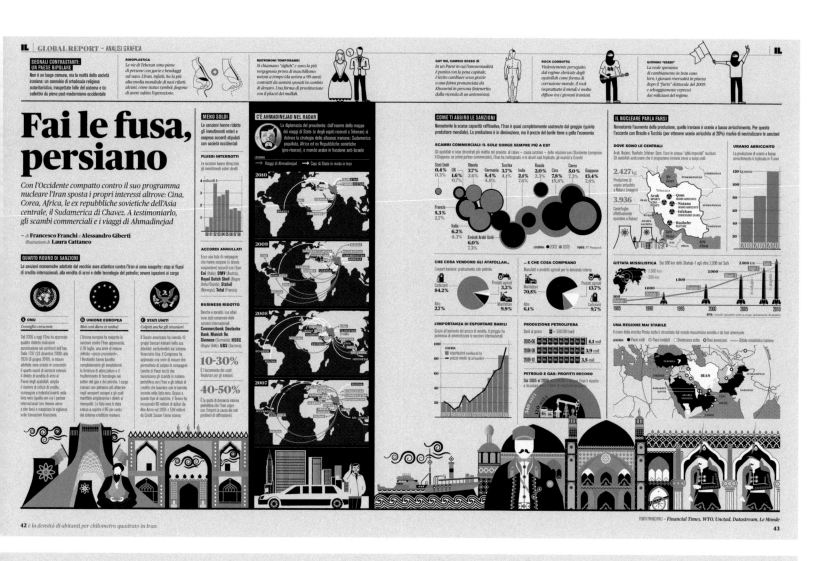

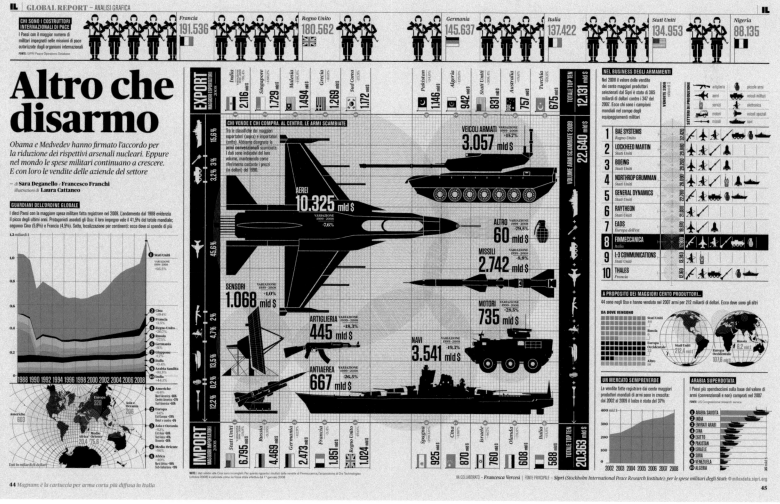

1 — Various Sketches

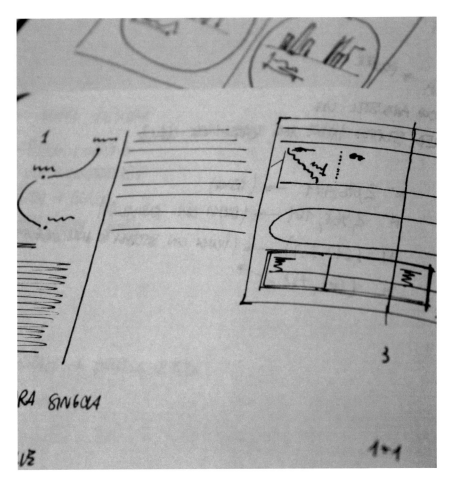

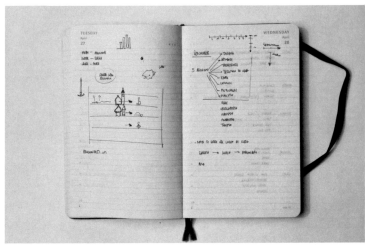

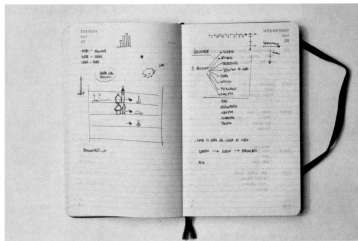

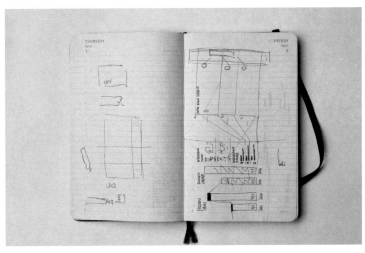

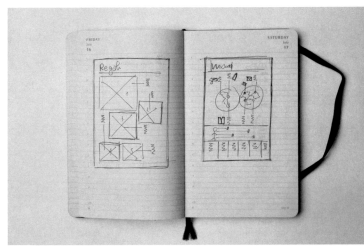

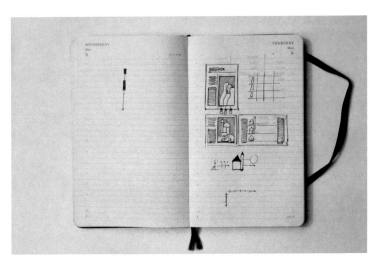

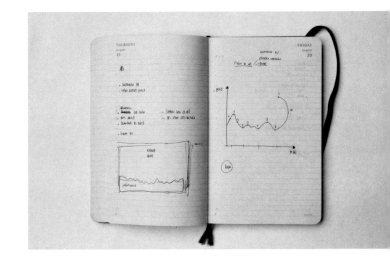

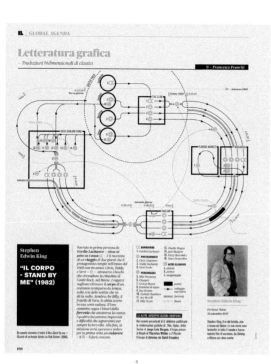

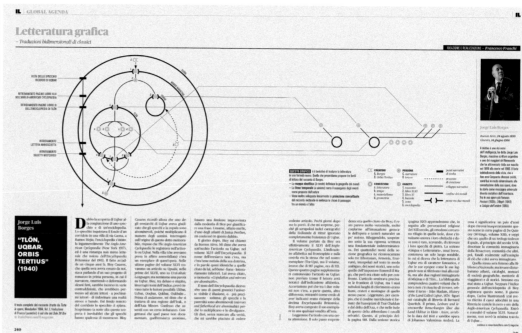

1

2

1,2 Letteratura Grafica
The column *Letteratura Grafi-ca,* published in the journal *IL – Intelligence in Lifestyle,* is an attempt to translate some works of classical literature into a nonlinear format using two dimensional graphics and maps. The goal is to produce synoptic maps, which allow the relationships between the elements of literary narrative to be easily seen, revealing the complex relationships in a clear format.
Year: 2008–2009—Client: *IL—Intelligence in lifestyle*

3 Partitura Grafica
An attempt to translate music into a two-dimensional graphic.
Year: 2009—Client: *IL—Intelligence in lifestyle*—Designer: Davide Di Gennaro—Illustrator: Laura Cattaneo—Editor: Giovanni Albini

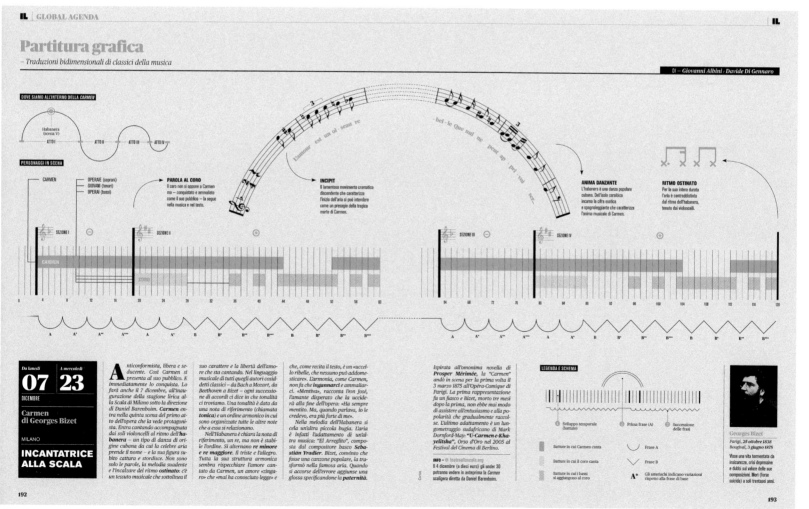

3

Part

B

Visual

STORIES

26%
Have changed their behaviour because
of gang related crime

55%
Have not changed behaviour because
of the gang related crime

Peter Ørntoft, *Information Graphics In Context,* 2010

Seeing the News

Chapter

1

Seeing

the NEWS

To people whose minds go blank when they hear something ending in "illion", all big numbers are the same, so exponential explosions make no difference. Such an inability to relate to large numbers is clearly bad for society. It leads people to ignore big issues on the grounds that they are incomprehensible.

○ Douglas HOFSTADLER, *Metamagical Themas*

1

GARETH HOLT /
BEN BRANAGAN
1   Human Development Index
Rank: Picturing the Social Order
1516–2009
The United Nations developed a ranking system for every country in the world that incorporates life expectancy and adult literacy with economic welfare and well-being. The countries at the top and bottom of this scale are graphically shown using campaign badges, which can be used as tools of democracy or injustice. → 74–75
Year: 2009—Client: Northern Gallery of Contemporary Art

XAVIER BARRADE
2   Le Spectacle
One thousand fluorescent retail pricing labels were used to create this dynamic, graph-like sculpture, which hangs suspended from the ceiling.
Year: 2010—Support from: Apli-Agipa

2

Our relationship with news reporting has changed fundamentally over the past decade. Today, we often learn about events via a variety of unconfirmed social media sources, turning to the mainstream in order that it summarize, analyze and validate the information.

This means that the mainstream media, in particular in print, now has to work harder to find original ways of interpreting an event. In many cases, large news publishers are devoting increasing resources to produce highly crafted visuals on a regular basis, providing context and explanation in ways that citizen journalists can't match—albeit also having to satisfy publishers' demands for print, online and iPad-compatible graphics.

The *New York Times,* which contains one of the largest and most highly lauded news visualization operations in the world, labels its visual storytellers not by their tools (designer, illustrator) but as graphic editors. It has on occasions sent its staff out on assignment, alongside text-based journalists and photographers, to newsworthy locations including Afghanistan. The visual journalist's remit is to gather data, and to report, just like the others, on what is happening. The only difference is the nature of their output—and the time and budget often required to produce quality work.

However, the field of news-themed visual storytelling is not only populated by those with the backing of a fully-staffed newsroom. Using many of the same visualization tools as the professionals, and often basing their work on the same publicly available data sets, unaffiliated designers are tackling stories in their own way, revealing new narratives through different visual interpretations without the limitations of an in-house style.

Some of these visualizations are side projects, centered on a personally significant theme that they feel deserves more attention. Others may be primarily aimed towards bringing attention to their own talents.

A great piece of visual storytelling, particularly one whose accompanying text is written in English, can reach a wide audience, no matter what its origin. Just as we may learn about a newsworthy event on Facebook or Twitter, so successful visualizations of whatever provenance are themselves circulated, blogged, Tumblred, Flickred. The news belongs to nobody, and to everybody.

The visualizations in this chapter use a broad range of imagery, aimed towards very different audiences.

Some, such as *National Geographic's* stunning map of oil exploration in the Gulf of Mexico following the Deepwater Horizon tragedy, adopt a formal visual style, as befits the nature of their publication.

This particular infographic, which showcases the enormous scale of oil-based activity in the region, reframes the Deepwater Horizon oil platform as a tiny dot among hundreds. It allows the viewer to impose their own emotion on the facts, its principle role being to give a new understanding to the event's wider, near-overwhelming context. The graphic was awarded Best in Show at the Malofiej infographics awards in 2011.

A different emotional reaction comes from reading Jan Hartwig's *50 Days—Interrogation Log Detainee 063*. He has taken a single person's story, as related in the prisoner reports from Guantanamo Bay, and abstracted it into a series of dehumanising graphs. A simple plotting of time against frequency of the words "The detainee began to cry" is more chillingly effective than any attempt to add further emotion to the already traumatic source material.

Simplicity is used to political ends in Pitch Interactive's *US Federal Contract Spending, 2009,* 2010. It manages a neat double trick—showing first how much money was spent on defense, and then with a deft flip of the graph, it makes another societal model seem entirely feasible.

Visual complexity, however, is a feature of Lorenzo Petrantoni's typically elaborate piece on the Middle East, a feast of surface visual decoration with a depth of news-related content almost hidden in plain sight. The overwhelming confusion of words and images, surrounded by more traditional decoration, convey some of the hopelessness of the situation. His work has been featured in many publications around the world, including the cover of *Time* and *Newsweek* magazines.

A growing trend in visual explanation seems to be the exploration of using real-world objects to represent precise data. A single headscarf cleverly hides within it a precise graph about immigration. A series of forks are in fact a carefully measured bar chart on wealth and food. Bread, standing on end, is a way of discussing the market for grain and baking. A feast table laid out with vessels red liquid is a stomach-churning showcase of blood spilt in 20th-century wars. The real world, seen through a particular lens, can be an abstraction itself.

Finally, Sosolimited's *Prime Numbers* point towards a dynamic future for visual storytelling. Projected live during the prime ministerial debate in the UK, it grabbed the words and phrases from each participant, showing how the use of abstract nouns avoided clear argument.

Though the narrative was automatically generated, it succeeded in achieving the higher goal of news-related visual storytelling: giving the viewer a whole new way of seeing the world around them.

69

57%
Are very afraid of being in specific places because of gang related crime

26%
Are somewhat afraid of being in specific places because of gang related crime

16%
Are not afraid of being in any specific places in spite of gang related crime

18%
Have changed their behaviour a lot because of gang related crime

26%
Have changed their behaviour because of gang related crime

55%
Have not changed behaviour because of the gang related crime

PETER ØRNTOFT
Information Graphics In Context
This project illustrates a ranked list of social concerns in Denmark. Using data from a poll conducted by a major Danish consultancy company, the diagrams were shaped and designed according to the context of specific polls within each concern. Providing context allows the reader to understand multiple layers of information about the data. The usual use of photography for the infographic creates a direct link from abstract data to everyday life.

Year: 2010—University project—Client: The Danish Design School, Copenhagen, Denmark

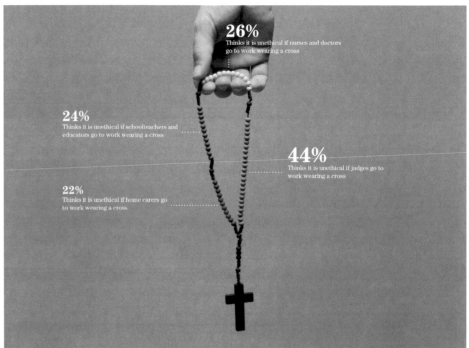

26%
Thinks it is unethical if nurses and doctors go to work wearing a cross

24%
Thinks it is unethical if schoolteachers and educators go to work wearing a cross

44%
Thinks it is unethical if judges go to work wearing a cross

22%
Thinks it is unethical if home carers go to work wearing a cross

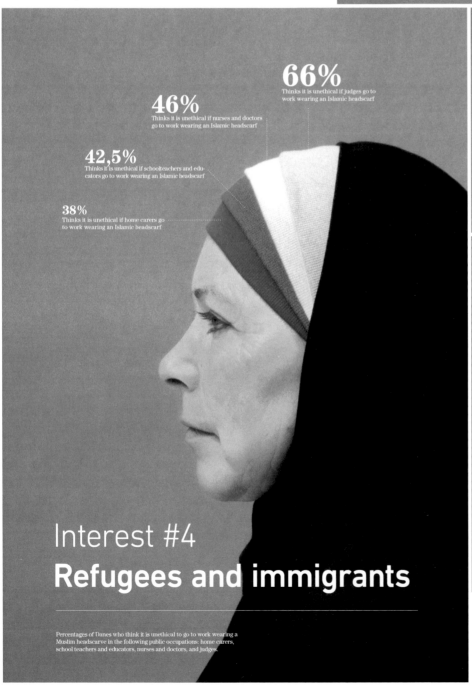

66%
Thinks it is unethical if judges go to work wearing an Islamic headscarf

46%
Thinks it is unethical if nurses and doctors go to work wearing an Islamic headscarf

42,5%
Thinks it is unethical if schoolteachers and educators go to work wearing an Islamic headscarf

38%
Thinks it is unethical if home carers go to work wearing an Islamic headscarf

Interest #4
Refugees and immigrants

Percentages of Danes who think it is unethical to go to work wearing a Muslim headscarve in the following public occupations: home carers, school teachers and educators, nurses and doctors, and judges.

64%
Thinks it is unethical if judges go to work wearing a Jewish yarmulke

46,5%
Thinks it is unethical if nurses and doctors go to work wearing a Jewish yarmulke

40%
Thinks it is unethical if home carers go to work wearing a Jewish yarmulke

42%
thinks it is unethical if schoolteachers and educators go to work wearing a Jewish yarmulke

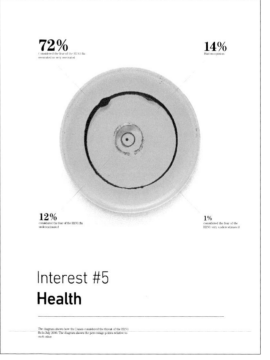

72%
Considered the fear of the H1N1 flu overstated or very overstated

14%
Had no opinion

12%
considered the fear of the H1N1 flu understated

1%
considered the fear of the H1N1 flu very understated

Interest #5
Health

The diagram shows how the Danes considered the threat of the H1N1 flu in July 2010. The diagram shows the percentage points relative to each other.

CLARA KAYSER-BRIL,
NICOLAS KAYSER-BRIL,
MARION KOTLARSKI
100 Years of World Cuisine

100 Years of World Cuisine attempts to visualize the deaths caused by wars and conflicts throughout history. The data is represented by glass containers filled with blood, set out on a kitchen table. Studio photography emphasized the realism of the image, giving new meaning to numbers that had lost their significance. The picture went viral; it was viewed 40,000 times in 10 days.

Year: 2011

100 years of world cuisine

38,000,000 deaths   25 conflicts   1915 - present

100yearsofworldcuisine.com

Sudanese civil war
1983-2005
2,200,000 †

Biafran war
1967-70
1,000,000 †

Nor▓
1990-
2,000

Congo wars
1998-2003
3,900,000 †

Gulag system
1929-53
1,600,000 †

Wars in Indo
1945-75
6,000,000 †

Korea war
1950-53
3,500,000 †

Armenian genocide
1915-16
1,500,000 †

Afghanistan
2001-ongoing
40,000 †

Immigration to Europe
1988-ongoing
15,000 †

Mexican drug war
2006-ongoing
30,000 †

Europe 36%

Africa 24%

Visualized
38m

Not visualized
162m

...mine

Stalingrad
1942-43
1,520,000 †

Iraq
2003-2010
100,000 †

Khmer genocide
1975-79
3,000,000 †

Romas
1941-45
200,000 †

Holocaust
1941-45
5,000,000 †

Expulsion of Germans after WW2
1944-45
500,000 †

...eli conflict
950-ongoing
51,000 †

...n wars
...-ongoing
...0,000 †

Yugoslav wars
1991-95
130,000 †

Algeria war
1954-62
960,000 †

9/11 attacks
2001
2,997 †

Rwandan genocide
1994
1,000,000 †

Iran-Iraq war
1980-88
500,000 †

Partition of India
1947
500,000 †

BREAKING NEWS

GARETH HOLT,
BEN BRANAGAN
1   Rich List
2   Socio-Professional Classification
3   Socio-Economic Classification of
     Working Population
   These images are part of a series
of 13 charts and graphs created for the
traveling exhibition *Rank: Picturing
The Social Order 1516 – 2009*. Each image was created in response to statistical data exploring different aspects of
social hierarchies. The data was visually presented with objects that reference ways of signifying social groups
such as clothing and silverware.
   Year: 2009——Client: Northern Gallery of
Contemporary Art

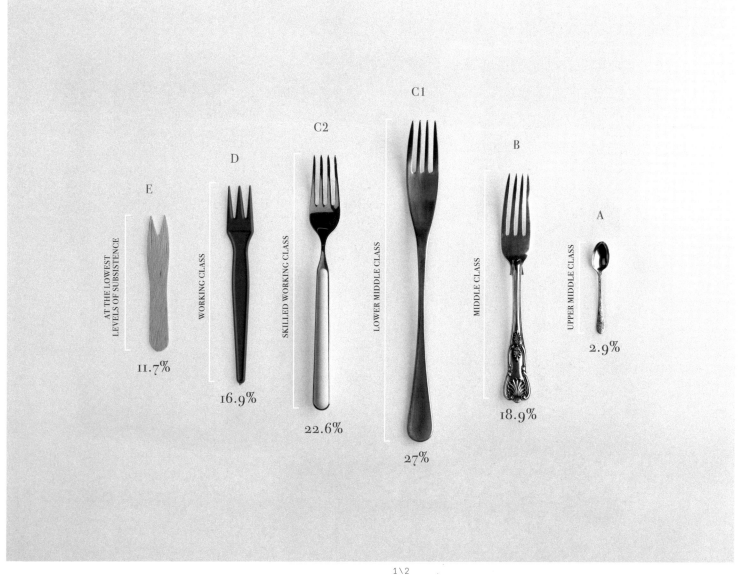

1 \ 2

HIGHER
MANAGERIAL
& PROFESSIONAL
OCCUPATIONS

10.2%

LOWER
MANAGERIAL
& PROFESSIONAL
OCCUPATIONS

21.9%

INTERMEDIATE
OCCUPATIONS

10.4%

SMALL EMPLOYERS
& OWN ACCOUNT
WORKERS

7.3%

LOWER SUPERVISORY
& TECHNICAL
OCCUPATIONS

9.6%

SEMI ROUTINE
OCCUPATIONS

13.0%

ROUTINE
OCCUPATIONS

10.2%

LONG TERM
UNEMPLOYED

17.5%

SARAH ILLENBERGER
Campaign for PSC,
Socialist Party of Catalonia
Year: 2010—Client: PSC,
Socialist Party of Catalonia

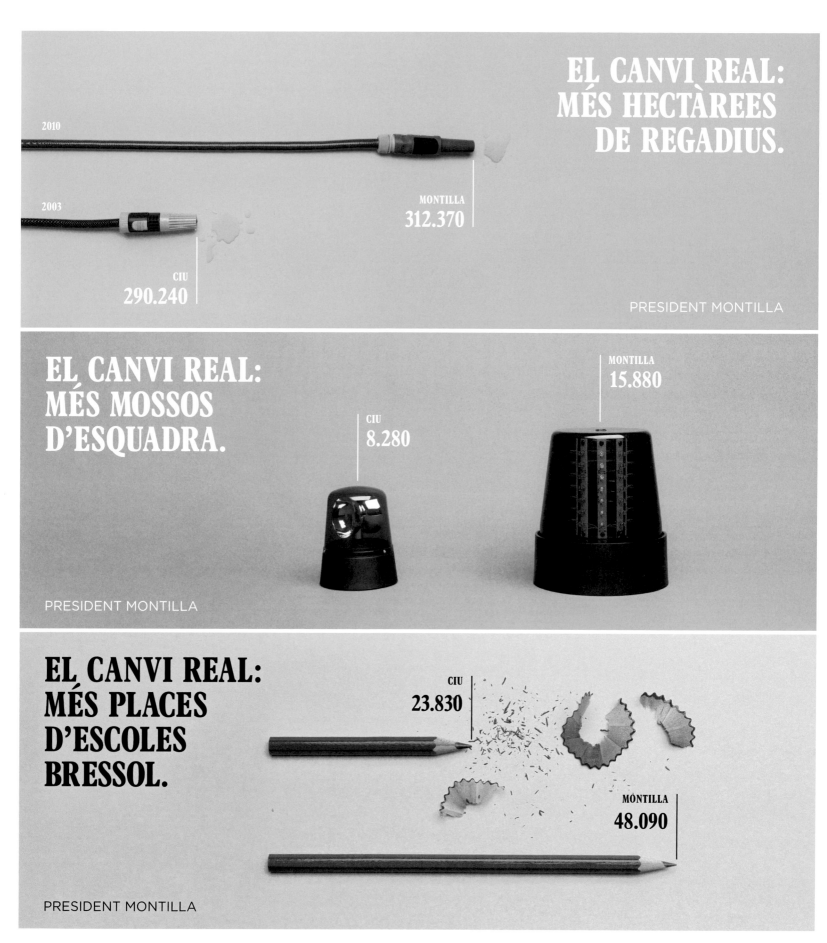

**EL CANVI REAL:
MÉS HECTÀREES
DE REGADIUS.**

2010

2003

MONTILLA
312.370

CIU
290.240

PRESIDENT MONTILLA

**EL CANVI REAL:
MÉS MOSSOS
D'ESQUADRA.**

MONTILLA
15.880

CIU
8.280

PRESIDENT MONTILLA

**EL CANVI REAL:
MÉS PLACES
D'ESCOLES
BRESSOL.**

CIU
23.830

MONTILLA
48.090

PRESIDENT MONTILLA

This campaign for the Socialist Party of Catalonia was built on their slogan "a real change." The colors red and blue run consistently through the images, coloring objects that represent the records of the PSC and the Catalan Nationalist Coalition, the CiU (Convergència i Unió).

EL CANVI REAL: MÉS MILIONS D'EUROS PACTATS AMB L'ESTAT.

CIU
290

MONTILLA
2.150

PRESIDENT MONTILLA

EL CANVI REAL: MÉS QUILÒMETRES DE METRO.

MONTILLA
52

CIU
24

2010

2003

PRESIDENT MONTILLA

EL CANVI REAL: MÉS KM D'AUTOVIES SENSE PEATGE.

MONTILLA
250

CIU
170

PRESIDENT MONTILLA

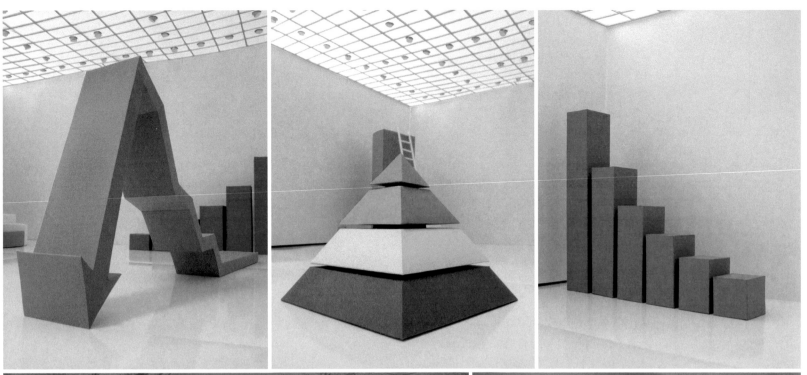

XAVIER BARRADE
Retrospective
Retrospective is an art practice that only exists through pictures made from 3D imaging software and textures and images found on the internet. *Retrospective* is also a book that presents the work in this practice.
Year: 2010 – ongoing

Visual Stories

KIRCHERBURKHARDT

1   The Lonely President (detail)
     The dominoes at the periphery are starting to topple, symbolizing the erosion of the United States as a super power as it is in deep crisis and in danger of collapse.
     Year: 2010—Client: *Handelsblatt*

BREAKING NEWS

XAVIER BARRADE

2   Diagrams
     An American flag created as part of a series of diagrams.
     Year: 2009

1

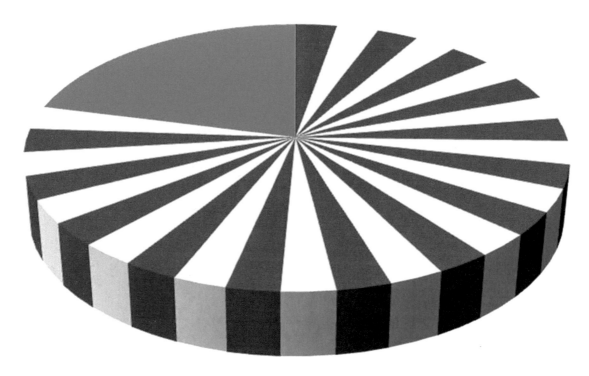

2

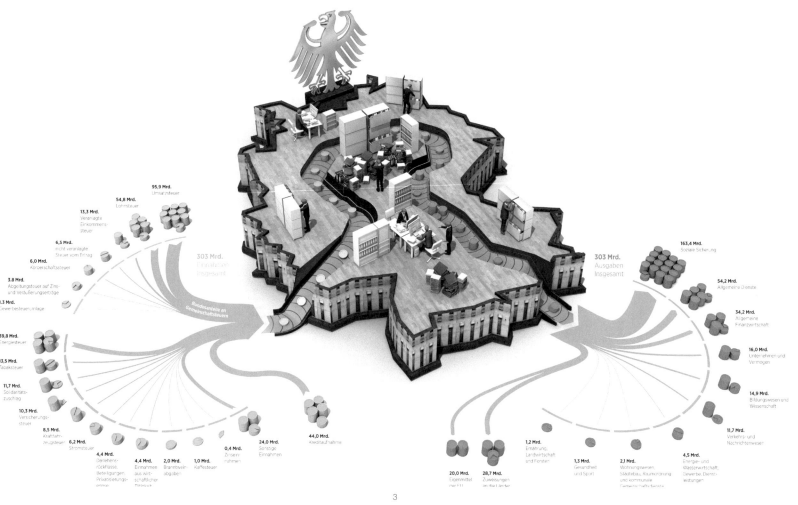

3

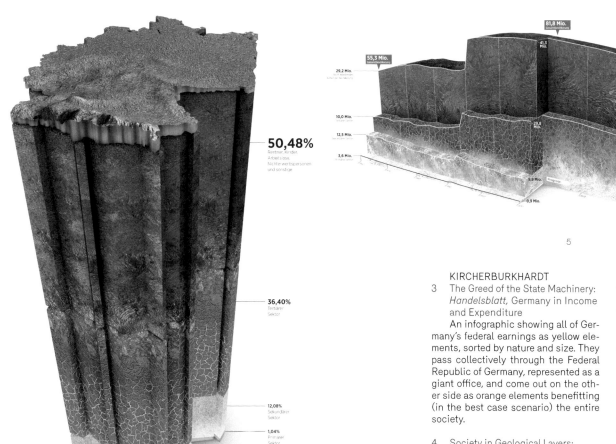

50,48%
Rentner, Kinder,
Arbeclose,
Nichterwertspersonen
und sonstige

36,40%
Tertiärer
Sektor

12,08%
Sekundärer
Sektor

1,04%
Primärer
Sektor

KIRCHER
BURKHARDT
KONZEPT/GRAFIK: Handelsblatt/
KircherBurkhardt Infografie
QUELLE: Handelsblatt Research

4

5

KIRCHERBURKHARDT

3 The Greed of the State Machinery: *Handelsblatt,* Germany in Income and Expenditure

An infographic showing all of Germany's federal earnings as yellow elements, sorted by nature and size. They pass collectively through the Federal Republic of Germany, represented as a giant office, and come out on the other side as orange elements benefitting (in the best case scenario) the entire society.

4 Society in Geological Layers: *Handelsblatt,* Germany Extruded

This image attempts to use geological layers as a metaphor for Germany's job sectors. Manufacturing, considered to be the most important element, is represented by the molten core. The service sector and agriculture and forestry industries are in the middle because of their important but subordinate roles to manufacturing. The non-productive populace, seen as supported by the sectors below it, is illustrated as the outer crust.

5 The Fight for Expansion Pays-off: *Handelsblatt,* 3D Line Drawing

The graphic shows the present day German job market and its prognosis for the coming decades. The yellow layer represents many people work in the agriculture, forestry, and manufacturing industries. These fuel the lava, or red layer, which represents the service sector. The cool lava, represented in black, symbolizes the portion of the populace such as pensioners and children that are not economically productive and rely on the other layers for economic support.

Year: 2011—Client: *Handelsblatt*

81

PITCH INTERACTIVE
U.S. Federal Contract
Spending in 2009

"Visualizing America", a contest hosted by The Sunlight Foundation, challenged participants to explore new ways to visualize government data. Using information from the website USAspending.gov, Pitch Interactive created two graphics that show just how much America's defense spending dwarfs all other contract spending.

Year: 2010—Client: Sunlight Foundation—Concept, Creative Direction: Wesley Grubbs—Programming: Nick Yahnke

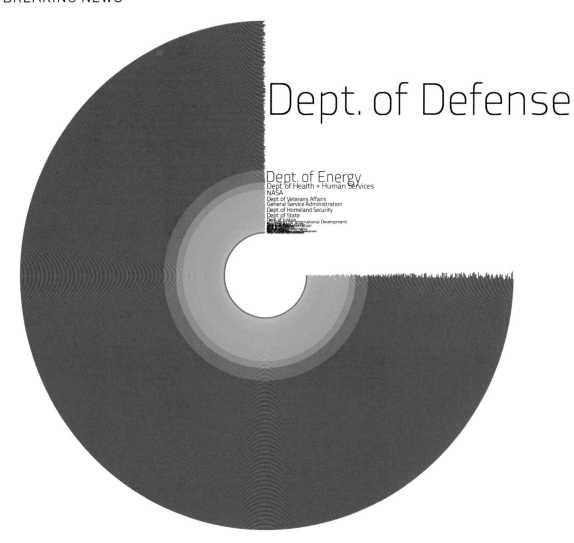

Dept. of Defense

Dept. of Energy
Dept. of Health + Human Services
NASA
Dept. of Veterans Affairs
General Service Administration
Dept. of Homeland Security
Dept. of State

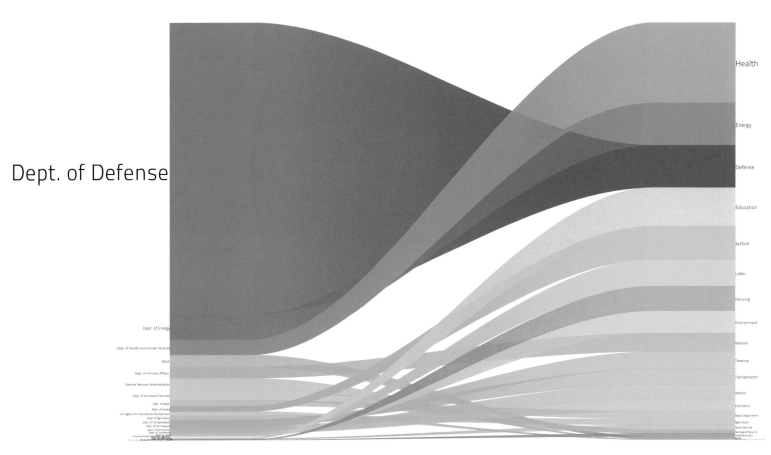

Dept. of Defense

Health
Energy
Defense
Education
Justice
Labor
Housing
Environment
Veteran
Treasury
Transportation
Interior
Commerce
State Department
Agriculture
Social Security
Homeland Security
Small Business

COPING WITH CRISIS
As Income Declines

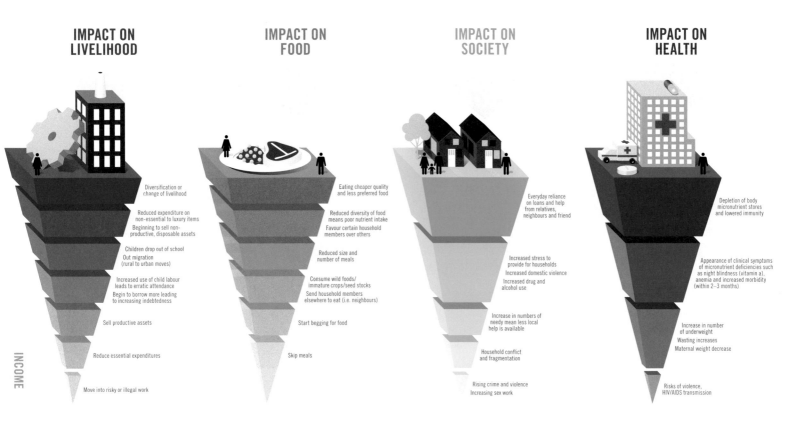

IMPACT ON LIVELIHOOD

INCOME

Diversification or change of livelihood

Reduced expenditure on non-essential to luxury items

Beginning to sell non-productive, disposable assets

Children drop out of school

Out migration (rural to urban moves)

Increased use of child labour leads to erratic attendance

Begin to borrow more leading to increasing indebtedness

Sell productive assets

Reduce essential expenditures

Move into risky or illegal work

IMPACT ON FOOD

Eating cheaper quality and less preferred food

Reduced diversity of food means poor nutrient intake

Favour certain household members over others

Reduced size and number of meals

Consume wild foods/ immature crops/seed stocks

Send household members elsewhere to eat (i.e. neighbours)

Start begging for food

Skip meals

IMPACT ON SOCIETY

Everyday reliance on loans and help from relatives, neighbours and friend

Increased stress to provide for households

Increased domestic violence

Increased drug and alcohol use

Increase in numbers of needy mean less local help is available

Household conflict and fragmentation

Rising crime and violence

Increasing sex work

IMPACT ON HEALTH

Depletion of body micronutrient stores and lowered immunity

Appearance of clinical symptoms of micronutrient deficiencies such as night blindness (vitamin a), anemia and increased morbidity (within 2–3 months)

Increase in number of underweight

Wasting increases

Maternal weight decrease

Risks of violence, HIV/AIDS transmission

HYPERAKT
UN Voices of the
Vulnerable Visualizations

The UN's "End Poverty 2015 Millennium Campaign" aims to improve the lives of the world's poorest citizens. The approach created a campaign that educates people about poverty using surprising statistics. Information about how poverty affects basics such as diet, health, and society are illustrated to show the downward spiral of poverty. In turn, they hope to inspire anyone in a position to help to join an international effort to end the cycle of poverty.

Year: 2007——Client: *GOOD*——
Creative Direction & Design: Deroy Peraza——Design: Jason Lynch

THE INFORMATION GAP
Making Decisions in a Vacuum

CRISIS   STIMULUS PACKAGE BEING ENACTED   INFORMATION GAP

WAVES OF RECESSION

MACROECONOMIC IMPACT
Growth, trade, FDI, credit contract

ECONOMIC IMPACT ON PEOPLE
Job losses, household income squeezed
Livelihood diversification

WAVE 1

FISCAL IMPACT
Government revenues decline
Public deficits increase
Public spending squeezed

SOCIAL IMPACT
Harder work, tougher job competition
Household spending on health and education squeezed
Families and societies

WAVE 2

WAVE 3

UNEVEN RECOVERY

EXPERIENCES OF RECOVERY
Contracts renegotiated
Some groups emerge stronger
Lasting effects on health and schooling

0 months   6 months   12 months   18 months   24 months   30 months

THE TIMBER TRADE

In this high-tech world of metal and plastic, it's easy to forget that many things are still made with good, old-fashioned wood. Countries with lots of forest stand to benefit from the lucrative timber trade, but at what cost to their Ecological Footprint? Here are five major timber exporters, and which countries are buying their wood.*

Figures in global hectares.

*Figures show legal trade only. Illegal timber trade remains a serious threat to forests, wildlife, and communities.

http://wwf.panda.org/lgr

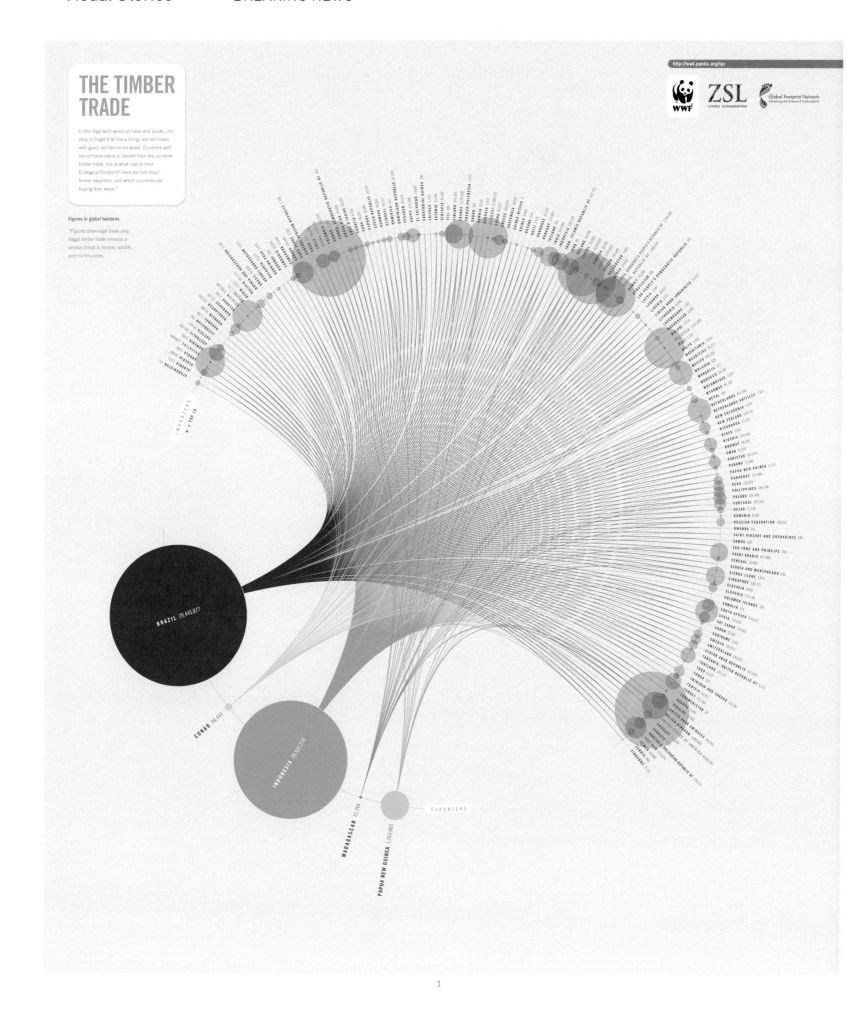

Parteispenden über 50.000 €

Zeitraum: Juli 2002 bis Januar 2011

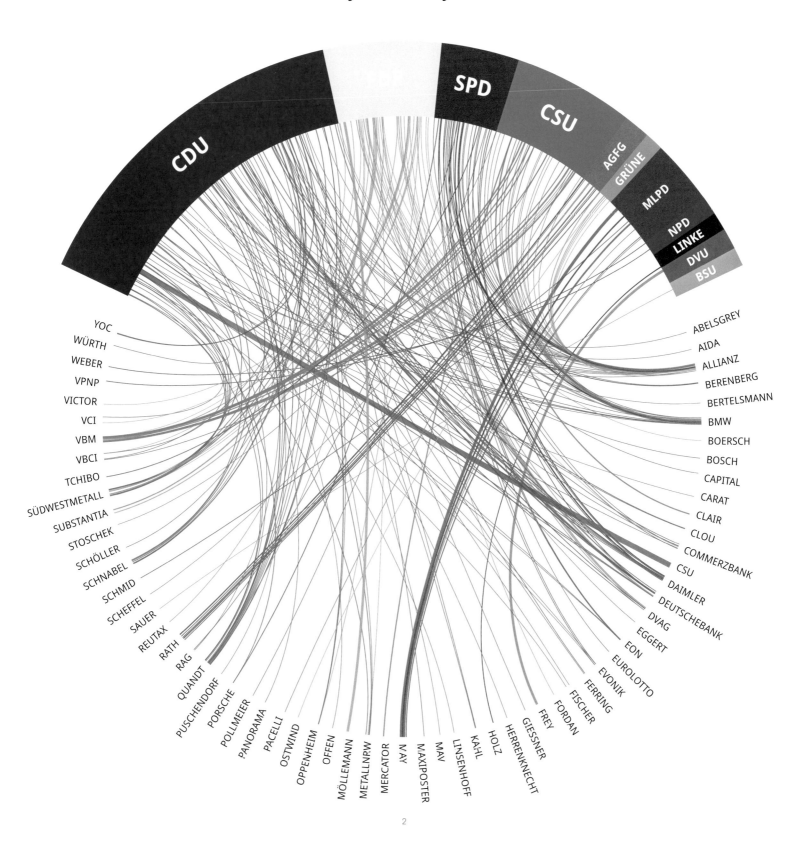

SECTION DESIGN
o Paul Butt
1 The Timber Trade
The illegal timber trade is a major environmental threat to many regions of the world. The legal timber trade, despite its legitimate status, also poses serious risks to the environment. Here the world's five major legal timber exporters are visually connected to the countries that import their wood. Each country's relative level of consumption is shown; the top ten importers are highlighted in red.
Year: 2011—Client: WWF/GOOD magazine

DRIVEN BY DATA
o Gregor Aisch
2 German Party Donations
Since 2002, all German political parties are required to publish received donations in excess of 50,000 € on the website of the German Bundestag. This graphic captures all recipients and their donors in a single image.

Year: 2010—Client: driven-bydata. net—Data source: www.bundestag. de/bundestag parteienfinanzierung/ fundstellen50000/2011

DOMINGO, 6 DE JUNIO DE 2010

WWW.PUBLICO.ES

PÚBLICO 31

Dinero

Así funciona la especulación bursátil

Cómo actúan los especuladores

Quiénes son

1 Diseñan la estrategia

2 Apuestan a la baja

3 Hunden el mercado

4 Recompran a la baja

5 Pagan las comisiones

Fondos de alto riesgo, grandes bancos de inversión y fondos de pensiones

Eligen un objetivo y **solicitan prestados productos financieros** por los que pagarán una prima y devolverán después de la operación.

Se dan **órdenes masivas de venta** en los mercados para hacer caer el precio de los productos financieros

El pánico se extiende y hay una **venta en masa de productos financieros** relacionados con el objetivo atacado. Se hunde la bolsa y la renta fija

Recompran los productos financieros que pidieron prestados a un precio mucho más bajo

Cuando ya han obtenido la ganancia devuelven los productos financieros a los prestamistas y les **pagan la prima prometida**

Recreación de una jornada tipo

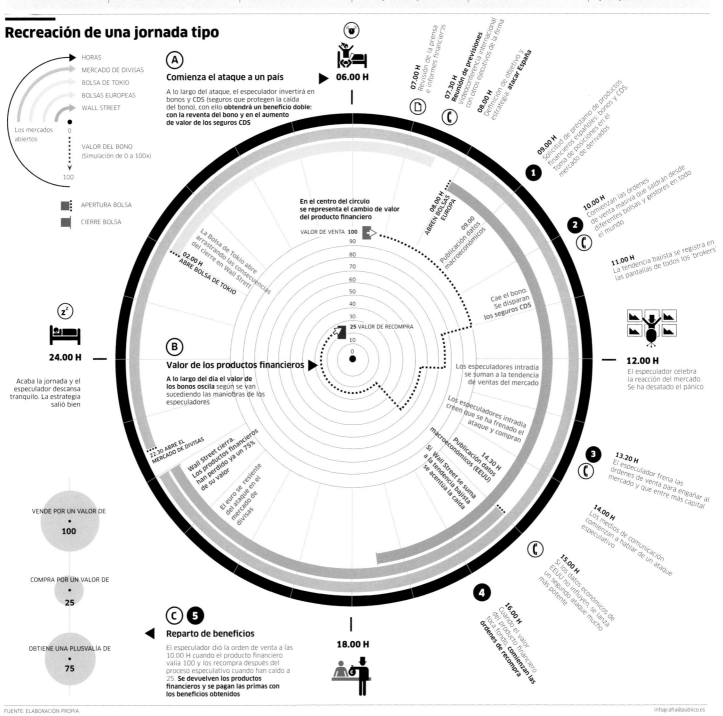

HORAS

MERCADO DE DIVISAS

BOLSA DE TOKIO

BOLSAS EUROPEAS

WALL STREET

Los mercados abiertos   0

VALOR DEL BONO
(Simulación de 0 a 100x)

100

APERTURA BOLSA

CIERRE BOLSA

A Comienza el ataque a un país

A lo largo del ataque, el especulador invertirá en bonos y CDS (seguros que protegen la caída del bono), con ello **obtendrá un beneficio doble: con la reventa del bono y en el aumento de valor de los seguros CDS**

06.00 H

07.00 H Revisión de la prensa e informes financieros

07.30 H Reunión de previsiones Videoconferencia internacional con otros ejecutivos de la firma

08.00 H Definición de objetivo y estrategia: **atacar España**

09.00 H Solicitud de préstamo de productos financieros españoles: bonos y CDS. Toma de posiciones en el mercado de derivados

1

10.00 H Comienzan las órdenes de venta masiva que saldrán desde diferentes bolsas y gestores en todo el mundo

2

11.00 H La tendencia bajista se registra en las pantallas de todos los 'brokers'

En el centro del círculo se representa el cambio de valor del producto financiero

VALOR DE VENTA **100**

90
80
70
60
50
40
30
25 VALOR DE RECOMPRA
10
0

La Bolsa de Tokio abre arrastrando las consecuencias del cierre en Wall Strett

02.00 H ABRE BOLSA DE TOKIO

08.00 H ABREN BOLSAS EUROPA

09.00 Publicación datos macroeconómicos

Cae el bono. Se disparan **los seguros CDS**

Los especuladores intradía se suman a la tendencia de ventas del mercado

12.00 H El especulador celebra la reacción del mercado. Se ha desatado el pánico

B Valor de los productos financieros

A lo largo del día el valor de **los bonos oscila** según se van sucediendo las maniobras de los especuladores

24.00 H

Acaba la jornada y el especulador descansa tranquilo. La estrategia salió bien

22.30 ABRE EL MERCADO DE DIVISAS

Wall Street cierra. Los productos financieros han perdido ya un 75% de su valor

El euro se resiente del ataque en el mercado de divisas

Los especuladores intradía creen que se ha frenado el ataque y compran

Publicación datos macroeconómicos (EEUU) 14.30 H Si Wall Street se suma a la tendencia bajista se acentúa la caída

3

13.20 H El especulador frena las órdenes de venta para engañar al mercado y que entre más capital

14.00 H Los medios de comunicación comienzan a hablar de un ataque especulativo

15.00 H Si los datos económicos de EEUU no influyen se lanza un segundo ataque mucho más potente

4

16.00 H Cuando el valor del producto financiero toca fondo **comienzan las órdenes de recompra**

VENDE POR UN VALOR DE
100

COMPRA POR UN VALOR DE
25

OBTIENE UNA PLUSVALÍA DE
75

C 5 Reparto de beneficios

El especulador dió la orden de venta a las 10.00 H cuando el producto financiero valía 100 y los recompra después del proceso especulativo cuando han caído a 25. **Se devuelven los productos financieros y se pagan las primas con los beneficios obtenidos**

18.00 H

FUENTE: ELABORACIÓN PROPIA

infografia@publico.es

1

PÚBLICO

o   Samuel Granados
1   How Financial Speculation Works
    How do speculators bet to get the most money from borrowed stocks? This cycle diagram, which doubles as a clock face, recreates a typical day in the life of the Japanese, European, and American stock markets.
    Year: 2010—Client: *Público*

SECTION DESIGN

2   Footprint vs. Biodiversity
    As low income countries see a decrease in their ecological footprint, high income countries are experiencing the opposite. This infographic illustrates these opposing trends and the *Living Planet Index,* which measures the health of a country's natural resources and shows how low income countries are paying the most for consumption by high-income countries.
    Year: 2010—Client: WWF/*GOOD* magazine

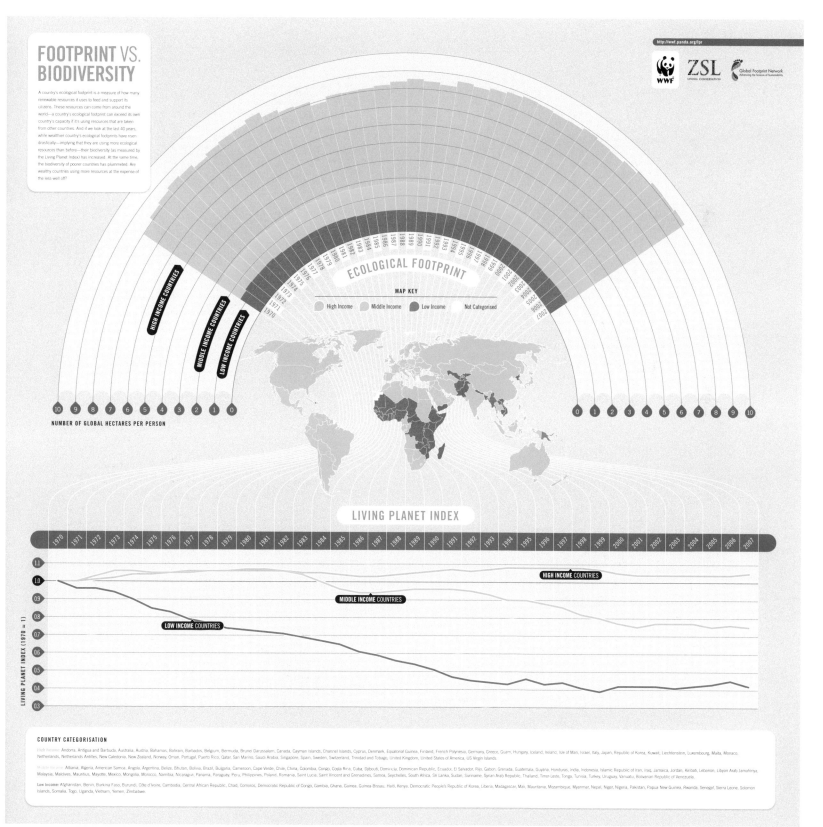

2

Visual Stories

CARL DETORRES

1 A Tale of Three Markets
This infographic depicting the history of and difference between the three major US stock indexes: the Dow Jones industrial average, the Standard & Poor's 500, and the Nasdaq composite. Each was designed with a different goal and market in mind
Year: 2009—Client: *Money* magazine

2 Fortune's Best Networker
An infographic for *Fortune* magazine's profile of entrepreneur Adam Rifkin, the most connected person on LinkedIn when the article was published. It offers information about where the majority of his LinkedIn connections live, what fields they work in, and what companies they work for. This data is supplemented by profiles of some of his most successful connections, such as Evan Williams, the co-founder of Twitter, and statistics for the other social media sites he uses.
Year: 2011—Client: *Fortune* magazine

3 CSI:Wall Street
When the US Securities and Exchange Commission (SEC) goes to court, they must search through millions of files to located the files needed

BREAKING NEWS

to support their case. This infographic illustrates how investigation techniques are used to find the necessary files.
Year: 2010—Client: *Fortune* magazine

NICHOLAS FELTON

4 Ideas Economy
A poster to promote the people, ideas, and information involved in the The *Economist's* Ideas Economy event, which assembles experts working in business, government, academia, and the non-profit sectors to discuss solutions to global challenges and contribute to human progress.
Year: 2010—Client: The *Economist*

FAUNA DISEÑO

o Fernando Costa
5 Chile Infográfico |
Pueblos Originarios
Population, education, and economic condition were analyzed to visualize the current and past situation of indigenous cultures present in Chile.
Year: 2011—Client: Instituto Libertad y Desarrollo—Illustration: Alejandro Leiva—Design: Romina Rubulotta, Fredy Valencia

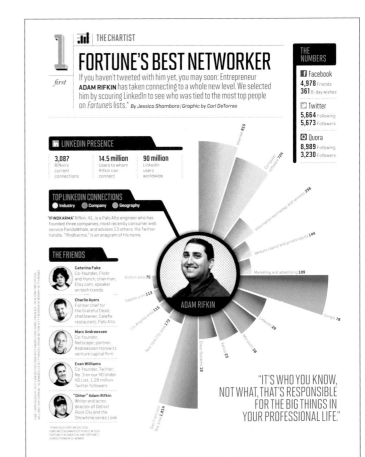

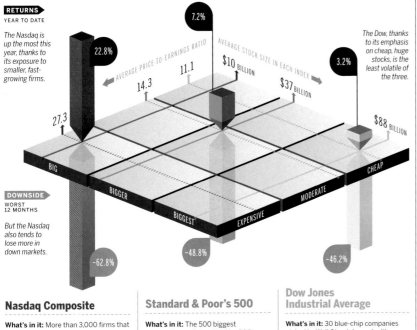

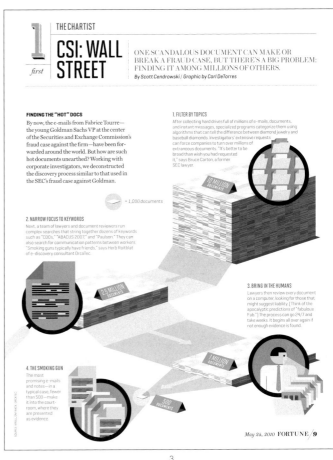

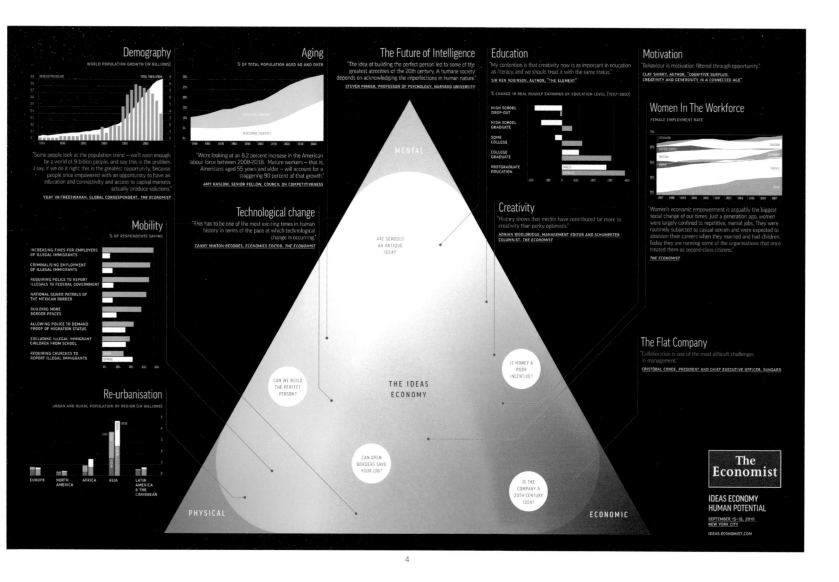

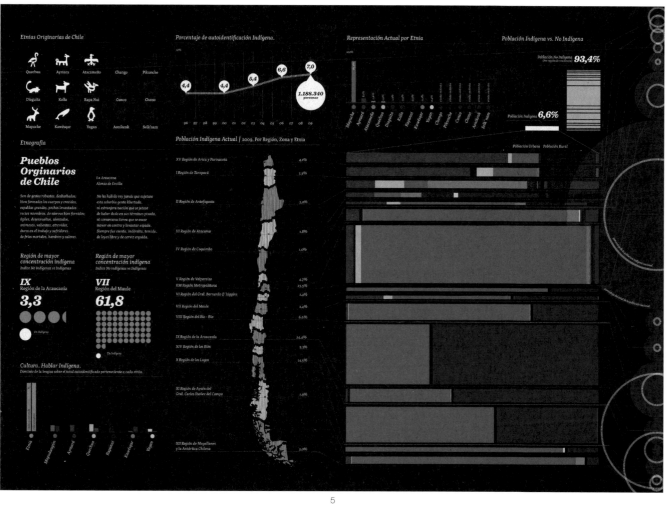

PITCH INTERACTIVE

1   Flight Patterns:
    Where the Money Goes
    The rapid rise in the cost of flight tickets begs the question as to what, exactly, that additional cost is covering. A jet stream serves as a visual metaphor for the stacked bar chart that breaks down the costs behind an average flight ticket.
    Year: 2011—Client: *FORTUNE* Magazine—Creative Direction: Wesley Grubbs—Designer: Mladen Balog

PÚBLICO

o   Artur Galocha, Mónica Serrano, Álvaro Valiño
2   The Power Triangle in Iran
    The hierarchical operation of the political and religious systems in the land of ayatollahs is highlighted in this piece focusing on the Grand Ayatollah Khamenei, Ali A. Hashemi Rafsanyani, and president-elect Mahmoud Ahmadinejad. The complicated differences and similarities that intertwine them are broken down into a simple diagram that uses arrows and colors to show how the power triangle is connected: elected institutions and positions are indicated with green, while designated institutions and positions are in red; black arrows show who or which institutions hold the right to veto the others.
    Year: 2009—Client: *Público*—Documentation: Óscar Abou-Kassem

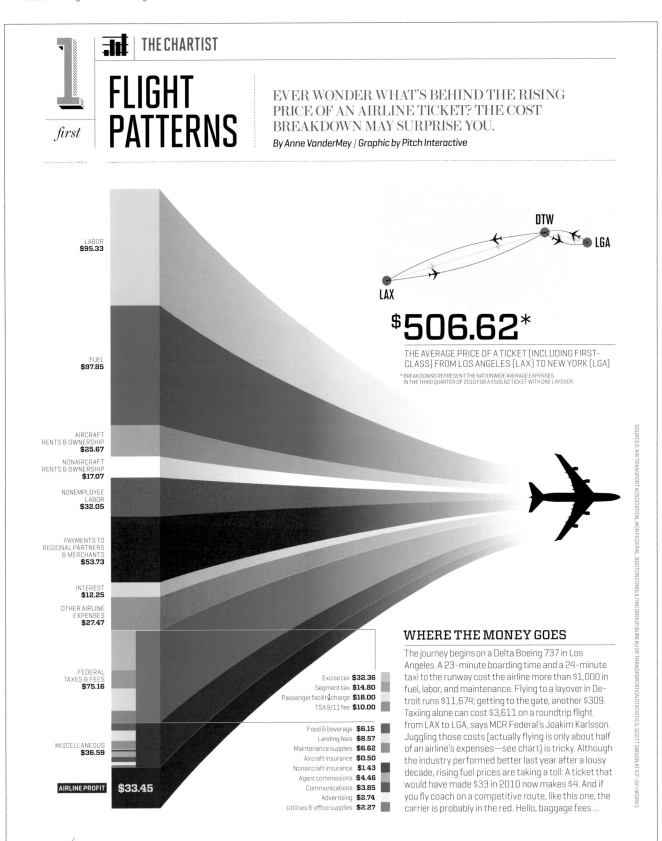

THE CHARTIST

FLIGHT PATTERNS

first

EVER WONDER WHAT'S BEHIND THE RISING PRICE OF AN AIRLINE TICKET? THE COST BREAKDOWN MAY SURPRISE YOU.

By Anne VanderMey / Graphic by Pitch Interactive

DTW   **LGA**   **LAX**

$506.62*

THE AVERAGE PRICE OF A TICKET (INCLUDING FIRST-CLASS) FROM LOS ANGELES (LAX) TO NEW YORK (LGA)

* BREAKDOWNS REPRESENT THE NATIONWIDE AVERAGE EXPENSES IN THE THIRD QUARTER OF 2010 FOR A $506.62 TICKET WITH ONE LAYOVER.

LABOR **$95.33**

FUEL **$97.85**

AIRCRAFT RENTS & OWNERSHIP **$25.67**

NONAIRCRAFT RENTS & OWNERSHIP **$17.07**

NONEMPLOYEE LABOR **$32.05**

PAYMENTS TO REGIONAL PARTNERS & MERCHANTS **$53.73**

INTEREST **$12.25**

OTHER AIRLINE EXPENSES **$27.47**

FEDERAL TAXES & FEES **$75.16**

Excise tax	**$32.36**
Segment tax	**$14.80**
Passenger facility charge	**$18.00**
TSA 9/11 fee	**$10.00**

Food & beverage	**$6.15**
Landing fees	**$8.57**
Maintenance supplies	**$6.62**
Aircraft insurance	**$0.50**
Nonaircraft insurance	**$1.43**
Agent commissions	**$4.46**
Communications	**$3.85**
Advertising	**$2.74**
Utilities & office supplies	**$2.27**

MISCELLANEOUS **$36.59**

AIRLINE PROFIT   **$33.45**

WHERE THE MONEY GOES

The journey begins on a Delta Boeing 737 in Los Angeles. A 23-minute boarding time and a 24-minute taxi to the runway cost the airline more than $1,000 in fuel, labor, and maintenance. Flying to a layover in Detroit runs $11,674; getting to the gate, another $309. Taxiing alone can cost $3,611 on a roundtrip flight from LAX to LGA, says MCR Federal's Joakim Karlsson. Juggling those costs (actually flying is only about half of an airline's expenses—see chart) is tricky. Although the industry performed better last year after a lousy decade, rising fuel prices are taking a toll: A ticket that would have made $33 in 2010 now makes $4. And if you fly coach on a competitive route, like this one, the carrier is probably in the red. Hello, baggage fees …

SOURCES: AIR TRANSPORT ASSOCIATION, MCR FEDERAL, BOSTON CONSULTING GROUP, BUREAU OF TRANSPORTATION STATISTICS, SCOTT GIBSON AT CF-SKYWORKS

Crisis política en Irán

El triángulo de poder en el sistema político-religioso iraní

● DESIGNADOS   ● ELEGIDOS   — DESIGNA   — ELIGE   — VETA

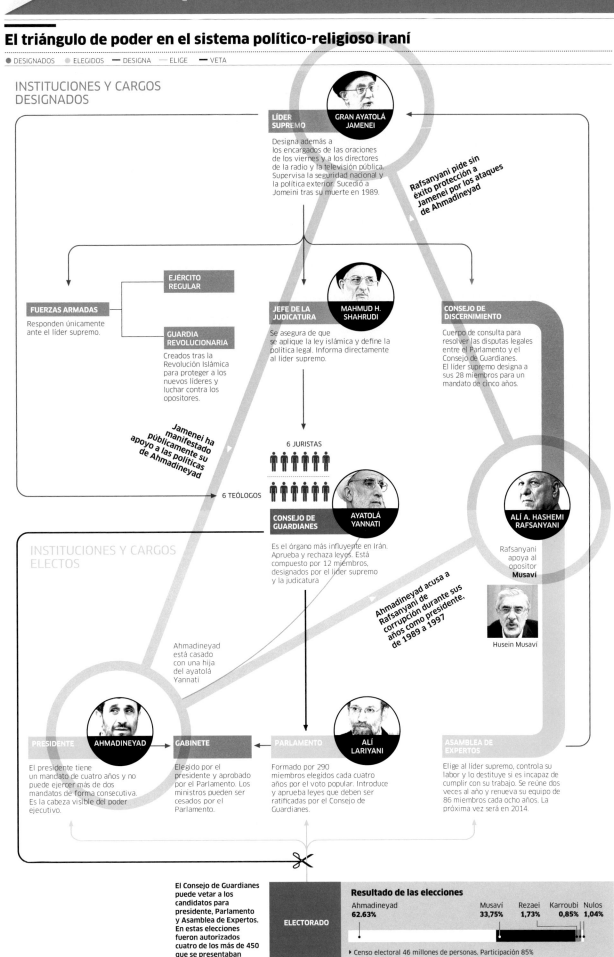

INSTITUCIONES Y CARGOS DESIGNADOS

GRAN AYATOLÁ JAMENEI

LÍDER SUPREMO

Designa además a los encargados de las oraciones de los viernes y a los directores de la radio y la televisión pública. Supervisa la seguridad nacional y la política exterior. Sucedió a Jomeini tras su muerte en 1989.

Rafsanyani pide sin éxito protección a Jamenei por los ataques de Ahmadineyad

EJÉRCITO REGULAR

FUERZAS ARMADAS

Responden únicamente ante el líder supremo.

GUARDIA REVOLUCIONARIA

Creados tras la Revolución Islámica para proteger a los nuevos líderes y luchar contra los opositores.

MAHMUD H. SHAHRUDI

JEFE DE LA JUDICATURA

Se asegura de que se aplique la ley islámica y define la política legal. Informa directamente al líder supremo.

CONSEJO DE DISCERNIMIENTO

Cuerpo de consulta para resolver las disputas legales entre el Parlamento y el Consejo de Guardianes. El líder supremo designa a sus 28 miembros para un mandato de cinco años.

Jamenei ha manifestado públicamente su apoyo a las políticas de Ahmadineyad

6 JURISTAS

6 TEÓLOGOS

AYATOLÁ YANNATI

CONSEJO DE GUARDIANES

Es el órgano más influyente en Irán. Aprueba y rechaza leyes. Está compuesto por 12 miembros, designados por el líder supremo y la judicatura.

ALÍ A. HASHEMI RAFSANYANI

Rafsanyani apoya al opositor **Musaví**

Husein Musaví

Ahmadineyad acusa a Rafsanyani de corrupción durante sus años como presidente, de 1989 a 1997

Ahmadineyad está casado con una hija del ayatolá Yannati

INSTITUCIONES Y CARGOS ELECTOS

AHMADINEYAD

PRESIDENTE

El presidente tiene un mandato de cuatro años y no puede ejercer más de dos mandatos de forma consecutiva. Es la cabeza visible del poder ejecutivo.

GABINETE

Elegido por el presidente y aprobado por el Parlamento. Los ministros pueden ser cesados por el Parlamento.

PARLAMENTO

Formado por 290 miembros elegidos cada cuatro años por el voto popular. Introduce y aprueba leyes que deben ser ratificadas por el Consejo de Guardianes.

ALÍ LARIYANI

ASAMBLEA DE EXPERTOS

Elige al líder supremo, controla su labor y lo destituye si es incapaz de cumplir con su trabajo. Se reúne dos veces al año y renueva su equipo de 86 miembros cada ocho años. La próxima vez será en 2014.

El Consejo de Guardianes puede vetar a los candidatos para presidente, Parlamento y Asamblea de Expertos. En estas elecciones fueron autorizados cuatro de los más de 450 que se presentaban

ELECTORADO

Resultado de las elecciones

Ahmadineyad	Musaví	Rezaei	Karroubi	Nulos
62.63%	**33,75%**	**1,73%**	**0,85%**	**1,04%**

▸ Censo electoral 46 millones de personas. Participación 85%

INFORMACIÓN: ÓSCAR ABOU-KASSEM   infografia@publico.es

La cara pragmática del sistema

Perfil

Rafsanyani no ha podido frenar el ascenso de Ahmadineyad

Ó. A.
MADRID

Ali Akbar Hashemi Rafsanyani lo ha sido casi todo en el sistema político-religioso iraní. Su destino natural era acabar relevando algún día al líder supremo Alí Jameneí. Pero su estrella se está apagando de manera inversamente proporcional al ascenso de su archienemigo Mahmud Ahmadineyad.

Rafsanyani nació en Bahraman, sureste de Irán, en 1934. Con 14 años sus padres lo enviaron a la ciudad santa de Qom, el Vaticano iraní, donde tuvo al imán Jomeini de profesor. Entre los años sesenta y setenta fue detenido en varias ocasiones por sus actividades relacionadas contra el régimen del Sha.

Tras la Revolución Islámica se convirtió en uno de los dirigentes del movimiento destacando por su pragmatismo. Rafsanyani ostenta el rango de hojatoleslam, uno menor al de ayatolá, y dirige la Asamblea de Expertos. Este *pata negra* del *establishment* iraní prefiere acompañar sus sermones de los viernes con estadísticas más que con frases del Corán.

La prioridad en sus dos mandatos como presidente (1987-95) fue la reconstrucción del país tras la guerra con Irak. Mientras progresaba en la jerarquía política del país, florecían sus negocios, típicamente iraníes: petróleo y pistachos. En la leyenda negra sobre el origen de su fortuna, Ahmadineyad ha encontrado un filón. El presidente ha decidido hacer la crítica a Rafsanyani una de sus banderas. Lo acusa de corrupto y de dirigir una familia de mafiosos que controlan la riqueza de Irán. La derrota de Mir Hosein Musaví también fue la de Rafsanyani. ●

91

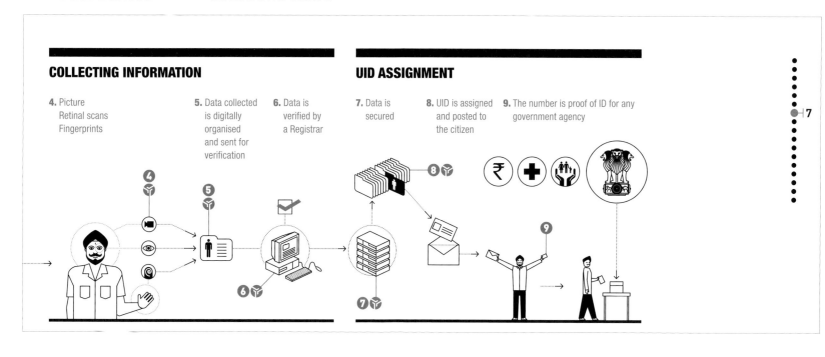

COLLECTING INFORMATION

4. Picture
Retinal scans
Fingerprints

5. Data collected
is digitally
organised
and sent for
verification

6. Data is
verified by
a Registrar

UID ASSIGNMENT

7. Data is
secured

8. UID is assigned
and posted to
the citizen

9. The number is proof of ID for any
government agency

7

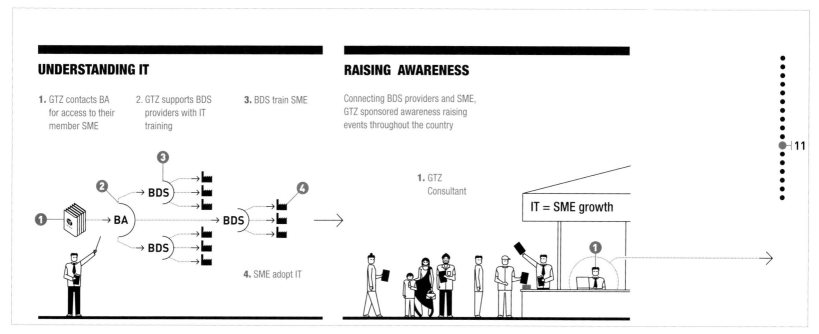

UNDERSTANDING IT

1. GTZ contacts BA
for access to their
member SME

2. GTZ supports BDS
providers with IT
training

3. BDS train SME

4. SME adopt IT

RAISING AWARENESS

Connecting BDS providers and SME,
GTZ sponsored awareness raising
events throughout the country

1. GTZ
Consultant

IT = SME growth

11

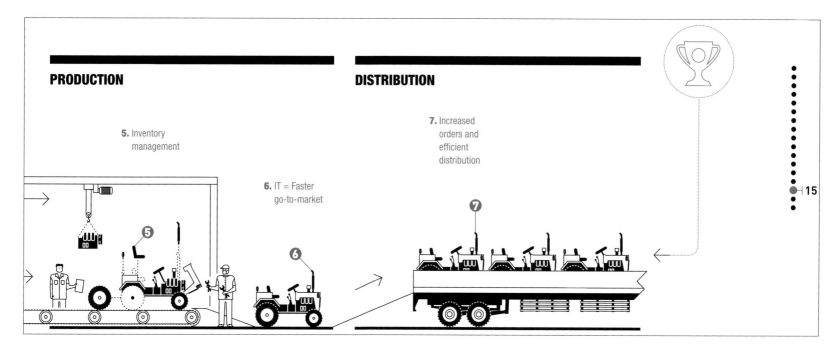

PRODUCTION

5. Inventory
management

6. IT = Faster
go-to-market

DISTRIBUTION

7. Increased
orders and
efficient
distribution

15

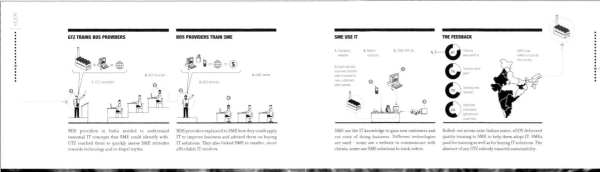

GTZ TRAINS BDS PROVIDERS

BDS providers in India needed to understand essential IT concepts that SME could identify with. GTZ coached them to quickly assess SME attitudes towards technology and to dispel myths.

BDS PROVIDERS TRAIN SME

BDS providers explained to SME how they could apply IT to improve business and advised them on buying IT solutions. They also linked SME to smaller, more affordable IT vendors.

SME USE IT

SME use the IT knowledge to gain new customers and cut costs of doing business. Different technologies are used - some use a website to communicate with clients, some use SMS solutions to track orders.

THE FEEDBACK

Rolled-out across nine Indian states, eGOV delivered quality training to SME to help them adopt IT. SMEs paid for training as well as for buying IT solutions. The absence of any GTZ subsidy ensured sustainability.

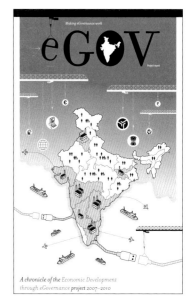

A chronicle of the *Economic Development* through eGovernance **project** 2007–2010

INFONAUTS
eGovernance Magazine

In 2007, the German Technical Cooperation (GTZ) and the Standardization Testing and Quality Certification Directorate (STQC) joined forces for the eGov project. The project's goal was to achieve higher quality electronic public services by creating the Quality Assurance Framework to be used by all eGovernance projects in India. Captain Tractors, an SME featured in eGov, went on to win the Prime Minister's Award for Excellence. This magazine is a chronicle of eGov from its inception to its completion in 2010, with simple graphics that illustrate various processes that were implemented including data collection and UID assignments.

Year: 2010—Client: German Technical Cooperation

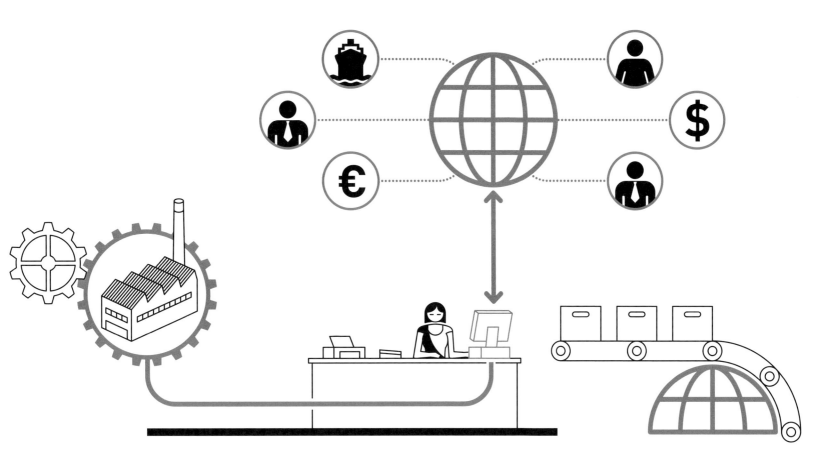

■ STATE of the UNION ■
THE NATION   IN NUMBERS

How the Recession Changed Us

WHAT A DIFFERENCE TWO YEARS MAKES.

By Timothy Lavin
Graphics by Amanda Buck

OFFICIALLY, THE GREAT Recession lasted from December 2007 to June 2009. A mere 18 months—about average, as recessions go. Yet if the trauma this time feels deep and lasting, that may be because, as the figures on these pages show, so many disruptions have upended national life at once.

Millions of Americans have lost their jobs, nearly every state faces a budget shortfall, and hundreds of banks have shut their doors. The young are

unemployed, living at home, and playing video games. The ranks of third-party candidates have swollen, militias have proliferated, and national leaders of both parties have seen their support decline. Of course, times of flux are often times of anxiety and unrest. But as the economy begins its slow and stuttering recovery, the vast changes wrought by this recession will continue to reverberate for many years—in ways predictable and otherwise. ◢

Timothy Lavin is an Atlantic senior editor.

DAILY CONSUMER SPENDING
2006 $$$$$ 2010 $$$$$
$$$$$ $:
$59 $62

U.S. BOOK SALES
2007   2009
$275.0 billion $23.9 billion

PERCENTAGE INCREASE in NYT ARTICLES mentioning the WORD "uncertainty," 2007 vs. 2010
31%

TAX COLLECTED by the TREASURY on sales of FIREARMS and AMMUNITION
2007   2009
$267,836,000 $452,692,000

PERCENT who believe it's more important to preserve GUN OWNERS' RIGHTS than to control GUNS
2008 37%   2010 46%

FEATURE-LENGTH MOVIES released in 3D
2007 3
2010 23

AVERAGE MINUTES SPENT READING per WEEKEND DAY, 15-19 year olds
2007 16   2009 5

AVERAGE MINUTES SPENT PLAYING A GAME or USING A COMPUTER per WEEKEND DAY, 15-19 year olds
2007 27   2009 60

DOMESTIC AUTO-INDUSTRY PROFITS (in billions of dollars)
8.4
0
-13.5
-48.0
YEAR BY QUARTER '07 '08 '09 '10

UNEMPLOYMENT RATE, national
2007 5.0%   2010 9.6%

PERCENTAGE of UNEMPLOYED WHO HAVE BEEN UNEMPLOYED for 27 WEEKS or MORE
2007 19.7%   2010 43.2%

FEDERAL UNEMPLOYMENT BENEFITS PAID
2007 $41.43 billion   2010 $162 billion

PERCENTAGE of 18-29 year olds WHO MOVED BACK IN WITH THEIR PARENTS during recession
24%

PERCENT WHO THINK AMERICA IS STILL a land of prosperity
70%

NUMBER of PEOPLE in POVERTY
2007 37.3 million   2010 43.6 million

FOOD STAMP RECIPIENTS by state

	2007	2009	% increase
FLORIDA	192,534	415,608	113%
NEVADA	17,434	47,599	173%
NEW YORK	170,330	338,989	99%

RESIDENTIAL PROPERTIES in FORECLOSURE
2008 858,994   2010 2,054,693

MORTGAGES HELD by FEDERAL AGENCIES
2007 725,455   2010 5,148,130

AVERAGE RATE on 30-YEAR FIXED MORTGAGE
2007 6.10%   2010 4.23%

MEDIAN SALE PRICE of EXISTING HOMES
2007 $219,000
2010 $177,500

STATES facing BUDGET SHORTFALLS
2007 1
2010 46

FEDERAL BUDGET DEFICIT
2007 $161 billion   2010 $1.3 trillion+

DEFICIT as PERCENTAGE of GDP
2007 1.2%   2010 9.1%

NUMBER of FEDERAL EMPLOYEES
2007 1,888,000
2009 2,094,000
Percent Change: +10.9%

BANK failures
2000-2007 26   2008-2010 308

MARKET CAP of EBAY
2008 $45.516 billion   2010 $40.23 billion

MARKET CAP of 99¢ only STORES
2008 $528.9 million   2010 $1.06 billion

INTEREST RATE, 2-year TREASURY NOTE
2007 3.625%   2010 0.375%

TOTAL ASSETS of the FEDERAL RESERVE
2007 $886 billion   2010 $2.3 trillion

CURRENCY in CIRCULATION
2007 $819 billion   2010 $9.60 trillion

ACTIVE MILITIAS
2007 23   2009 127

SECRET SERVICE AGENTS
2007 3,365   2009 3,542

SAVINGS RATE, as percentage of disposable income
2007 0.8%   2010 5.3%

AVERAGE INTEREST PAID on DOMESTIC DEPOSITS
2008 2.45%   2010 0.80%

PERSONAL BANKRUPTCIES
2007 226,413   2010 422,061

VIOLENT CRIMES per 100,000 PEOPLE
2007 472   2008 457.5   2009 429.4

PERCENT of AMERICANS who think PRESIDENT OBAMA is a MUSLIM
2008 12%   2010 18%

FAVORABLE VIEWS of SARAH PALIN
2008 43%   2010 22%

APPROVAL RATING for PRESIDENT OBAMA
2009 68%   2010 45%

THIRD PARTY CANDIDATES
2008 311   2010 **443**

1

RISING AND RECEDING

COMPILED BY MICHAEL ZELENKO AND AIDAN GARDINER / DESIGNED BY NICHOLAS FELTON

In 2001, Leonard Lauder, chairman of a lipstick firm, detected a possible correlation between lipstick sales and hard times. Lauder believed lipstick sales climbed, not insignificantly, during an economic slump. When women skimp on everything else, he posited, they find lipstick an allowable luxury. Economists disagree on whether Lauder overstated the case or not—though a few have actually started tracking lipstick sales as an indicator of calamity.

In any case, an economy is a staggeringly complex thing, with more levers of cause and effect than most of us can fathom. What follows here is a snapshot of a few largely unnoticed shifts in american commerce and industry that have surfaced recently. While these numbers won't tell you when to buy stock, they might give some insight into just how far the fingers of the recession reach.

FAMILICIDE

'09

20   AVG.
      4–6
FAMILICIDE RATE

Our research indicates that so far in 2009, there have been at least 20 familicide or filicide cases—cases in which a parent kills his or her child, or his or her entire family.

FAMILICIDE

+333%

-85%
POLLUTION

POLLUTION

Fewer factories around the world are able to stay afloat during this economic downturn. The closure of steel mills around delhi, india has dropped levels of sulfur dioxide, which forms acid rain, by 85%. At least in part because of diminished production, by the end of 2009 carbon dioxide emissions are forecasted to drop by 100 million tons each in both europe and the united states. Beef prices have fallen 51% in the past 12 months, hindering cattle farming in brazil, primary cause of amazonian deforestation. Less cattle farming has, in turn, caused the rate of deforestation to drop by 70%.

EGG & SPERM DONATIONS

More men and women are choosing to donate their eggs or sperm to donor agencies. Health News, a national referral service for donors, says that they've seen a 40% spike since February. USA Today reports that before the recession, a donor coordinator at North Hudson IVF in Englewood Cliffs, N.J., Got around eight calls a week from potential egg donors. She now receives that many calls daily.

SMART PHONES

'08   '09

31.5M   40M
SMART PHONE SALES

A Gartner report released in August 2009 suggests that the smart phone is still roaring forward, with 40 million units sold in the second quarter of 2009.

EGG & SPERM DONATIONS
+40%   *SMART PHONES* **+27%**

-9%
NEW JERSEY DIVORCE RATES

NEW JERSEY DIVORCE RATES

Q1/Q2 '08   Q1/Q2 '09

31,400   28,579
NEW JERSEY DIVORCES

Couples in New Jersey are divorcing at a lower rate this year as the recession takes its toll on family finances and raises the cost of splitting up. The number of new divorce cases filed during the first six months of the year fell 9 percent—to 28,579—compared with the same period a year ago, according to the latest figures from the state administrative office of the courts.

SLEEP ISSUES

2001   2009
38%   **28%**
PEOPLE SLEEPING EIGHT HOURS OR MORE

According to a study released by the National Sleep Foundation, almost one-third of Americans say their sleep has been disturbed at least a few nights a week because of financial concerns, employment concerns, and the general economy. The foundation also reports that the number of people having sleep problems has increased 13% since 2001. The number of people who sleep less than six hours a night has risen from 13% to 20% and the number of people who report sleeping eight hours or more has dropped from 38% to 28%. The Pew Research Center reports that there isn't a hard correlation between income and sleep, but that those who are dissatisfied with their financial situation are 40% more likely to report having trouble sleeping.

SLEEP ISSUES
+13%

-3%
TOYS   **-30%**
BICYCLE SALES

TOYS

According to market research firm NPD Group, overall U.S. toy sales were down 3 percent in 2008. While more expensive products such as video games have seen record setting sale declines, dropping as much as 19 percent in october 2009 compared to a year ago, more traditional toys such as dolls, building sets, and puzzles are either holding their own or showing sales gains.

BICYCLE SALES

First quarter sales of bicycles in 2009 were the lowest they've been in 11 years. This means 1.1 million less bikes imported into the country—a drop in 30% when compared to first quarter sales in 2008.

COUNTY FAIRS

The Alameda County Fair, held July 1 to 19, attracted 432,000 people. Attendance was up by almost 87,000 visitors over 2008, and 2009 broke the 1997 record of 431,000 attendees. An increase in "staycations" and tighter budgets have encouraged families to seek entertainment closer to home. County fairs from Milwaukee to Missouri to Santa Barbara have logged strong attendance numbers this year.

BEER SALES

'06   '07   '08
                  +0.5%
         +1.3%
+2.1%
SALES GROWTH

Beer sales have seen better years, but sales have continued to grow. Growth in 2006 and 2007 was 2.1 and 1.3 percent, respectively. This slowdown in growth looks a lot like a decline. 2008 beer sales grew only 0.5 percent.

COUNTY FAIRS
+25%   *BEER SALES* **+0.5%**

-4.5%
POSTAL SERVICE

POSTAL SERVICE

677 POSTOFFICES WILL SOON CLOSE OR BE CONSOLIDATED

The United States Postal Service reported that it will be facing $7 billion deficit due to a decrease in pieces of mail delivered (the USPS says this is mostly because people increasingly rely on email). Mail volume fell by 9 billion pieces in 2008 and experts believe volume delivered could drop by as much as 28 billion pieces by 2010.

CONDOM SALES

As if spurred on by impending puns, condom sales are rising. Nielsen Co. reports that sales of condoms rose 5% in the fourth quarter of 2008. Economists say that more people are staying home and looking for cheap ways to entertain themselves and fewer people are growing their families. People generally want to avoid unintended pregnancies which become all the more "burdensome" in economic downturns. The rise in condom sales tells us that people are having more sex (or just more safe sex) and fewer women are getting pregnant.

KELLOGG

As budgets tighten, and families become more frugal, meals are more likely to be eaten at home rather than at restaurants. For Kellogg—makers of cereals, crackers, Pop-Tarts, granola bars, waffles, and many other marginally healthy food products—this trend translated into higher than expected quarterly profits throughout 2009. The company's third quarter profit this year, for instance, was $361 million, as opposed to the $342 million profit it posted during the same period in 2008.

CONDOMS **+5%**   *KELLOGG* **+5.5%**

-2.9%
BOTTLED WATER

BOTTLED WATER

Water bottle sales have dropped off for the first time in a decade. According to the consulting firm Beverage Marketing Corp., Americans drank 1 hundred million less gallons of bottled water in 2008 than they did in 2007—a drop from 8.8 billion gallons in 2007 to 2.7 billion gallons in 2008. Nestle, for instance, sells a variety of bottled water brands, such as Poland Spring, Deer Park, sparkling Pellegrino and Perrier. Bottled water was the only sector in Nestle's food and beverage group to post a decline in global sales during the first half of the year, down 2.9 percent due—according to Nestle—to economic "weakness" across the U.S. and western Europe.

DATING

Both Match.com and eHarmony noticed that whenever the dow drops more than 100 points in a single day, site traffic rises about 2%. According to a study by eHarmony, a quarter of female respondents said that, "stress about the state of the economy made them more inclined to seek a long-term relationship."

ONLINE UNIVERSITIES

Q3 '08   Q3 '09

340,800   420,000
ONLINE ENROLLMENT

Phoenix university, one of the largest online universities, has seen incredible growth recently. Earlier this year, apollo group inc., The operators, has seen its stock hover consistently at about $84 this year, near its 52-week high of $89.68 And well above its 52-week low of $37.92.

DATING **+2%**   *ONLINE UNIVERSITIES* **+18%**

-1.6%
BIRTHS

BIRTHS

'07   '08

14.3   13.9
BIRTH RATES PER THOUSAND

Although numbers aren't in for 2009, the United States experienced a decline in birthrates in 2008. This followed a steady rise through the last decade and 50-year record high in 2007. About 4,247,000 babies were born last year, down roughly 68,000 from 2007. According to the New York Times, economists agree that this is because of economic hard times. During the prior two major economic downturns in the united states—the great depression and the 1970s oil embargo—birth rates also dipped.

DIAGRAM III
»THE DETAINEE BEGAN TO CRY.«

The Diagram shows number and time of the detainee's crying during the 50 days of interrogation. Altogether this emotional reaction is documented 21 times.

Das Diagramm zeigt, wie oft und wann der Häftling während der 50 Tage des Verhörs weinte. Insgesamt kam es 21-mal beim Gefangenen zu dieser emotionalen Reaktion.

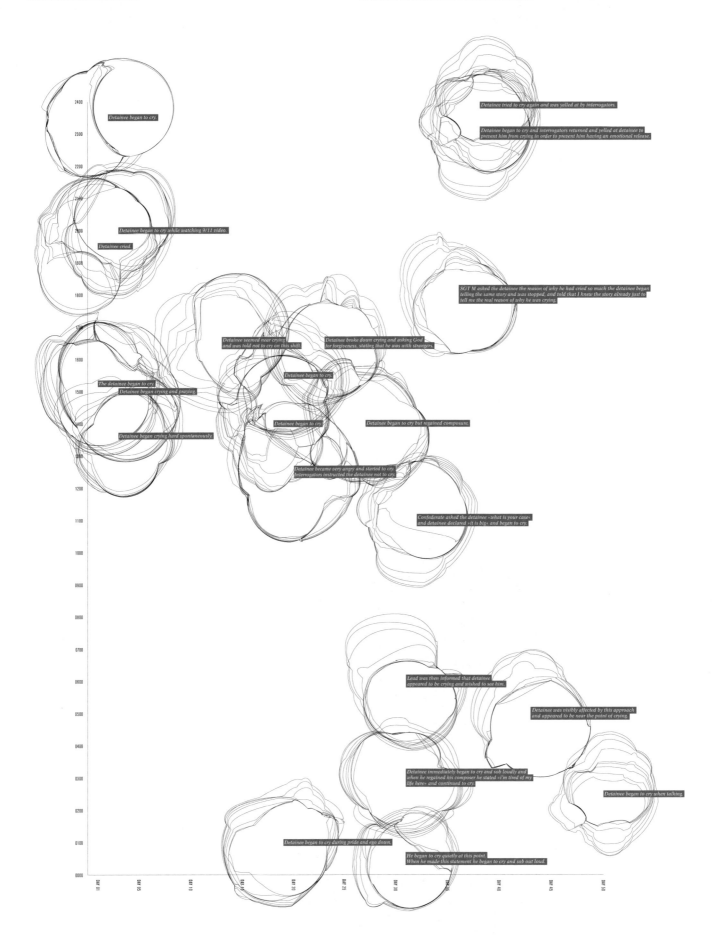

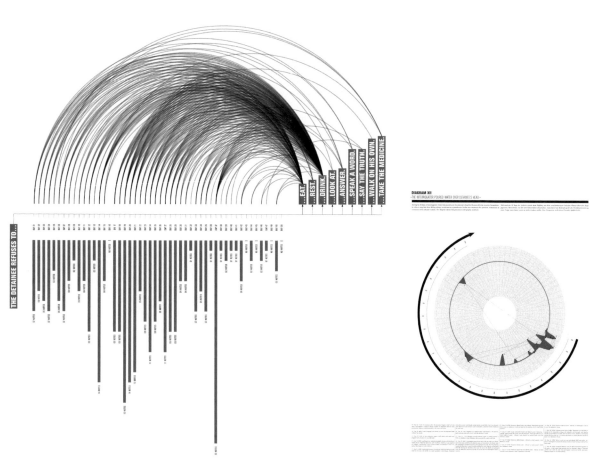

THE DETAINEE REFUSES TO...

...EAT
...REST
...DRINK
...LOOK AT
...ANSWER
...SPEAK A WORD
...SAY THE TRUTH.
...WALK ON HIS OWN.
...TAKE THE MEDICINE.

DIAGRAM XII
– THE INTERROGATOR POURED WATER OVER DETAINEE'S HEAD –

JAN HARTWIG
50 Days — Interrogation Log
Detainee 063

The piece is based on the 84-page *Secret Orcon—Interrogation Log Detainee 063,* which documents 50 days in the life of detainee 063 in the Guantánamo Bay detention camp, showing the complex psychological relationships during interrogation and providing a unique insight life inside the cells of Guantánamo Bay. The log is structured in the form of diagrams, which refer to individually logged circumstances. They also illustrate the existing contradiction between human emotion and objectivity in the log.

Year: 2008—Self-published newspaper—This work is based on an interrogation log published in *Time* magazine

DIAGRAM I
– INTERROGATION TIMETABLE –

DIAGRAM V
– THE INTERROGATOR OCCURRENCE –

DIAGRAM VIII
– LOUD MUSIC (WHITE NOISE) WAS PLAYED. –

DIAGRAM XIII
– THE INTERROGATOR GAVE A LAST CHANCE TO TELL THE WHOLE TRUTH. –

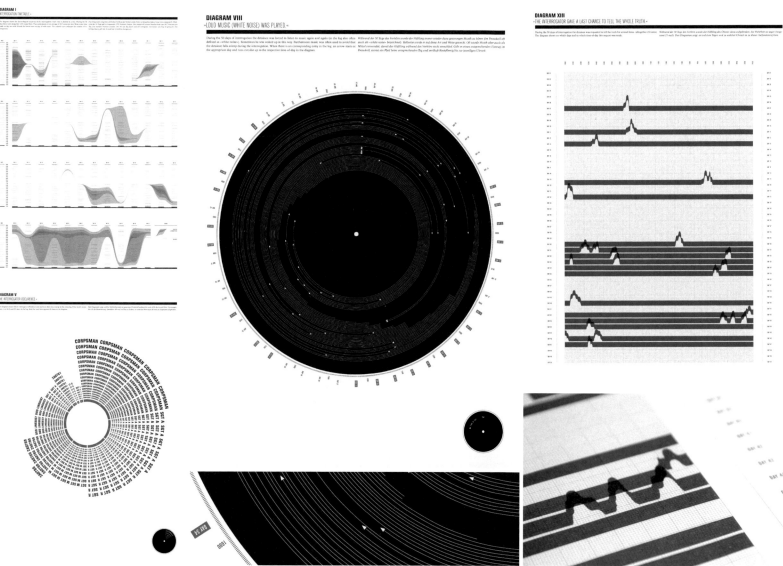

WEST BANK

SYRIA

OBAMA

INDEPENDENCE

HAMAS

PALESTINIANS

ROBERT GATES

IRAN

IRANIAN BOMB

MUSLIM NATIONS

LEBANON

LORENZO PETRANTONI

1   Guerra
This piece was commissioned by the *Wall Street Journal* for an article about the countries, themes, and characters involved in the Gulf crisis.

Year: 2009—Client: *Wall Street Journal*—Additional credits: Banche immagine

2   The New Global
Globalization was the theme for this 2008 *Newsweek* cover illustration. Within the piece are the names of the most discussed people of the year, including US President Barack Obama. The image of Obama is easily recognizable, while the symmetrically arranged elements that surround him make reference to money. All of the graphics in the image—with the obvious exception of the photograph of Obama—are engravings found in books dating from the years 1860–1905.

Year: 2008—Client: *Newsweek*—Additional credits: Banche immagine

2

DAVID VON BASSEWITZ
Krise (*Crisis*)
A campaign promoting the Ger-
man political magazine *Der Spiegel* as
Germany's best investigative political
magazine commissioned this illustration. The magazine's unique journalistic qualities were translated into a large
image made up of numerous smaller
details that provide more information
upon closer investigation.
Year: 2009—Client: Jung von Matt/*Der
Spiegel*—Creative Direction:
Dörte Spengler-Ahrens, Jan Rexhausen

101

SOSOLIMITED
o Justin Manor
   Prime Numerics

Sosolimited created a software that can deconstruct and analyze live TV broadcasts in realtime for immediate display. This project was a live remix of the final 2010 UK Prime Minister debate held in Manchester, England. The audio, video, and text of the debates were fed into Sosolimited's software system, which then found and displayed patterns within the data. The software detects popular themes and graphically displays them with charts, graphs, and dynamic word clouds.

Year: 2010—Medium: Live remix of 2010 UK Prime Minister debates

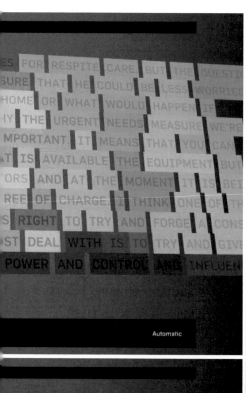

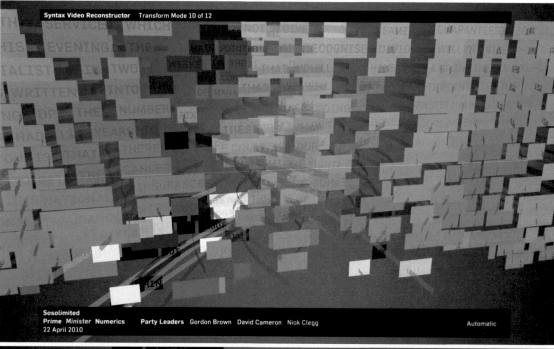

Automatic

Sosolimited
Prime *Minister* **Numerics**
22 April 2010

Party Leaders Gordon Brown David Cameron Nick Clegg

Automatic

Automatic

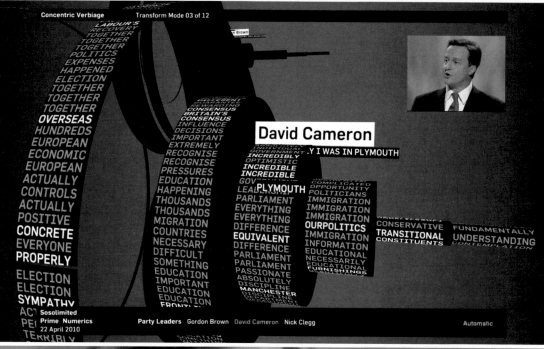

Sosolimited
Prime Numerics
22 April 2010

Party Leaders Gordon Brown David Cameron Nick Clegg

Automatic

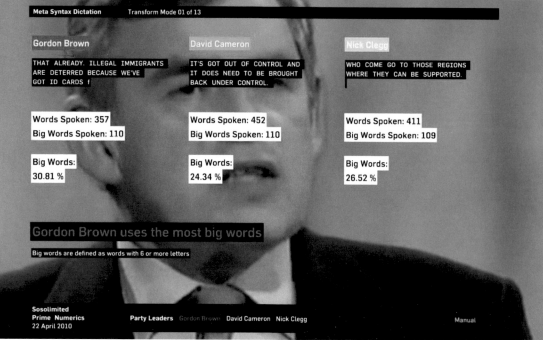

Gordon Brown

THAT ALREADY. ILLEGAL IMMIGRANTS ARE DETERRED BECAUSE WE'VE GOT ID CARDS f

Words Spoken: 357
Big Words Spoken: 110

Big Words:
30.81 %

David Cameron

IT'S GOT OUT OF CONTROL AND IT DOES NEED TO BE BROUGHT BACK UNDER CONTROL.

Words Spoken: 452
Big Words Spoken: 110

Big Words:
24.34 %

Nick Clegg

WHO COME GO TO THOSE REGIONS WHERE THEY CAN BE SUPPORTED.

Words Spoken: 411
Big Words Spoken: 109

Big Words:
26.52 %

Gordon Brown uses the most big words

Big words are defined as words with 6 or more letters

Sosolimited
Prime Numerics
22 April 2010

Party Leaders Gordon Brown David Cameron Nick Clegg

Manual

103

THE LOOP CURRENT

The Gulf's largest current, the Loop Current, enters from the Caribbean as the Yucatán Current. Running to depths of 2,600 feet, it can swing directly east to join the Gulf Stream or surge north before curling back through the Straits of Florida. If it penetrates deeply into the Gulf, it often sheds a great eddy, which drifts westward. The Loop Current could carry oil from a Gulf spill up the Atlantic coast.

The Gulf holds more than 50,000 wells and some 43,000 miles of pipeline.

Perdido
Floating production platform operating in world-record 8,000 feet of water

Tiber well
World's deepest offshore well (art at left)

The maximum depth of the Gulf is unknown. Estimates range from 12,303 to 14,370 feet.

Map Legend

- Coastal wetland
- Coastal protected area

Active federal lease as of March 2010
- Shallow water
- Deep water (1,000 to 4,999 feet)
- Ultradeep water (5,000 feet or more)

- Oil or gas offshore platform
- Oil or gas well
- Crude oil or gas terminal
- Oil refinery
- Oil- or gas-related pipeline
- Maritime boundary
- Planning area boundary

OFFSHORE WELL PROFILES

- TIBER Water depth 4,132 ft
- MACONDO (Deepwater Horizon) Water depth 5,000 ft
- PERDIDO Operating in deepest water 8,000 ft
- MACONDO Total depth 18,000 ft
- TIBER Total depth 35,050 ft

U.S. PLATFORMS

A waterborne city of oil rigs rises off the coasts of Texas, Louisiana, Alabama, and Mississippi—but not Florida. Exploration off the Florida coast, starting in the 1940s, yielded largely dry holes, and the potential threat to the state's top industry, tourism, has been considered too great a risk.

NATIONAL GEOGRAPHIC

Gulf of Mexico

A GEOGRAPHY OF OFFSHORE OIL

For the past half century, oil has driven the economy of the Gulf of Mexico. A third of U.S. oil production flows from nearly 3,500 platforms in the Gulf, with thousands of miles of pipeline delivering oil and natural gas to shore. Since the first Gulf well was drilled off Louisiana in 1938, in less than 15 feet of water, close-in reserves have been depleted and exploration has marched off the continental shelf, onto the continental slope, and beyond. Today Gulf oil is deep oil; the bulk of U.S. production draws from wells in more than a thousand feet of water. U.S. Gulf oil reserves are estimated at 44.9 billion barrels, but as the *Deepwater Horizon* disaster showed, the challenges of deep drilling are formidable.

U.S. Gulf oil from federal leases by depth

350 million barrels
300
250 — Shallow water
200
150
100
50
0
1965 1970 1975 1980 1985 1990 1995 2000 2005 2009
Deep   Ultradeep

NEW DEPTHS

The world's deepest offshore well, the Tiber well (art, above) reaches nearly six miles below the Gulf's seafloor. Not yet operational, it was drilled in late 2009 by the rig *Deepwater Horizon*, which was destroyed months later drilling the Macondo well. Other record holders in the Gulf: The floating production platform *Perdido* operates in the deepest water—8,000 feet—and the Petronius tower, the tallest fixed platform, stands in 1,754 feet of water.

MEXICO'S OIL DROP

Daily output of Pemex, the state-owned oil monopoly, hit 3.4 million barrels in 2004 but has fallen to 2.6 million. The drop is blamed on poor management and declining close-in reserves. Three-quarters of the oil comes from the Gulf, where Mexico has estimated reserves of at least 11.3 billion barrels. Oil and gas sales fund a third of the federal budget; the U.S. is the top importer.

IXTOC I OIL SPILL

Mexico's Ixtoc I well blew out in the Bay of Campeche in 1979 and flowed for 295 days. Some 3.5 million barrels of oil fouled hundreds of miles of shore as far as Padre Island, Texas. Most habitat recovered, but three-inch-thick tar mats remain in some lagoons. Ixtoc I ranked as the world's largest accidental marine spill until it was surpassed by Macondo.

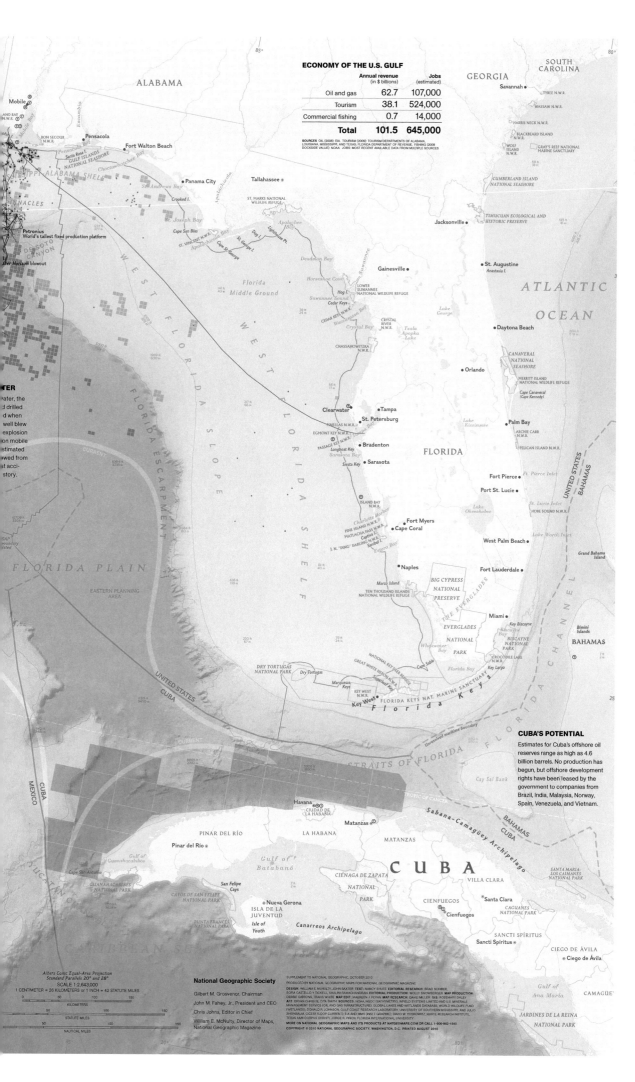

ECONOMY OF THE U.S. GULF

	Annual revenue (in $ billions)	Jobs (estimated)
Oil and gas	62.7	107,000
Tourism	38.1	524,000
Commercial fishing	0.7	14,000
Total	**101.5**	**645,000**

SOURCES: OIL (2008): EIA. TOURISM (2009): TOURISM DEPARTMENTS OF ALABAMA, LOUISIANA, MISSISSIPPI, AND TEXAS; FLORIDA DEPARTMENT OF REVENUE. FISHING (2008 DOCKSIDE VALUE): NOAA. JOBS: MOST RECENT AVAILABLE DATA FROM MULTIPLE SOURCES

CUBA'S POTENTIAL

Estimates for Cuba's offshore oil reserves range as high as 4.6 billion barrels. No production has begun, but offshore development rights have been leased by the government to companies from Brazil, India, Malaysia, Norway, Spain, Venezuela, and Vietnam.

National Geographic Society

Gilbert M. Grosvenor, Chairman

John M. Fahey, Jr., President and CEO

Chris Johns, Editor in Chief

William E. McNulty, Director of Maps,
National Geographic Magazine

SUPPLEMENT TO NATIONAL GEOGRAPHIC, OCTOBER 2010
PRODUCED BY NATIONAL GEOGRAPHIC MAPS FOR NATIONAL GEOGRAPHIC MAGAZINE

DESIGN: WILLIAM E. MCNULTY, JOHN BAXTER. TEXT: NANCY SHUTE. EDITORIAL RESEARCH: BRAD SCRIBER, SOFIA CASTELLO Y TICKELL, SHALINI RAMACHANDRAN. EDITORIAL PRODUCTION: MOLLY SNOWBERGER. MAP PRODUCTION: DEBBIE GIBBONS, TRAVIS WHITE. MAP EDIT: MAUREEN J. FLYNN. MAP RESEARCH: DAVID MILLER. GIS: ROSEMARY DALEY. ART: BRYAN CHRISTIE, DAN TRAPP. SOURCES: NOAA, MSGC BATHYMETRY; MMS (LEASES AND U.S. MINERALS MANAGEMENT SERVICE OIL AND GAS INFRASTRUCTURE); GLOBAL LEASES AND MARITIME DATABASE, WORLD WILDLIFE FUND (WETLANDS); DONALD R. JOHNSON, GULF COAST RESEARCH LABORATORY, UNIVERSITY OF SOUTHERN MISSISSIPPI, AND JULIO SHEINBAUM, CICESE (LOOP CURRENT); E4 AND MMS (WEST CURRENT); DAVID W. YOSKOWITZ, HARTE RESEARCH INSTITUTE, TEXAS A&M–CORPUS CHRISTI; JORGE R. PIÑON, FLORIDA INTERNATIONAL UNIVERSITY.
MORE ON NATIONAL GEOGRAPHIC MAPS AND ITS PRODUCTS AT NATGEOMAPS.COM OR CALL 1-800-962-1643
COPYRIGHT © 2010 NATIONAL GEOGRAPHIC SOCIETY, WASHINGTON, D.C. PRINTED AUGUST 2010

Albers Conic Equal-Area Projection
Standard Parallels 20° and 28°
SCALE 1:2,643,000
1 CENTIMETER = 26 KILOMETERS or 1 INCH = 42 STATUTE MILES

NATIONAL GEOGRAPHIC

Gulf of Mexico. A Geography of Offshore Oil

One-third of all US oil production comes from the Gulf of Mexico; oil extraction drives the economy of the Gulf. The map shows the complete infrastructure of oil production in the region—including all 3,500 platforms, thousands of miles of pipelines, active federal leases—as well as its fragile wetlands and protected areas.

Year: 2010—Designer and Map Director: William McNulty—Designer: John Baxter—Copywriter: Nancy Shute—Map Producer: Debbie Gibbons—GIS: Rosemary Daley—Publisher: *National Geographic*

CAN WE KEEP UP?

DOMESTIC WATER USE IN URBAN AREAS WILL INCREASE AS A RESULT OF POPULATION GROWTH AND URBANISATION.

THIS WILL REQUIRE NEW WATER INFRASTRUCTURE IN MANY COUNTRIES.

INCREASE IN URBAN DOMESTIC WATER USE BY 2030

⑤ BRAZIL 298
④ MEXICO 323
③ CHINA 691
② INDIA 1139
① USA 1500

TOP 5 NEED IN MILLION CUBIC METERS OF WATER

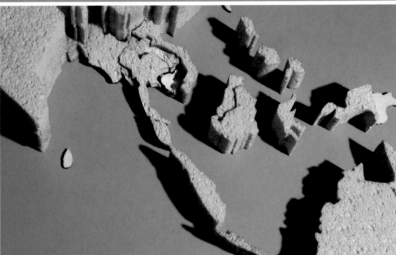

HAL WATTS & MATTHEW LAWS
Urban Water Needs: Can We Keep Up?

Combining their precision as engineers with creativity honed at the London Royal College of Art, Matthew Laws and Hal Watts designed a world map out of cheap kitchen sponges. Water was poured onto each country in amounts proportional to its expected urban water consumption in 2030. The sponges then grew in height according to how thirsty the country will be, generating a stark topography of future needs for urban domestic water. As more people crowd into cities over the next 20 years, those cities will experience huge increases in the demand for domestic water for cooking,

cleaning, and sanitation—as opposed to industry and agriculture. It is easy to see that the needs will not be equitably distributed.

Year: 2011—Client: Runner up in Visualising the World Water Day Challenge hosted by Visualization.org and Circle of Blue—Materials: Cellulose Sponge, water, photography—Photography, Image Processing, and Support: Luke Bennett

106

PAUL MAY
From Over Here

From Over Here is a physical representation of articles from the *New York Times* that mention Ireland. The piece is assembled from 228 cards. The size of each card represents the number of articles published in one month. People and topics mentioned in the articles are etched on each card, which stack vertically to build a tactile, interactive picture of coverage spanning the years 1992–2010. The data on which the piece is based was pulled from the *Times'* article search API and then parsed using the Processing framework. A vector graphic was generated for each card and given to a laser cutter for etching.
Year: 2009

107

A person's CO$_2$ emmisions and how to reduce them
C: Consumers CO$_2$ emissions represent 70% of all USA human generated CO2
O$_2$: Tips for reducing CO2 and facts about trees

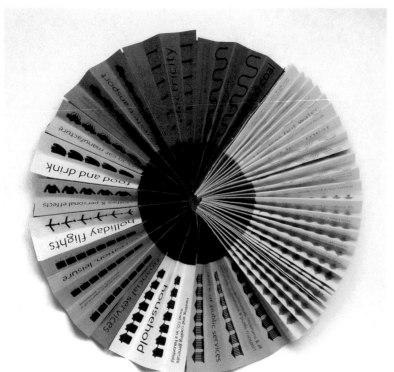

the pollution

the solution

ALEXANDRA MURESAN
P. 108 The Paper Pie Chart
Various paper products such as tissue, cardboard, writing paper, and newsprint are used in corresponding amounts to make a pie chart representing the breakdown of paper production in the United States in 2000.

Year: 2010—Personal project—Material: Paper assemblage, photography, poster—Photography: Alexandra Muresan—Data Source: American Forest and Paper Association

CO$_2$ Paper Pie Chart
Alexandra Muresan constructed the *CO$_2$ Paper Pie Chart* using data from cutco2.org, erasecarbonfootprint.com, eoearth.org, American Forest, and Paper Association. The pie chart is a three-dimensional piece that uses colors and an accordion style folding technique to create either the letter "C" or "O." When folded as a "C," the viewer sees the multiple ways in which CO$_2$ is polluting the atmosphere including airplane travel and manufacturing. When refolded, the pie becomes the letter "O," which reveals tips for reducing carbon emissions.

Year: 2010—Personal project—Paper assemblage, photography, poster

PATTERN MATTERS
Lim Siang Ching
Pattern Matters—Tangible Paper
Infographics
Year: 2011—Client: Pattern Matters: An
Experimental Design Response—Pho-
tography: Lim Siang Ching—Additional
credits: LASALLE College of the Arts

This project investigates the possibilities for augmenting the role of the pattern in design. It explores tactility through pattern-making and aims to demonstrate how pattern is not merely a decorative tool, but an essential element in graphic design. The outcome consists of an experimentation on patterns and its tactile qualities as a visual representation of information based on three different topics. Since humans are naturally drawn to patterns, it could be acquired as a tool to enhance the experience of information by visualizing pattern as a metaphor for information.

ABO

FREQUENCY OF BLOOD GROUPS IN SINGAPORE DONOR POPULATION

B- 1%

6%

A-

7%

O-

AB-

1%

40% O+

B+

8%

A+ 34%

AB+

3%

MICHAEL NAJJAR
Bionic Angel
Future engineering of the human body as an interface will abolish any distinction between inner and outer body and lead to the development of new forms of communication and interconnectivity. *Bionic Angel* shows a portrait of a woman surrounded by the nerve fibers of her own brain. The woman's brain was scanned in a laboratory using diffusion tensor imaging (DTI) technology. The measurement data of its fiber tracks was then computed and visualized as a three dimensional model.

Year: 2006—Courtesy of the artist

Chapter

2

Viewing Science
AND TECHNOLOGY

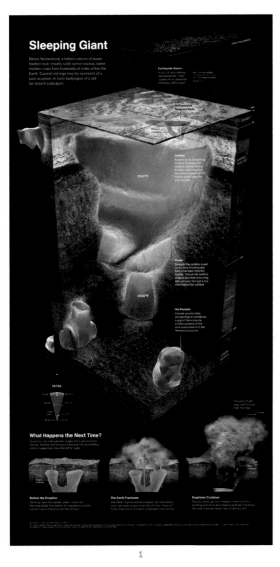

1

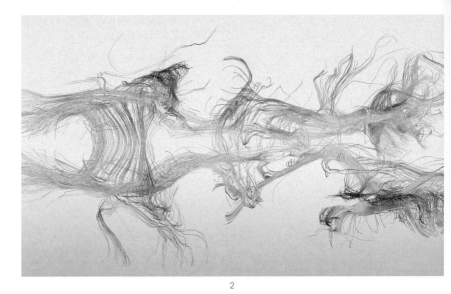

2

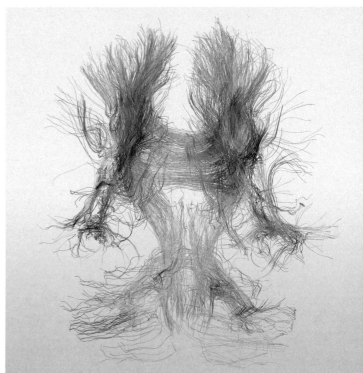

3

NATIONAL GEOGRAPHIC
1   Sleeping Giant
A plume of magma 400-miles deep lies beneath Yellowstone National Park in the United States. Recent seismic activity in the area has caused reason for worry about the gigantic supervolcano.
    Year: 2009—Senior Graphics Editor: Alejandro Tumas —Research and text: Shelley Sperry—Publisher: National Geographic

MICHAEL NAJJAR
2   The Sublime Brain [of Sherin + Michael]
3   The Sublime Brain [of Jonathon]
    The Sublime Brain [of Jonathon] is an example of a neuronal portrait. A special scanning technology was used to capture all the nerve fiber networks in the human brain in the form of numerical measurement data. The data was then converted into a three-dimensional model using software developed by the artist. Viewers see a frontal view of the neuronal structure in the same way they would see the face in a portrait. This represents a new kind of portraiture by presenting an elusive aspect of personality that remains hidden to the human eye and the camera: the subject's neuronal identity.
    Year: 2008—Courtesy of the artist

Scientists need to tell stories to nonscientists, because science stories have to compete with other stories about how the universe works, and how it came to be. Some of those other stories—Bible stories, movie stories, myths—can be very beautiful and very compelling. But to protect science and scientists—and this is not a gentle competition—you've got to get in there and tell your version of how things are, and why things came to be.

o   Robert KRULWICH, Commencement speech at the California Institute of Technology

Science and technology have visual storytelling at their heart. The Lewis structure, invented by Gilbert Norton Lewis in 1916, is how chemists explain the bonds between atoms and electrons. Circuit diagrams are how printed circuit boards are planned. No successful web page gets made without a wireframe.

Sometimes, abstracted diagrams are needed because they represent things that nobody has ever seen, either because it's too small, such as the structure of the atom, or too big, such as the solar system. Other times, visualizations are applied because they can help people see patterns in the data, such as when, famously, a spot map of London was used in 1854, to help prove the link between water supply and cholera. Visuals can also communicate an idea with more precision than words, without the need for translation.

Sketches in notebooks are often how the most complex scientific experiments begin. And then, on the other end of the process, there is the challenge of visualising the work in as clear a way as possible, in order to communicate important information to non scientists, including politicians and the general public: a vital part of securing funding. The need for clear, uncomplicated explanations of scientific information is also a fundamental part of being human: at some point in your adult life, a doctor is going to have to explain something unfortunate about your body, or that of someone close to you. Visual storytelling helps us truly understand the answers to some of the most urgent questions we have, including how could this happen, and will it happen again, without the need for a medical qualification.

On a more positive note, we also need visual storytelling in science and technology to help inspire the practitioners of tomorrow. Only by building a clear path to understanding can the different disciplines encourage people to walk along it.

And as we move towards a world of increased climate change, and increasing urgency to provoke changes in human behavior, we will increasingly look to visualizations to help us understand what is happening, and what our next steps as a society must be.

These are not simple problems, and they cannot be solved with a single graphic. However, the visualizations in this chapter may contain at least some of the tools that can help us comprehend the world around us, and our relationship to it, in a more fundamental way.

The Dynamikum science museum's mission is to make visible the basic laws that govern our world, through entertaining and engaging interactive visuals for people of all ages. A few of their methods are included in this chapter, including the ability to race different animals across a fixed distance, and a precise mapping of the parabola created by throwing a ball into the air.

Elsewhere, the *Immaterials* project takes a very specific piece of data and shows it through a beautiful piece of art, painting the fluctuations in WiFi signal around a building using LED rods, while Wataru Yoshida has created a form of photography overlaid with illustrated bone structures. The result feels like an eighteenth-century anatomy text book mixed in with some beautiful portrait photography, making these familiar creatures seem strangely mythological.

Kim Asendorf and Jana Lange's *Sumedicina* took scientific-style visualizations and used them to tell a fictional story about a laboratory from which a viruses were deliberately set loose in order to sell more vaccines. The story of one of the workers in the lab is told only through infographic and scientific visuals – as if they had been automatically generated for or by the laboratory through the only medium it understood.

Finally, Yuri Suzuki, Masi Kimura and Platform 21's *Breakfast Machine* is a move in the opposite direction to most visual storytelling. It uses complication and obfuscation in order to carry out a very simple and facile task.

Every part of its overengineering is visualized, in a Rube Goldberg fashion, teaching us that even the most useful and practical physical laws can be applied in a way that results in little exposition but plenty of pure entertainment.

Visual Stories

TIMO ARNALL,
JØRN KNUTSEN, EINAR
SNEVE MARTINUSSEN
Immaterials: Light Painting WiFi
This project explores the invisible
terrain of WiFi networks in urban spac-
es by light painting signal strength in
long exposure photographs. A four-me-
ter-long measuring rod with 80 points
of light reveals cross-sections of WiFi
networks. vimeo. com/20412632
Year: 2011——Location: Oslo, Norway——
Client: Yourban Project, Oslo School of
Architecture & Design

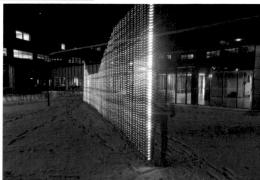

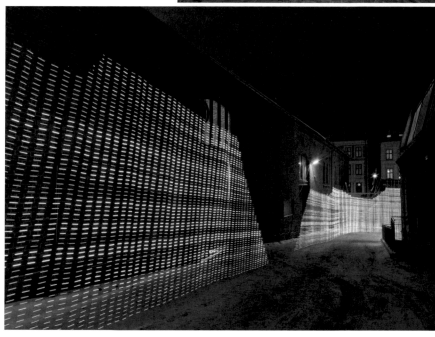

Visual Stories

SCIENCE

DAN PEARLMAN
Lufthansa Markenakademie
Tower 360° Projektion

The *360° projection,* created by Dan Pearlman for the Lufthansa Brand Academy, is a spatial experience created within a reproduced airport tower. It features a digital, interactive, 360° presentation that is based on an educational psychological concept. Brand knowledge is brought to life to train 25,000 employees and executives in an engaging and sustainable way.

Year: 2009—Client: Deutsche Lufthansa—Location: Seeheim, Germany—Photography: diephotodesigner.de

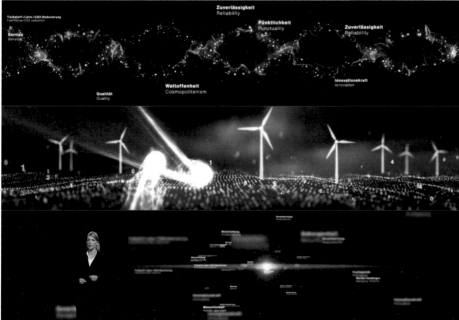

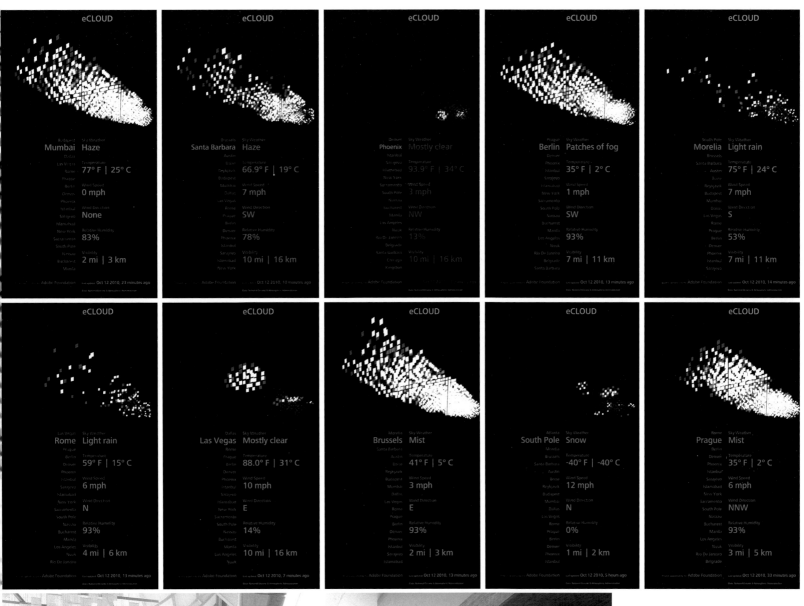

NIKOLAUS HAFERMAAS,
DAN GOODS, AARON KOBLIN
eCLOUD

The *eCLOUD* is a dynamic sculpture inspired by the volume and behavior of an idealized cloud. Made from about 3,000 polycarbonate tiles that can fade between transparent and opaque states, its moving patterns are influenced by real time international weather data pulled from from The National Oceanic and Atmospheric Administration. This data simulates weather from international locations, which is then visualized within the cloud sculpture and on the dynamic display along with the current location being visualized and the NOAA data driving each animation.

Year: 2010—Client: City of San José Office of Cultural Affairs—Creative Producer: Jamie Barlow, Uebersee, Inc— Photography: Spencer Lowell

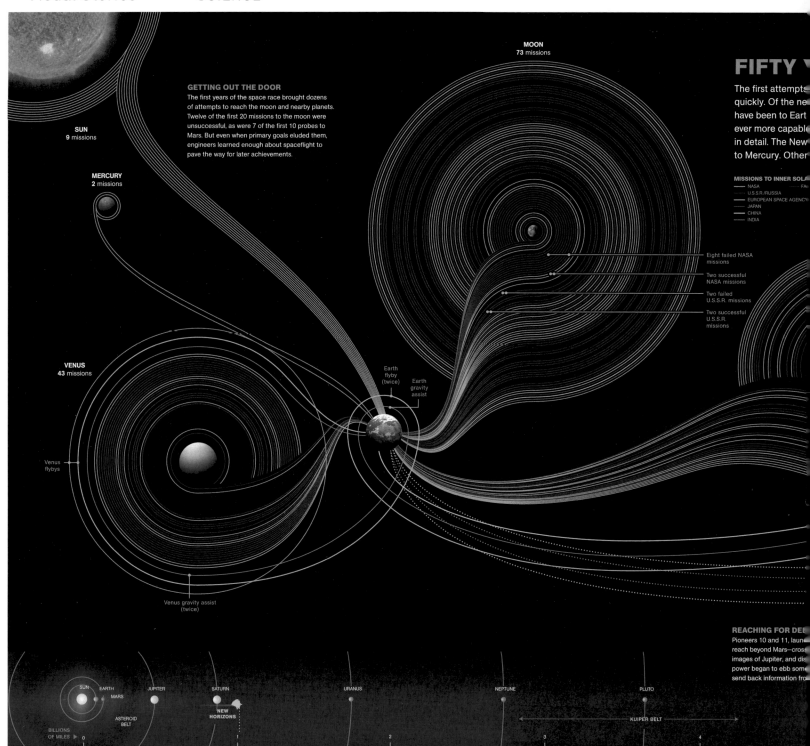

MOON
73 missions

SUN
9 missions

GETTING OUT THE DOOR
The first years of the space race brought dozens of attempts to reach the moon and nearby planets. Twelve of the first 20 missions to the moon were unsuccessful, as were 7 of the first 10 probes to Mars. But even when primary goals eluded them, engineers learned enough about spaceflight to pave the way for later achievements.

MERCURY
2 missions

FIFTY Y

The first attempts
quickly. Of the ne
have been to Eart
ever more capable
in detail. The New
to Mercury. Other

MISSIONS TO INNER SOL
NASA   FA
U.S.S.R./RUSSIA
EUROPEAN SPACE AGENCY
JAPAN
CHINA
INDIA

Eight failed NASA missions

Two successful NASA missions

Two failed U.S.S.R. missions

Two successful U.S.S.R. missions

VENUS
43 missions

Earth flyby (twice)

Earth gravity assist

Venus flybys

Venus gravity assist (twice)

REACHING FOR DEI
Pioneers 10 and 11, laun
reach beyond Mars—cros
images of Jupiter, and dis
power began to ebb some
send back information fro

SUN   EARTH
      MARS

JUPITER

SATURN

NEW
HORIZONS

URANUS

NEPTUNE

PLUTO

KUIPER BELT

ASTEROID
BELT

BILLIONS
OF MILES ▶   0   2   3   4

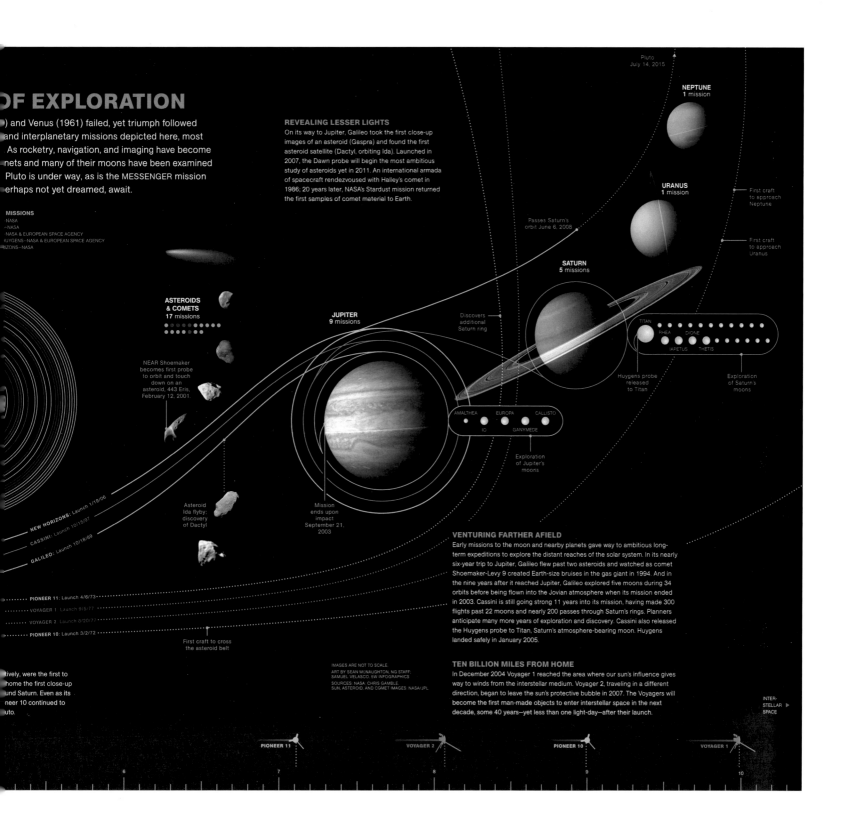

OF EXPLORATION

) and Venus (1961) failed, yet triumph followed
and interplanetary missions depicted here, most
As rocketry, navigation, and imaging have become
nets and many of their moons have been examined
Pluto is under way, as is the MESSENGER mission
erhaps not yet dreamed, await.

MISSIONS
-NASA
-NASA
-NASA & EUROPEAN SPACE AGENCY
UYGENS–NASA & EUROPEAN SPACE AGENCY
IZONS–NASA

REVEALING LESSER LIGHTS
On its way to Jupiter, Galileo took the first close-up
images of an asteroid (Gaspra) and found the first
asteroid satellite (Dactyl, orbiting Ida). Launched in
2007, the Dawn probe will begin the most ambitious
study of asteroids yet in 2011. An international armada
of spacecraft rendezvoused with Halley's comet in
1986; 20 years later, NASA's Stardust mission returned
the first samples of comet material to Earth.

Pluto
July 14, 2015

NEPTUNE
1 mission

URANUS
1 mission

First craft
to approach
Neptune

First craft
to approach
Uranus

Passes Saturn's
orbit June 6, 2008

SATURN
5 missions

ASTEROIDS & COMETS
17 missions

JUPITER
9 missions

Discovers
additional
Saturn ring

TITAN
RHEA   DIONE
IAPETUS   THETIS

NEAR Shoemaker
becomes first probe
to orbit and touch
down on an
asteroid, 443 Eris,
February 12, 2001.

Huygens probe
released
to Titan

Exploration
of Saturn's
moons

AMALTHEA   EUROPA   CALLISTO
IO   GANYMEDE

Exploration
of Jupiter's
moons

NEW HORIZONS: Launch 1/19/06

CASSINI: Launch 10/15/97

GALILEO: Launch 10/18/89

Asteroid
Ida flyby;
discovery
of Dactyl

Mission
ends upon
impact
September 21,
2003

VENTURING FARTHER AFIELD
Early missions to the moon and nearby planets gave way to ambitious long-
term expeditions to explore the distant reaches of the solar system. In its nearly
six-year trip to Jupiter, Galileo flew past two asteroids and watched as comet
Shoemaker-Levy 9 created Earth-size bruises in the gas giant in 1994. And in
the nine years after it reached Jupiter, Galileo explored five moons during 34
orbits before being flown into the Jovian atmosphere when its mission ended
in 2003. Cassini is still going strong 11 years into its mission, having made 300
flights past 22 moons and nearly 200 passes through Saturn's rings. Planners
anticipate many more years of exploration and discovery. Cassini also released
the Huygens probe to Titan, Saturn's atmosphere-bearing moon. Huygens
landed safely in January 2005.

PIONEER 11: Launch 4/6/73

VOYAGER 1: Launch 9/5/77

VOYAGER 2: Launch 8/20/77

PIONEER 10: Launch 3/2/72

First craft to cross
the asteroid belt

IMAGES ARE NOT TO SCALE.
ART BY SEAN MCNAUGHTON, NG STAFF;
SAMUEL VELASCO, 5W INFOGRAPHICS
SOURCES: NASA; CHRIS GAMBLE.
SUN, ASTEROID, AND COMET IMAGES: NASA/JPL

TEN BILLION MILES FROM HOME
In December 2004 Voyager 1 reached the area where our sun's influence gives
way to winds from the interstellar medium. Voyager 2, traveling in a different
direction, began to leave the sun's protective bubble in 2007. The Voyagers will
become the first man-made objects to enter interstellar space in the next
decade, some 40 years—yet less than one light-day—after their launch.

INTER-
STELLAR ▶
SPACE

ively, were the first to
home the first close-up
und Saturn. Even as its
neer 10 continued to
uto.

PIONEER 11   VOYAGER 2   PIONEER 10   VOYAGER 1

6   7   8   9   10

NATIONAL GEOGRAPHIC
Fifty Years of Space Exploration
This infographic shows every
space mission and destination in the
last 50 years, including manned and
unmanned, completed and failed.
Year : 2009—Credits: 5W Infographics—Client: *National Geographic
Magazine*—Designer: Sean McNaughton, Senior Graphics Editor, *National
Geographic Magazine*

Visual Stories

SCIENCE

GR/DD
Carbon Cycle

Carbon Cycle was created for the Atmosphere interactive gallery at the Science Museum in London. By interacting with a number of augmented reality tags that represent a carbon cycle component, visitors can directly influence an animated, on-screen carbon cycle. Visitors can also add factories, forests, roads, and more to the island grid in order to explore what effects the earth's carbon cycle.

Year: 2011—Client: Science Museum

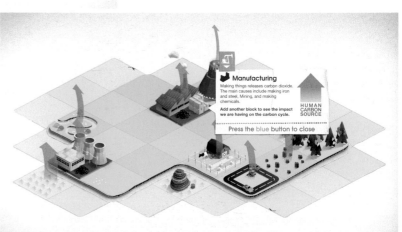

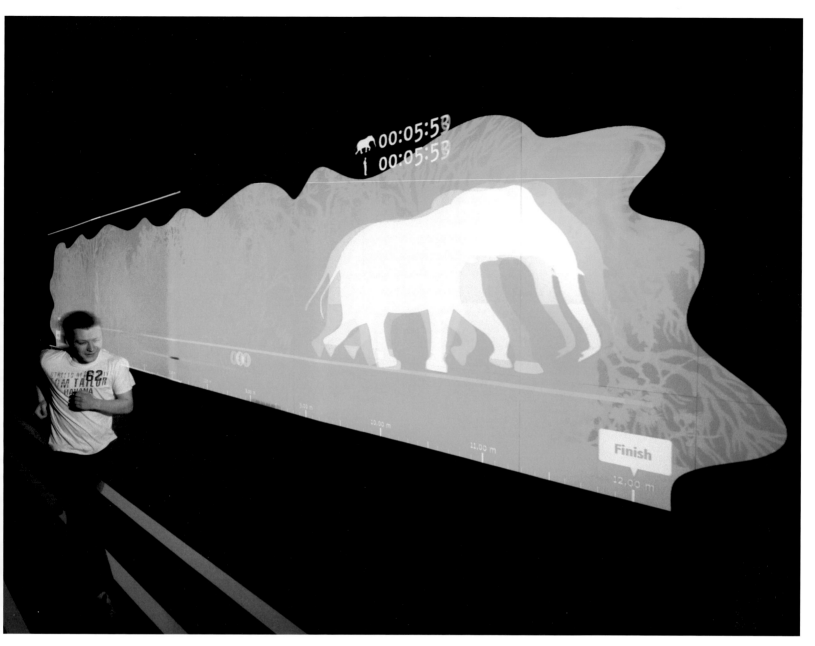

STUDIO KLV
Dynamikum Science Center

Footrace
Which is faster: human or animal? Users can step onto a track, race the animal of their choice, and answer that question. After the race, information about the animal, its habitat, and its predators are shown. The exhibit also aims to show that in the natural world, each living creature adapts itself to its habitat, which includes protecting itself from enemies and foraging strategies. Many animals are hunters, meaning they need to be able to move quickly to catch their prey; other animals can't move quite as quickly and have developed other methods of protection, such a a shell.

Flight Paths
The flight path of a ball and the physics behind it are illustrated in this interactive graphic for the Dynamikum science center. The graphic projection shows not only that the flight path is always curved, but that is contorted rather than circular. Color is used to show the various speeds at which the ball is traveling and to illustrate that once the ball has left the pitcher's hand, gravity exerts a growing influence on it and the path forms a parabola.

Planetary Orbits
In this interactive piece, the user experiences how the planets revolve around the sun in a very unique way: by stepping onto the projection surface, the user becomes the sun. A computer calculates the paths of the planets as if the user had the mass and gravitational force of the sun. The planets circle on colored paths, which denote the speed at which they are traveling; the closer a planet comes towards the sun, the quicker it moves and when it moves away, it slows down. If the user can capture one of the planets, it will revolve around them in an ellipsis.

Year: 2008—Client: Dynamikum—Location: Pirmasens Germany—Photography: Axl Klein

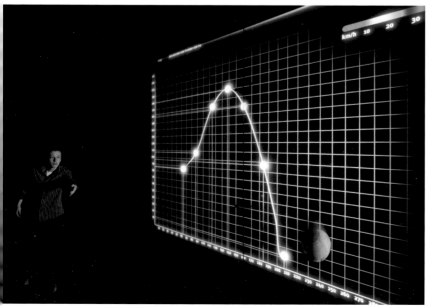

123

Visual Stories

SAM RENWICK
Astra—A User's Manual
Astra, Europe's largest satellite operator, commissioned a series of films explaining how satellites are launched and operated. The seven films—History, Physics, Control, Launch, Why We Need Satellites, Business, and The Future—explain their subjects in a simple and accessible way with colorful and evocative graphics.

Directed by: Sam Renwick and Chris Perry—Illustration: Sam Renwick—Animation: Chris Perry—Creative Director: Paul Belford—Agency: This is Real Art

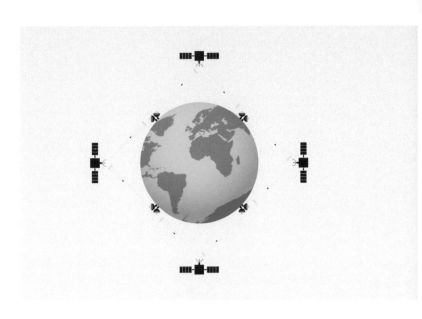

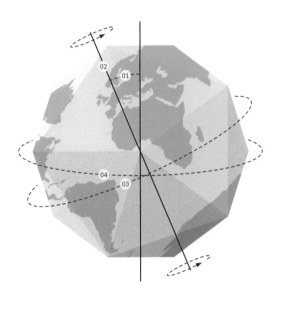

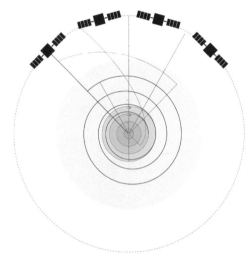

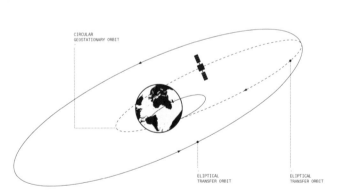

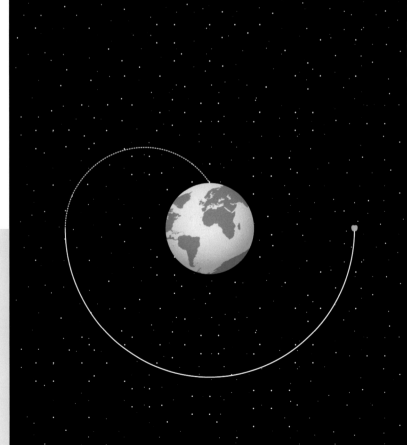

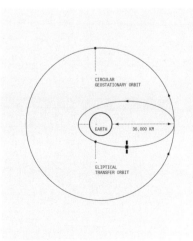

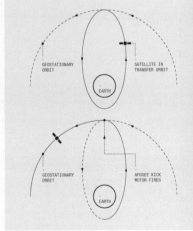

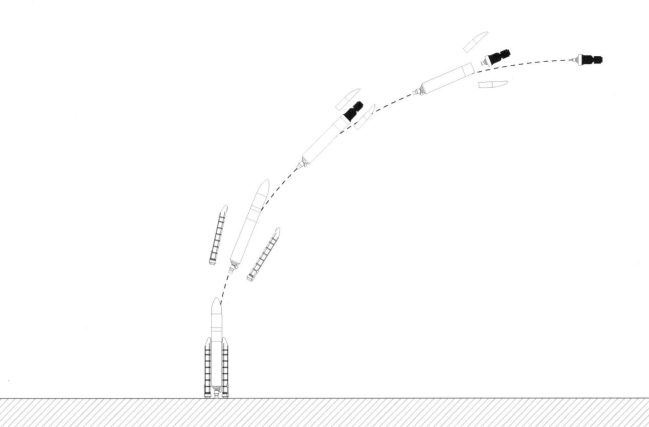

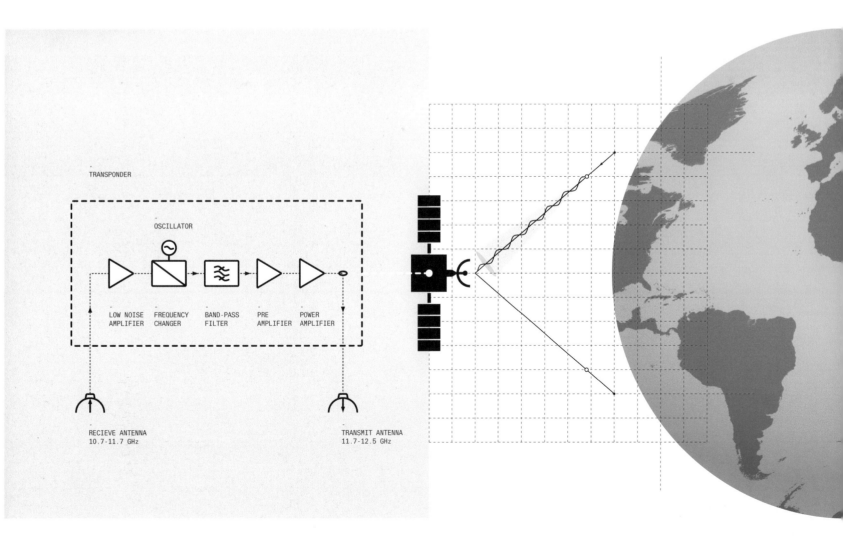

TRANSPONDER

OSCILLATOR

LOW NOISE
AMPLIFIER

FREQUENCY
CHANGER

BAND-PASS
FILTER

PRE
AMPLIFIER

POWER
AMPLIFIER

RECIEVE ANTENNA
10.7-11.7 GHz

TRANSMIT ANTENNA
11.7-12.5 GHz

125

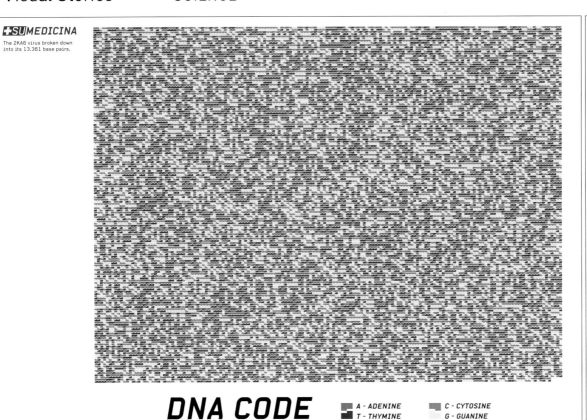

+SUMEDICINA

The 2KA6 virus broken down into its 13.361 base pairs.

DNA CODE

A - ADENINE
T - THYMINE
C - CYTOSINE
G - GUANINE

SOCIAL ACT

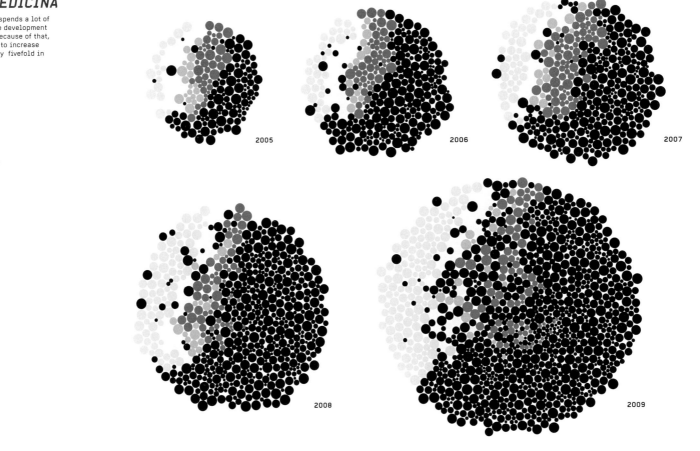

+SUMEDICINA

Sumedicina spends a lot of money for the development of viruses. Because of that, they made it to increase their capacity fivefold in four years.

2005

2006

2007

2008

2009

● ARCHIVED
● FURTHER INVESTIGATED
● TESTED ON ANIMALS
  TESTED ON HUMANS
  WIDESPREAD

· · ● ●
INFECTION DEGREE

VIRUS EVOLUTION

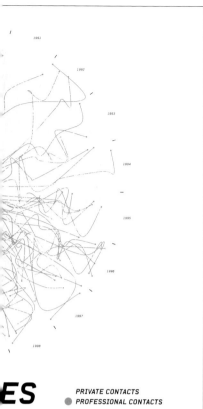

PRIVATE CONTACTS
PROFESSIONAL CONTACTS

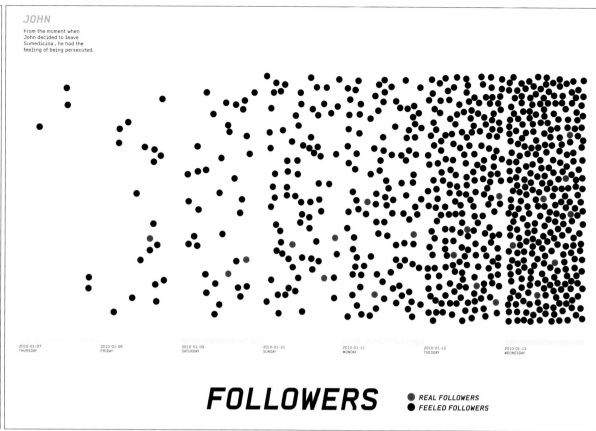

JOHN

From the moment when John decided to leave Sumedicina , he had the feeling of being persecuted.

FOLLOWERS

● REAL FOLLOWERS
● FEELED FOLLOWERS

2010-01-07
THURSDAY

2010-01-08
FRIDAY

2010-01-09
SATURDAY

2010-01-10
SUNDAY

2010-01-11
MONDAY

2010-01-12
TUESDAY

2010-01-13
WEDNESDAY

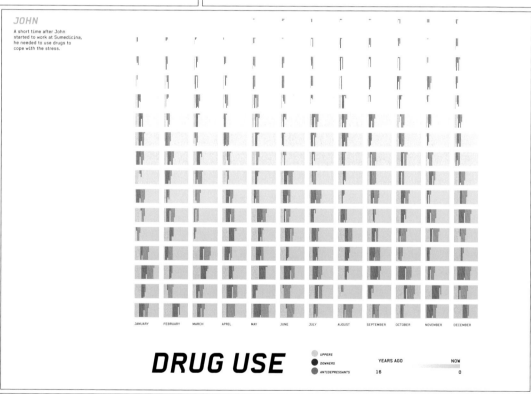

JOHN

A short time after John started to work at Sumedicina, he needed to use drugs to cope with the stress.

DRUG USE

○ UPPERS
● DOWNERS
● ANTIDEPRESSANTS

YEARS AGO
16

NOW
0

JANUARY FEBRUARY MARCH APRIL MAY JUNE JULY AUGUST SEPTEMBER OCTOBER NOVEMBER DECEMBER

JANA LANGE, KIM ASENDORF
Sumedicina

Jana Lange and Kim Asendorf created an alternate reality in which the H1N1 virus originated in the laboratories of Sumedicina, one of the biggest vaccine manufacturers in the world. According to Lange and Asendorf, if media hype is generated to boost the sale of vaccines, this could be a realistic scenario. Their fictional story continues with Sumedicina and one of its researchers, who breeds new viruses that are immune to current vaccines—except those of Sumedicina. When the new highly fatal 2KA6 virus is released, the researcher is tormented by his conscience, quits his job and is pursued by the Sumedicina's secret service. He disappears without a trace. The project contains 16 information graphics and a poster.

Year: 2010—Client: Artistic work

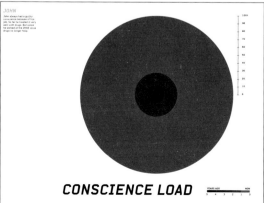

JOHN

CONSCIENCE LOAD

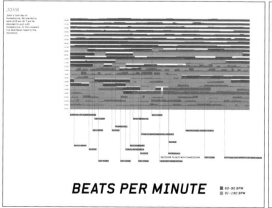

JOHN

BEATS PER MINUTE
■ 60-90 BPM
■ 91-180 BPM

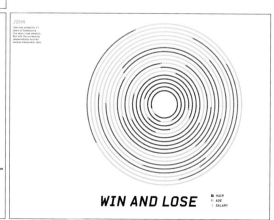

JOHN

WIN AND LOSE
■ HAIR
■ AGE
○ SALARY

Hivern
Invierno/Winter

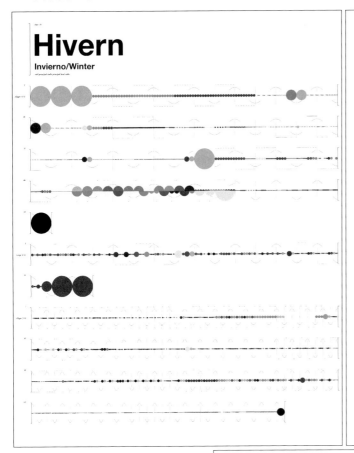

Primavera
Primavera/Spring

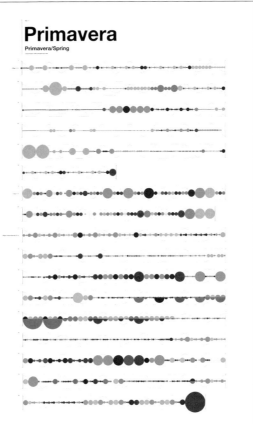

MOT
Lesquatrestacions

Lesquatrestacions, or *The Four Seasons,* refers to the musical composition of the eighteenth century Italian composer, Antonio Vivaldi. It is a graphic interpretation of the four violin concertos that constitute this baroque masterpiece. Mot designed a graphic notation system called SisTeMu that interprets musical texture and translates musical scores into simple, geometric forms. These colorful forms explore the rhythmic and melodic harmonies found in musical composition and simplify these complex mathematical structures so that they are accessible to the viewer as a visual narrative.

Year: 2010—Medium: Poster—Size: 594 × 840 mm—Client: Centre National des Arts Plastiques

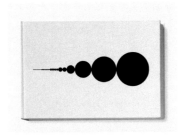

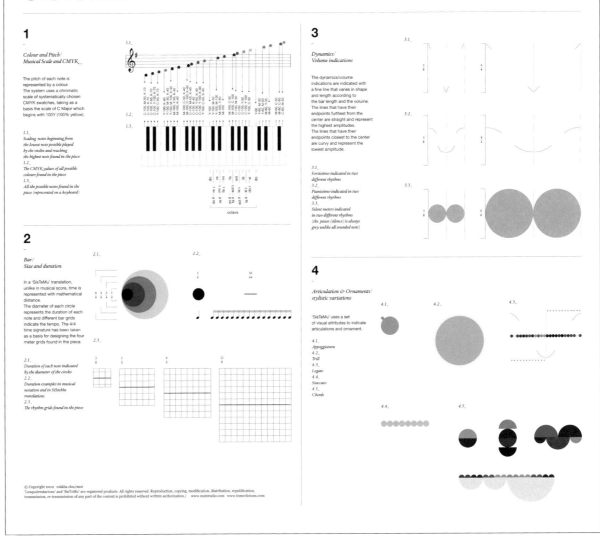

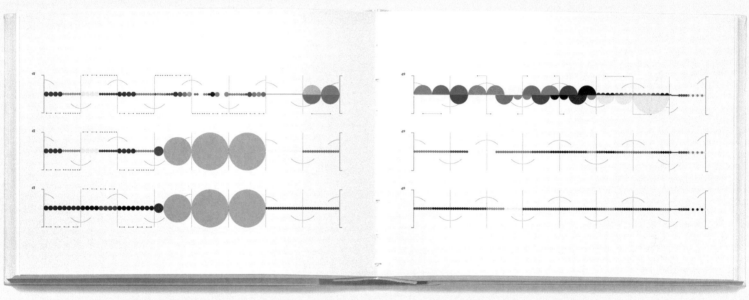

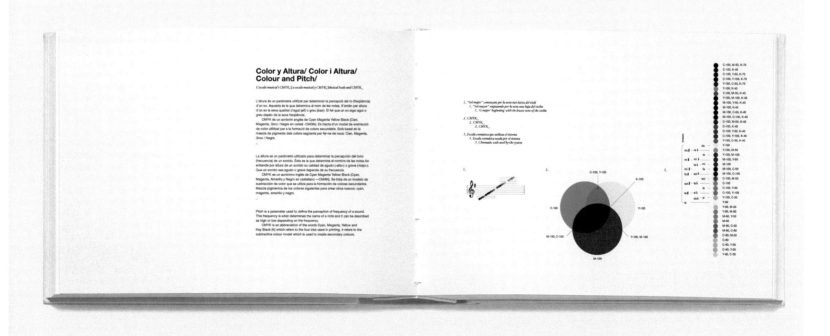

WATARU YOSHIDA
Composition of Mammals
Composition of Mammals, a fictional exhibition using fictional places, studied the anatomy of mammals with displays of taxidermy and skulls and accompanying informational posters. The posters show the complex structure of each mammal's body. Using diagrams of bone structures, photographs, and illustrations, the posters illustrate the mysterious and delicate qualities of the anatomy of mammals.

Year: 2011—Client: Personal project—
Photography: Wataru Yoshida © All rights reserved

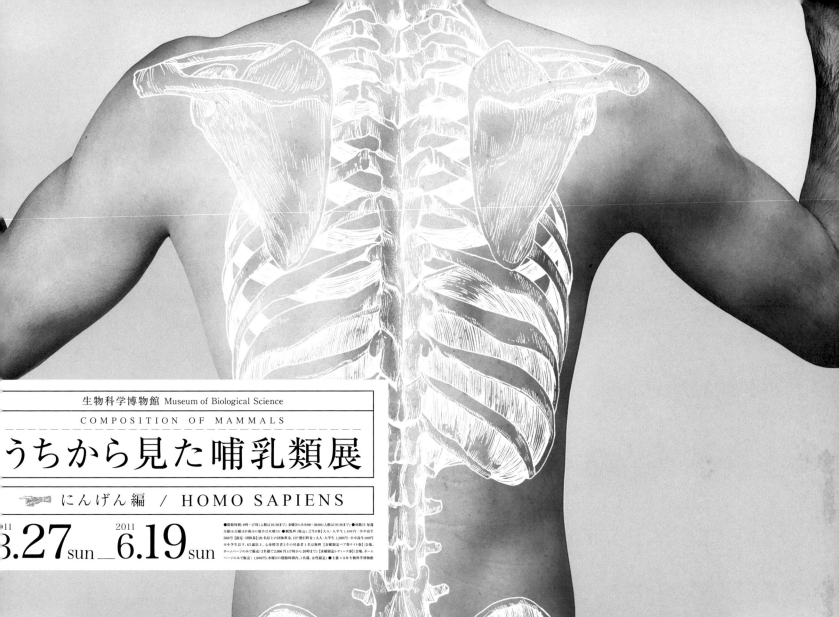

生物科学博物館 Museum of Biological Science

COMPOSITION OF MAMMALS

うちから見た哺乳類展

にんげん編 / HOMO SAPIENS

3.27 sun — 6.19 sun
2011 2011

●開館時間：9時〜17時（入館は16:30まで）金曜日のみ9:00〜20:00（入館は19:30まで）●休館日：毎週月曜日（月曜日が祝日の場合は火曜日）●観覧料（税込）：【当日券】大人・大学生 1,400円／小中高生 500円【前売・団体券】20名以上の団体料金、HP割引料金：大人・大学生 1,200円／小中高生 400円 ※小学生以下、65歳以上、心身障害者とその付添者1名は無料【金曜限定ペア券ナイト券】会場、ホームページにて販売／2名様で2,000円（17時から20時まで）【水曜限定レディース券】会場、ホームページのみで販売／1,000円（水曜日の開館時間内、1名様、女性限定）●主催＝日本生物科学博物館

生物科学博物館 Museum of Biological Science

COMPOSITION OF MAMMALS

うちから見た哺乳類展

陸の哺乳類編 / MAMMALS OF LAND

7.17 sun — 9.25 sun
2011 2011

●開館時間：9時〜17時（入館は16:30まで）金曜日のみ9:00〜20:00（入館は19:30まで）●休館日：毎週月曜日（月曜日が祝日の場合は火曜日）●観覧料（税込）：【当日券】大人・大学生 1,400円／小中高生 500円【前売・団体券】20名以上の団体料金、HP割引料金：大人・大学生 1,200円／小中高生 400円 ※小学生以下、65歳以上、心身障害者とその付添者1名は無料【金曜限定ペア券ナイト券】会場、ホームページにて販売／2名様で2,000円（17時から20時まで）【水曜限定レディース券】会場、ホームページのみで販売／1,000円（水曜日の開館時間内、1名様、女性限定）●主催＝日本生物科学博物館

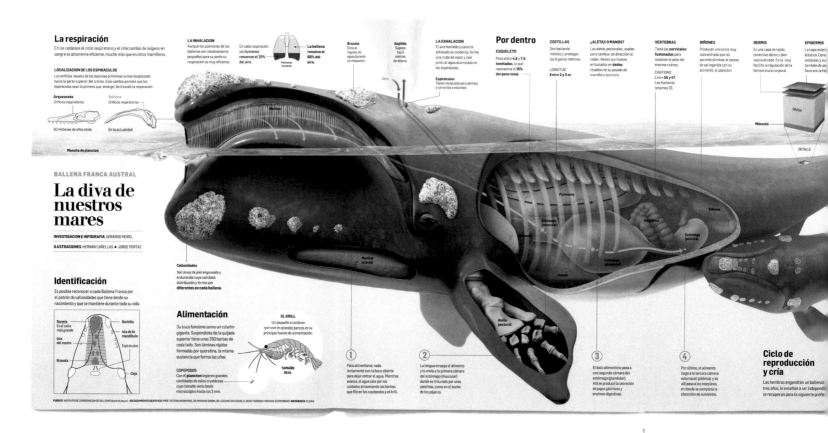

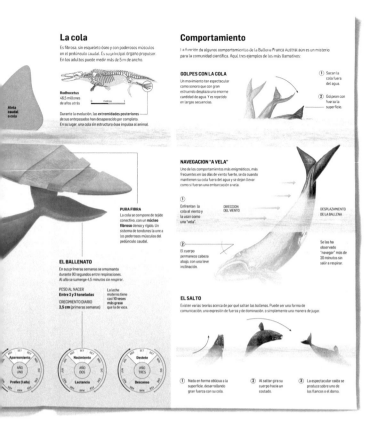

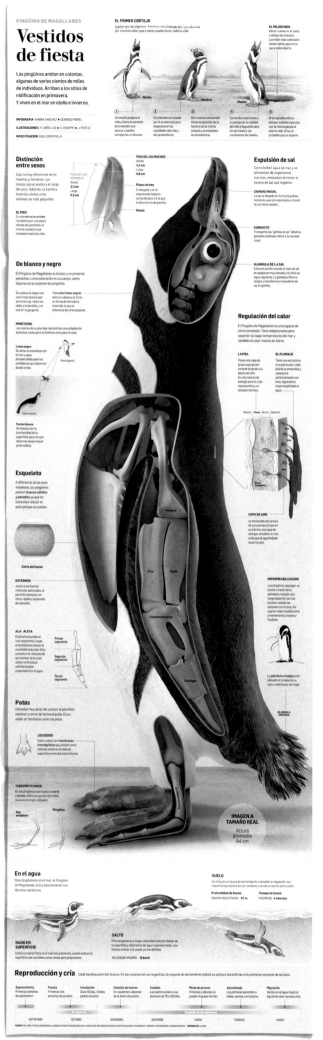

PABLO LOSCRI
○ with Gerardo Morel

1   Southern Right Whale

This image was included in a series of four fold-out posters printed in the *Sunday* magazine of the Argentinian newspaper *Clarín*. For this plate, the focus was on balancing historic information with the most recent scientific surveys about the southern right whale.

Year: 2008—Client: *Clarín*—Ilustration: Hernan Cañellas, Jorge Portaz—Researcher: Gerardo Morel

2   Twilight of the Artic Ice

Infographics for a poster printed in *National Geographic*. The graphic shows the last high resolution satellite image of the Arctic ice sheet and explains why the loss of ice takes place and what the consequences are of such a loss.

Year: 2009—Client: *National Geographic*—Graphic Editor: Alejandro Tumas—Illustrations: Hernan Cañellas, Pablo Loscri—Map Research: Kaitlin M. Yarnall—Text: Jane Vessels—Production: Mollie Bates—Satelite image: Robert Stacey, Worldsat International Inc.—GIS: Theodore A. Sickley

3   Magellanic Penguin

Four fold-out posters featuring animals native to Argentina were included in the *Sunday* magazine of the Argentinian newspaper *Clarín*. The *Magellanic Penguin* was able to be represented at its real size because of the size of the paper and the small size of the penguin.

Year: 2008—Client: *Clarín*—Codesigners: Vanina Sanchez, Gerardo Morel—Illustrations: Hernan Cañellas, Aldo Chiappe, Jorge Portaz—Researcher: Guillermo Milla

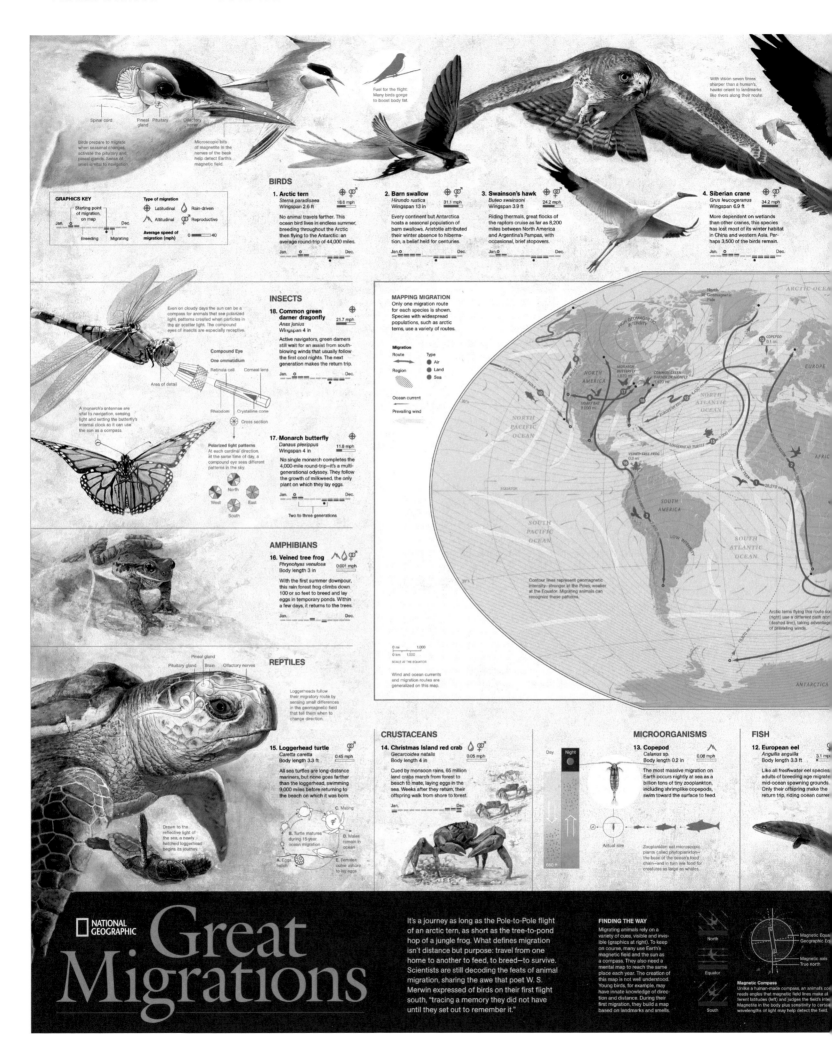

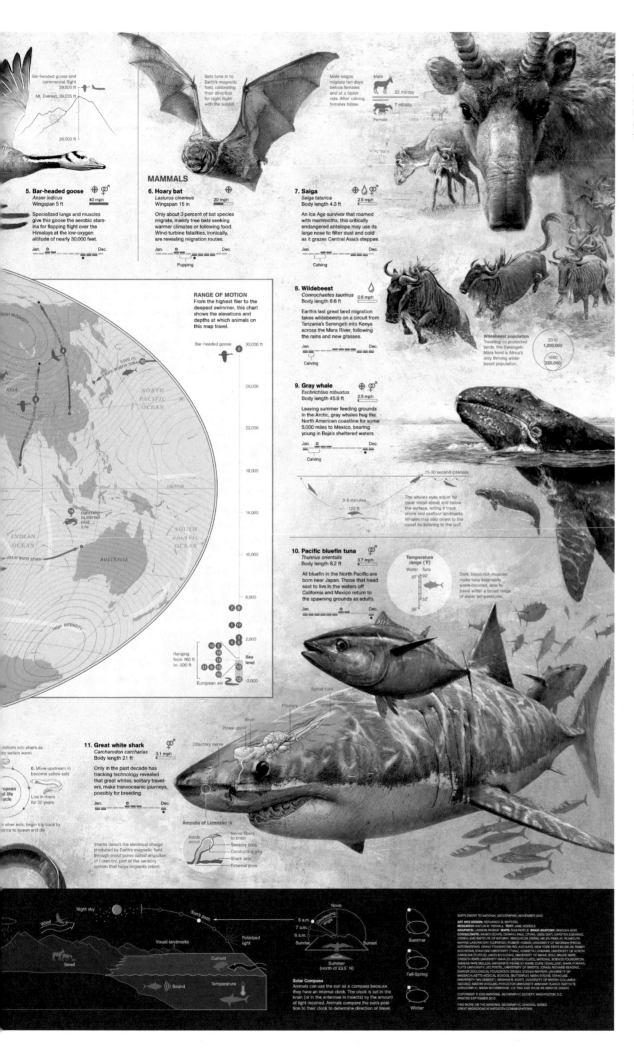

NATIONAL GEOGRAPHIC
Great Migrations
This poster shows the incredible feats of migrations undertaken by birds, insects, amphibians, fish, and microorganisms. Their routes, distances, and methods of orientation are plotted out on a map, with additional details given for the major migrating species.

Year: 2010—Designer and Senior Graphics Editor: Fernando Baptista——Designer: Elaine Bradley——Map and small graphics: Lawson Parker, Sam Pepple, Sizuka Aoki——Researcher: Kaitlin Yarnall——Copywriter: Jane Vessels——Publisher: *National Geographic Magazine*

MAMMALS

5. Bar-headed goose
Anser indicus
Wingspan 5 ft — 40 mph

Specialized lungs and muscles give this goose the aerobic stamina for flapping flight over the Himalaya at the low-oxygen altitude of nearly 30,000 feet.

Jan. — Dec.

6. Hoary bat
Lasiurus cinereus
Wingspan 15 in — 20 mph

Only about 3 percent of bat species migrate, mainly tree bats seeking warmer climates or following food. Wind-turbine fatalities, ironically, are revealing migration routes.

Jan. — Dec.
Pupping

7. Saiga
Saiga tatarica
Body length 4.3 ft — 2.5 mph

An Ice Age survivor that roamed with mammoths, this critically endangered antelope may use its large nose to filter dust and cold as it grazes Central Asia's steppes.

Jan. — Dec.
Calving

Male saigas migrate ten days before females and at a faster rate. After calving, females follow.
Male — 22 mi/day
Female — 7 mi/day

8. Wildebeest
Connochaetes taurinus
Body length 6.6 ft — 0.6 mph

Earth's last great land migration takes wildebeests on a circuit from Tanzania's Serengeti into Kenya across the Mara River, following the rains and new grasses.

Jan. — Dec.
Calving

Wildebeest population
Traveling on protected lands, the Serengeti-Mara herd is Africa's only thriving wildebeest population.
2010 1,200,000
1960 220,000

9. Gray whale
Eschrichtius robustus
Body length 45.9 ft — 2.5 mph

Leaving summer feeding grounds in the Arctic, gray whales hug the North American coastline for some 5,000 miles to Mexico, bearing young in Baja's sheltered waters.

Jan. — Dec.
Calving

15-30 second intervals
3-5 minutes
120 ft

The whale's eyes adjust for clear vision above and below the surface, letting it track shore and seafloor landmarks. Whales may also orient to the coast by listening to the surf.

10. Pacific bluefin tuna
Thunnus orientalis
Body length 8.2 ft — 3.7 mph

All bluefin in the North Pacific are born near Japan. Those that head east to live in the waters off California and Mexico return to the spawning grounds as adults.

Jan. — Dec.

Temperature range (°F)
Water — Tuna
87° — 90°
— 32°
36°

Dark, blood-rich muscles make tuna essentially warm-blooded, able to travel within a broad range of water temperatures.

11. Great white shark
Carcharodon carcharias
Body length 21 ft — 3.1 mph

Only in the past decade has tracking technology revealed that great whites, solitary travelers, make transoceanic journeys, possibly for breeding.

Jan. — Dec.

Sharks detect the electrical charge produced by Earth's magnetic field through snout pores called ampullae of Lorenzini, part of the sensory system that helps migrants orient.

Pituitary
Brain
Pineal gland
Olfactory nerve
Spinal cord
Ampulla of Lorenzini
Inside snout
Nerve fibers to brain
Sensory cells
Conducting jelly
Shark skin
External pore

RANGE OF MOTION

From the highest flier to the deepest swimmer, this chart shows the elevations and depths at which animals on this map travel.

Bar-headed goose	30,000 ft
	26,000
	22,000
	18,000
	14,000
	10,000
	6,000
	2,000
	Sea level
Ranging from 160 ft to -330 ft	
European eel	-2,000

Bar-headed goose and commercial flight — 29,500 ft
Mt. Everest, 29,035 ft
26,000 ft

Bats tune in to Earth's magnetic field, calibrating their direction for night flight with the sunset.

Solar Compass
Animals can use the sun as a compass because they have an internal clock. The clock is set in the brain (or in the antennae in insects) by the amount of light received. Animals compare the sun's position to their clock to determine direction of travel.

Night sky
Wind
Visual landmarks
Smell
Current
Sound
Temperature
Polarized light
Noon
Sun's path
8 a.m.
7 a.m.
6 a.m.
Sunrise
Sunset
Decreasing angle
South
Summer (north of 23.5° N)
Summer
Fall-Spring
Winter

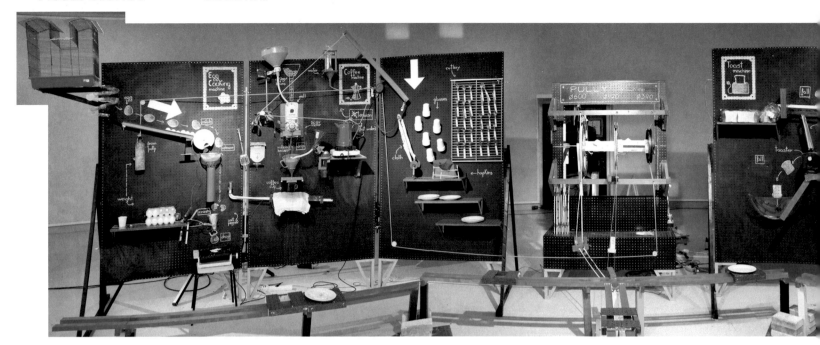

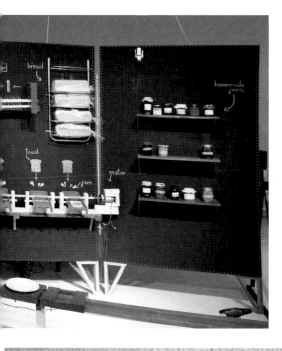

YURI SUZUKI, MASA KIMURA
Breakfast Machine

The cartoonist Rube Goldberg is famous for his cartoons of complex machines that perform uncomplicated jobs. For Platform 21 = Jamming in Amsterdam, Yuri Suzuki and Masa Kimura started to build the Breakfast Machine, which can serve an omelet, coffee, and toast with jam—a Rube Goldberg machine come to life. Because the machine's parts are fastened to a board and explained with drawings and notes, it retains a two-dimensional, cartoonish feel. When the machine was ready, it served breakfast all day to visitors.

Year: 2009—Material: Mixed media, wood, metal, plastic tube, oven, pan, coffee grinder, cooker, toaster, egg—Dimension: 18×2.5 m—Client: Platform 21 Amsterdam—Photography: Johannes Abeling—Illustration: Aurora Portillo—Project assistance: Aya Comori

137

1

JAN VON HOLLEBEN

1 Akkustische Kamera

For a photo shoot for *Geo* magazine, photographer Jan von Holleben was invited to explore the facilities of Berlin's Adlershof technology park as well as a radioactive particle accelerator, the blue-green algae laboratories of Cyano Biofuels, and newly invented acoustic cameras. He and his team used these places and props to do playful research and development of concepts for the future, even extending their narrative to homes, supermarkets, and playgrounds.

Year: 2009—Client: *Geo* magazine

2 Photosynthese

This series appeared in the magazine *Geo* to accompany an article on photosynthesis. It presents approaches taken by researchers to develop photosynthesis into a sustainable, energy-supplying technology.

Year: 2011—Client: *Geo* magazine—Concept/Art Direction/Photography: Jan von Holleben

2

LANG/BAUMANN
Street Painting #5
Using road paint, an intersection in Vercorin, a small village in the Swiss Alps, was turned into a public art piece reminiscent of a subway map.
Year: 2010— Photography: Robert Hofer

Looking at Control and Geography

Chapter

3

Looking at Travel
AND GEOGRAPHY

Eric Rodenbeck: *The most important carto-graphic innovation of the last 500 years is that the maps now have you on them… It's very ego-reinforcing. We are liter-ally the center of our world. In the future, reading maps won't be a separate activity from moving around. In fact, we won't call them "maps", they'll just be representa-tions of the world around us.*

Interviewer: *What information will feature on these representations?*

ER: *All of it*

o Interview for *Print* magazine, 2011

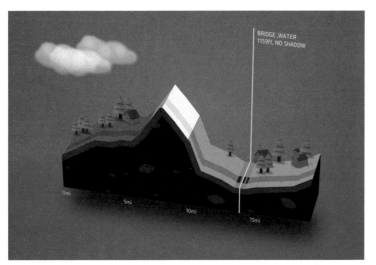

1

WE AIN'T PLASTIC
o Roland Loesslein
Komoot

Komoot is a small startup company which redefines interactive route plan-ning from scratch. This fully interactive three-dimensional height profile has been programmed as a part of the com-plex web application. GPS data could be dynamically displayed in a cross-section visualization. All textures are interchangeable at runtime and allow esthetic integration of the vertical pro-file in different environments.

Year: 2010—Client: komoot GmbH

NATIONAL GEOGRAPHIC
2 Barcelona's Natural Wonder

A look at Gaudí's masterpiece, the Sagrada Familia, in Barcelona, Spain. Construction on the basilica was be-gun in 1882 and is scheduled to be completed in 2026, marking the cen-tennial of Gaudí's death.

Year: 2010—Design: Oliver Uberti and Fernando G. Baptista—Research: Kaitlin Yarnall—Text: Jeremy Berlin—Senior Graphics Editor: Fernando G. Baptista—Publisher: National Geographic maga-zine—Location: Washington DC, USA

2

We can all draw a map. How do I get to the bank? Where is the wedding? Where exactly are you from? All we need is something to write with, something to write on, and a reason.

We become accustomed to the language and utility of two-dimensional geometric projections of our world at an early age. Although most people don't visualize the physical world in this way as they move through it, it isn't too difficult for them to apply their three-dimensional knowledge onto creating a basic overhead approximation of their surroundings, as if viewed from an angle (or series of angles) that they will never themselves see.

Like all abstractions, maps are themselves subjective. Though some of the data may be objective and verifiable, the decisions of what data to include, and how to represent it, make each map unique. Indeed, in order to protect the individuality of their creations, many professional mapmakers include trap streets in their creations: small fictional additions that allow them to prove definitively any breaches of copyright that may occur.

There is no perfect, accurate way of representing physical space in a two-dimensional form. We impose our own emotional vision of the world onto our landscapes—and have done for thousands of years. There be dragons and buried treasure wherever we look.

Vesa Sammalisto's beautiful maps for *Monocle* magazine are a prime example of the combining of emotional context and physical outline, a playful contrast to the more businesslike design of much of that publication's content. Not intended to be used as navigation tools, instead the shapes of the countries provide both a shorthand to the reader and a shape to the canvas. Many more such examples can be found in this chapter, including Lotta Nieminen's witty typographic survey of Italy, where carefully placed words comment on each part of the country, while also forming its shape.

The work of Ytje, Klas Ernflo, and Antoine Corbineau → 32 touch on similar visual and emotional cues, as does the three-dimensional creation of Katrin Rodegast, in which she carefully arranged local craftsmanship to make from their collective shape a proud map of the objects' origins.

A more literal example of placing personal emotion onto depictions of place emerged with Njenworks' city map in Sharjah, whose markings were sourced not from a list of tourist sights or useful amenities, but through surveys of local residents who revealed locations that made them happy and unhappy to be in.

Taking that theme to its logical next step, Julie Michel's ingenious *My Way* map encourages the user to personalise each copy with their own, place-based, thoughts and feelings, while the emotional power of the conventional map itself is manipulated through Judith Schalansky's fictional atlas, a piece of poetry which has at its heart both the visual and textual metaphors implicit in navigation.

Elsewhere, people are trying to rethink the conventional mapping aesthetic. *Komoot* took a height-based approach, the result of which is strikingly similar to that of the infographic, also in this chapter, that shows the fundamentals of water processing in the former GDR. Both appear like isometric line graphs, the peaks and valleys literal.

Others featured here have abstracted place through other, non-geographic visual vocabularies. Project Project's Istanbul guide is filled with hundreds of conventional-looking infographics, each interpreting the interplay of society and space through carefully chosen visuals and data. *Stadistik* took a similar approach by comparing nine German cities purely through the information generated by their activities. *Paris vs New York* is altogether more playful, a single, witty visual and phrase showing in each vignette how two of the world's great cities could not be more similar yet different.

It terms of pure utility, Martin Oberhäuser's rethinking of public transportation timetables is perhaps the most applicable of all the visuals in this chapter, a valiant attempt to standardise a perennial data problem inherent in the daily frustrations of millions of people.

However, as a way of connecting personality to place, it's hard to improve of the series of travel notebooks that appears in the Spanish newspaper *Público*. By taking the form of a lifesize reproduction of two pages in a Moleskine-like diary, the format speaks perfectly to itinerant writers and artists, while also providing a flexible canvas for the varied interactions of people and places. Perhaps it is the battered, well-worn sketchbook that is itself the perfect visual metaphor for travel.

1 \ 2 \ 3

DAVID GARCIA STUDIO

MAP (Manual of Architectural Possibilities) is a publication that aims to merge science and research with architectural design. Each issue deals with a single subject that is investigated from multiple perspectives, resulting in an architectural project as a response to the research.

1   MAP 001 Antarctica

The first issue of *MAP* dealt with Antarctica. Although its research stations appear to be robust in size and appearance, buildings are constantly being devoured by ice and spat out into the ocean. The climatic contradiction of Antarctica, which is larger than Europe, 70% ice, and a kind of desert, makes it an unavoidable subject to be studied.

Year: 2009—Architectural publication—Photography: NR 2154

2   MAP 002 Quarantine

Areas of containment in a quarantine can range from a single cell to an entire planet, from the political to the religious. Some geographies are so polluted that they would be considered quarantined landscapes if they were living beings. A public drinking fountain, for example, can hold 2.7 million bacteria per square inch. What are the implications of such landscapes? *MAP 002 Quarantine* examines the idea of containment and its spatial implications through research, projects, and the realm of architectural ideas. Four projects are investigated in this issue: a domestic isolation unit; an instantly quarantinable farm; a zoo of infectious species; and a quarantined library on a cargo ship.

Year: 2010—Architectural publication—Photography: David A. Garcia

3   MAP 003 Archive

Humans tend to systematically collect and reorganize what already exists in its own kind of order—or disorder. This desire for control over the environment has no doubt been beneficial for humankind. Some think, however, that archives have reached such epidemic proportions that not only has the digital revolution not been able to solve the problem, it has actually aggravated it. All of this occupies space—an increasingly huge amount of space. *MAP 003 Archive* takes a look.

Year: 2010—Architectural publication—Photography: NR 2154

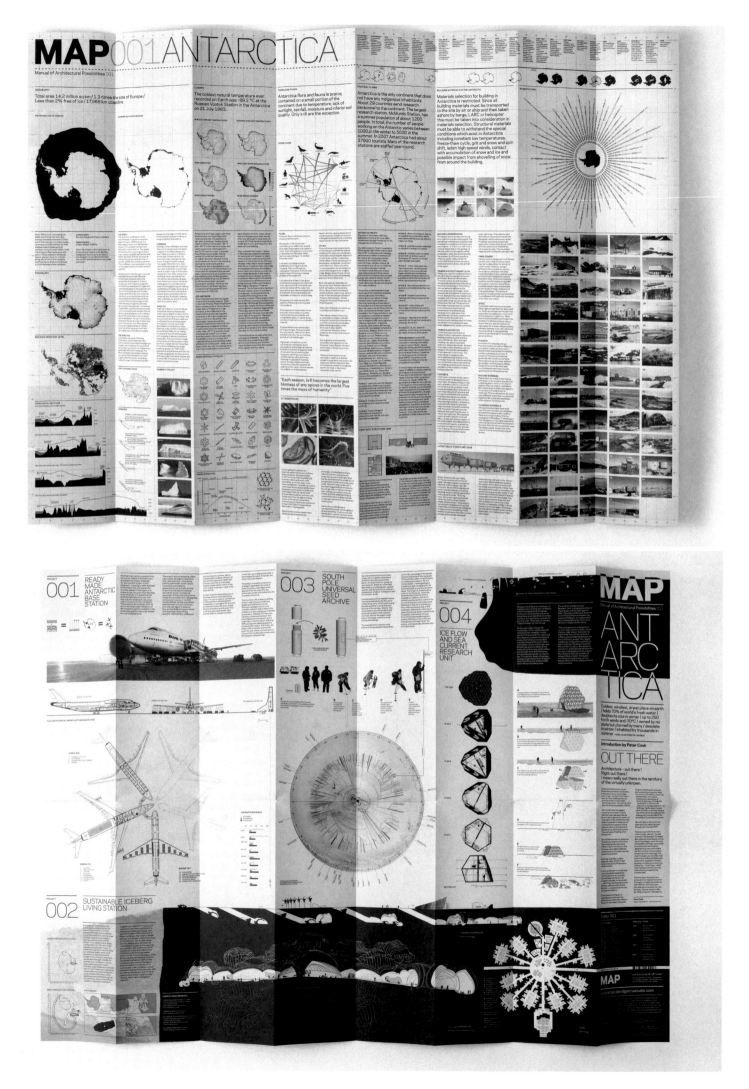

145

ONLAB
Beyroutes—A Guide To Beirut

Beyroutes is a guidebook to Beirut, one of the grand capitals of the Middle East. It presents a close-up and intimate view of the city with a design that reflects a subjective perspective through the use of snapshots, hand drawn maps, and hand written notes. *Beyroutes* was published as the first in the Archis city guide series *Never Walk A Lonely Planet*.

Year: 2010—Client: Archis Foundation—Art Direction: Jeanno Gaussi, Nicolas Bourquin—Design: Pascale Harès, Jeanno Gaussi, Nicolas Bourquin—Additional credits: Cover image and maps by Ran Rothuizen

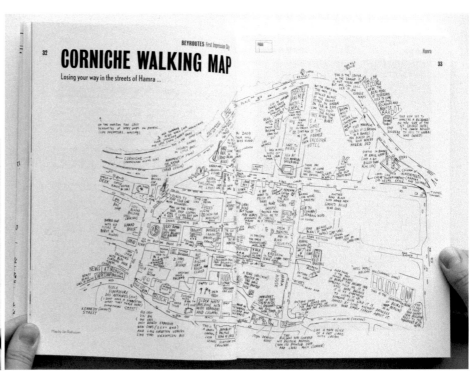

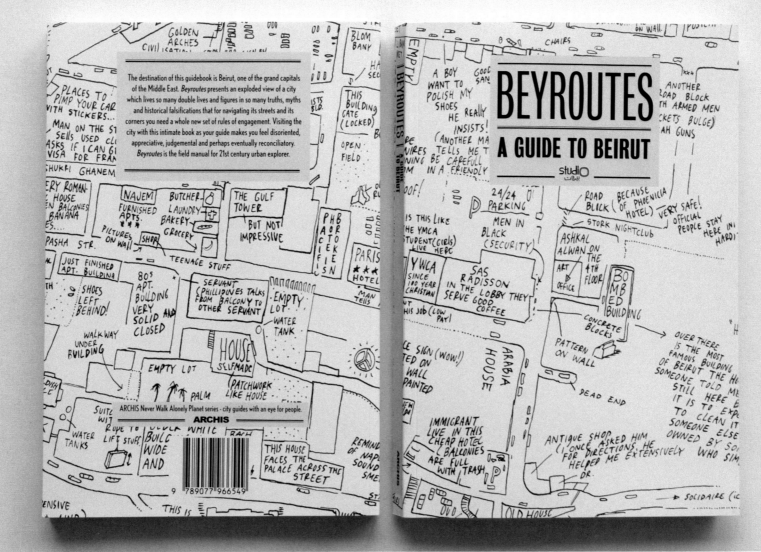

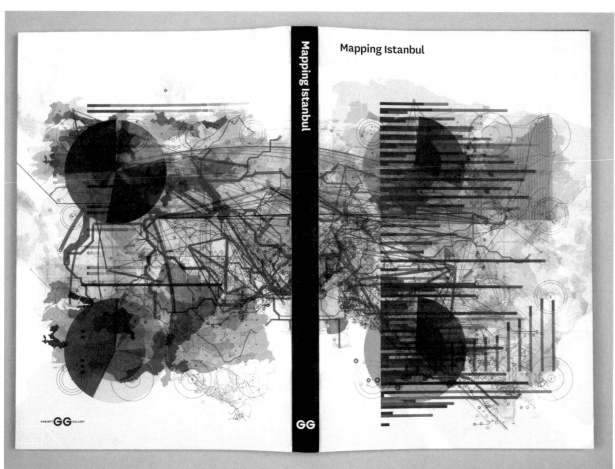

PROJECT PROJECTS
Mapping Istanbul
This book presents an effort to map the city of Istanbul, a city steeped in complexity. Working collaboratively with Garanti Galerie and the architects at Superpool, Project Projects established a uniform visual style for the hundreds of maps and information graphics included.

The book's design presents this information in an accessible, narrative sequence, creating a valuable resource for architects, planners, and policymakers invested in the city's future.

Year: 2009—Client: Garanti Galerie

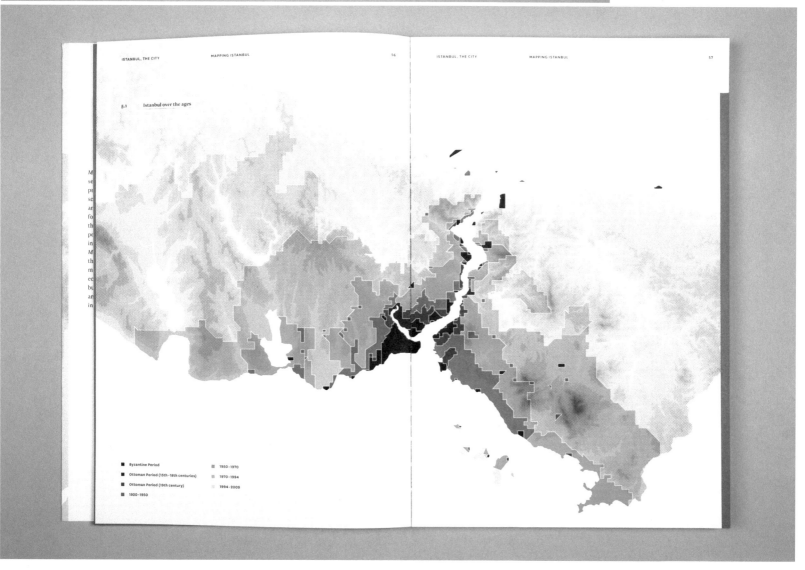

NJENWORKS
Sharjah CityMap

Sharjah InfoCart and *CityMap* is a site-specific project about Sharjah City in the United Arab Emirates. Designed by students at American University in Sharjah, the *InfoCart* traveled to malls and outdoor public spaces in Sharjah. Residents, workers, and visitors were asked about places that were important to their daily lives. This information was used to create the *CityMap*, an alternative representation of the city determined in part by the people

who live and work there. The *CityMap* is published in six languages (Arabic/ Urdu, English/Tagalog, and Malayalam/Bangla) and distributed for free from the *InfoCart* during the Biennial.

Year: 2011—Client: Lize Mogel and Lex Bhagat for the Sharjah Biennial 2011—Project Coordinators (Sharjah): Petra Matar, Ammar Savliwala—InfoCart Design Team (American University of Sharjah): Enayatollah Javad Ghaedi, Heba Helmy Hammad, Saeid Abdolaziz Khezri, Wasib Mahmood, Naji Muneer Mah'd and Professor Kevin Mitchell—Logo Design: Yasmin Mohammed—Photography: Alfredo Rubio (Sharjah Art Foundation)—Printer: Magnet in Dubai—Translators: Emna Zghal (Arabic), Mustafa Menai (Urdu), Sudeshna Sengupta (Bangla), Binoy Sebastian (Malayalam), and Beulah De Jesus (Tagalog).

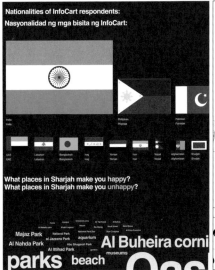

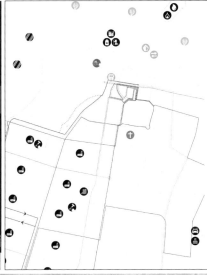

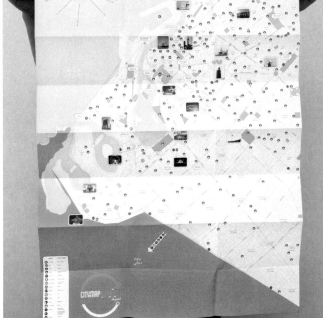

148

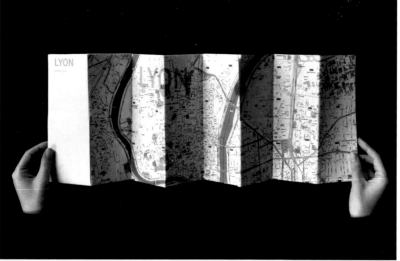

JULIE MICHEL
My Way

My Way, an object of personal cartography, is designed to give tourists a physical and mental experience of the space they are visiting. It is a city map that contains blank areas on which to write. Due to its folding system, these empty spaces do not interfere with the map's legibility because they are hidden behind the paper folds. The design reintroduces the idea of discovery, research, curiosity, and even getting lost. The map directs the tourist in space but also in time because it can be used to plan the trip before it even begins, during travel for writing and drawing, and back at home as a souvenir.

Year: 2009—Personal work

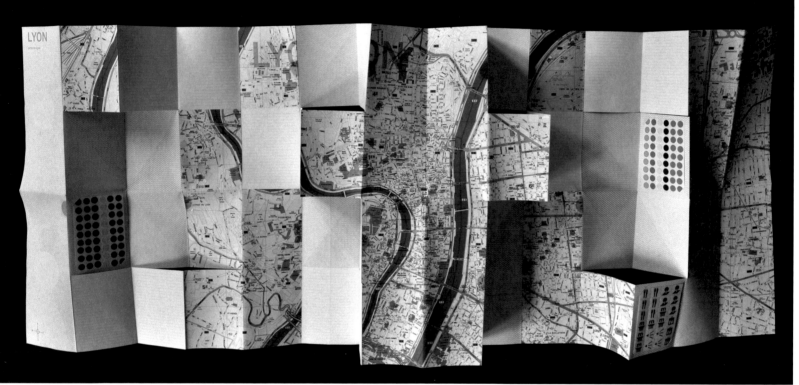

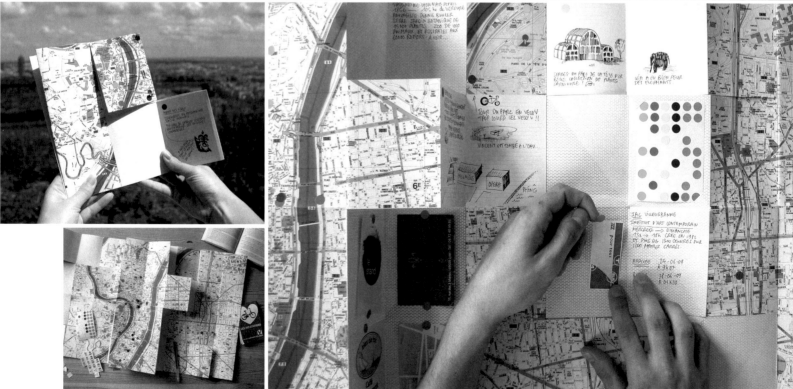

1

KATRIN RODEGAST
1   Ruhrgebietskarte
A map of the Ruhrgebiet area in Germany created from products by local designers. It was published as an editorial for the German magazine *Heimatdesign*.
    Year: 2010—Client: *Heimatdesign Magazin*—Photography: Anne Deppe

PÚBLICO
o   Samuel Granados, Covadonga F. Esteban, Mónica Serrano, Miriam Baña, Leif Steen, Artur Galocha, Álvaro Valiño
2   Cuadernos De Viaje— Travel Notebooks
The *Travel Notebooks* are taken from a daily section in the newspaper *Público* dedicated to summer. Each day a different topic is explained or illustrated using a notebook as the canvas.
    Year: 2010—Client: *Público*

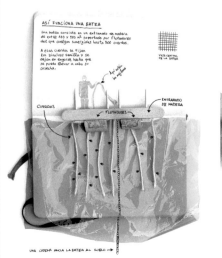
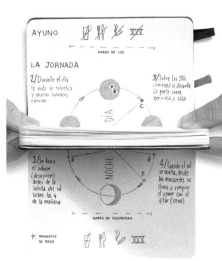

2

REINO UNIDO

ESPAÑA

⊙ Gibr

MARRUECOS

Aduar ve Europa desde África
Tiene 12 años y se sabe la alineación
del Barsa de memoria.

Señala el Estrecho. Luego se lleva el dedo
a la sien simulando una pistola.

⊙ Ceuta

⊙ Essaouira

SÁHARA OCCIDENTAL

Alí pasó varios veranos en Catalunya
cuando era niño. Su familia adoptiva
viene a visitarlo cada año porque
él ya no puede salir.

El gobierno le ha concedido un permiso
de dos meses para vender artesanía
a los turistas en Essaouira
Tendrá que volver a El Aaiún.

⊙ El Aaiún

⊙ La Agüera

MAURITANIA

Ocupa la ciudad saharaui de La Agüera desde 1976

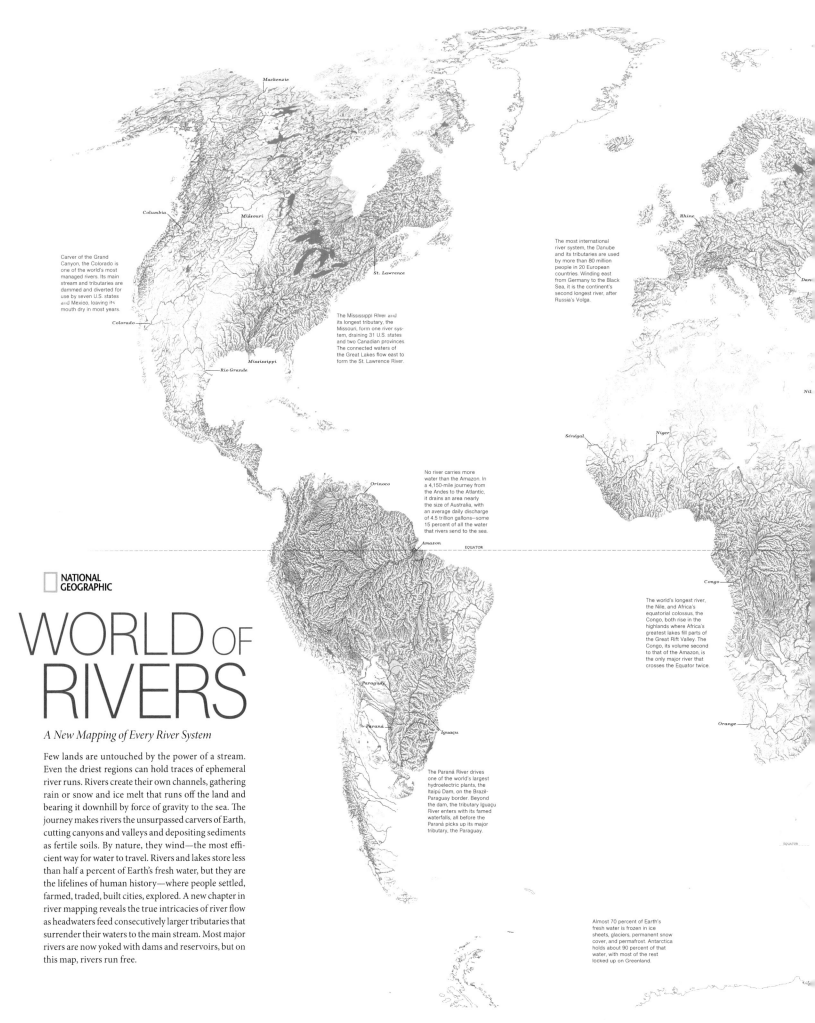

Mackenzie

Columbia

Missouri

Rhine

St. Lawrence

The most international river system, the Danube and its tributaries are used by more than 80 million people in 20 European countries. Winding east from Germany to the Black Sea, it is the continent's second longest river, after Russia's Volga.

Dan

Carver of the Grand Canyon, the Colorado is one of the world's most managed rivers. Its main stream and tributaries are dammed and diverted for use by seven U.S. states and Mexico, leaving its mouth dry in most years.

Colorado

The Mississippi River and its longest tributary, the Missouri, form one river system, draining 31 U.S. states and two Canadian provinces. The connected waters of the Great Lakes flow east to form the St. Lawrence River.

Nil

Mississippi

Rio Grande

Niger

Sénégal

No river carries more water than the Amazon. In a 4,150-mile journey from the Andes to the Atlantic, it drains an area nearly the size of Australia, with an average daily discharge of 4.5 trillion gallons—some 15 percent of all the water that rivers send to the sea.

Orinoco

Amazon   EQUATOR

Congo

NATIONAL GEOGRAPHIC

The world's longest river, the Nile, and Africa's equatorial colossus, the Congo, both rise in the highlands where Africa's greatest lakes fill parts of the Great Rift Valley. The Congo, its volume second to that of the Amazon, is the only major river that crosses the Equator twice.

WORLD OF RIVERS

A New Mapping of Every River System

Paraguay

Few lands are untouched by the power of a stream. Even the driest regions can hold traces of ephemeral river runs. Rivers create their own channels, gathering rain or snow and ice melt that runs off the land and bearing it downhill by force of gravity to the sea. The journey makes rivers the unsurpassed carvers of Earth, cutting canyons and valleys and depositing sediments as fertile soils. By nature, they wind—the most efficient way for water to travel. Rivers and lakes store less than half a percent of Earth's fresh water, but they are the lifelines of human history—where people settled, farmed, traded, built cities, explored. A new chapter in river mapping reveals the true intricacies of river flow as headwaters feed consecutively larger tributaries that surrender their waters to the main stream. Most major rivers are now yoked with dams and reservoirs, but on this map, rivers run free.

Paraná

Iguaçu

Orange

EQUATOR

The Paraná River drives one of the world's largest hydroelectric plants, the Itaipú Dam, on the Brazil-Paraguay border. Beyond the dam, the tributary Iguaçu River enters with its famed waterfalls, all before the Paraná picks up its major tributary, the Paraguay.

Almost 70 percent of Earth's fresh water is frozen in ice sheets, glaciers, permanent snow cover, and permafrost. Antarctica holds about 90 percent of that water, with most of the rest locked up on Greenland.

National Geographic Society

Gilbert M. Grosvenor, Chairman
John M. Fahey, Jr., President and CEO
Chris Johns, Editor in Chief
William E. McNulty, Director of Maps,
National Geographic Magazine

SUPPLEMENT TO NATIONAL GEOGRAPHIC: APRIL 2010
PRODUCED BY NATIONAL GEOGRAPHIC MAPS FOR NATIONAL
GEOGRAPHIC MAGAZINE
DESIGN: MOLLIE BATES AND ELAINE BRADLEY
TEXT: JANE VESSELS RESEARCH: CHRISTY ULLRICH
SCIENTIFIC ADVISERS: BERNHARD LEHNER, MCGILL UNIVERSITY;
BART WICKEL, WORLD WILDLIFE FUND GIS: TED SICKLEY
MAP PRODUCTION: DEBBIE GIBBONS AND DIANNE HUNT
MAP EDIT: MAUREEN FLYNN-STELMAN MAP DATA: WORLD
WILDLIFE FUND, HYDROSHEDS; AND USGS (RIVERS); THE
NATURE CONSERVANCY AND UNIVERSITY OF KASSEL, CENTER
FOR ENVIRONMENTAL SYSTEMS RESEARCH, WATERGAPS
(RIVER DISCHARGE); GLOBAL LAKES AND WETLANDS DATABASE,
WORLD WILDLIFE FUND; NATIONAL SNOW AND ICE DATA CENTER,
UNIVERSITY OF COLORADO GROUNDWATER MAP: KAITLIN
YARNALL (RESEARCH); BGR/UNESCO (DATA) RIVER LENGTHS:
SHAOCHUANG LIU, CHINESE ACADEMY OF SCIENCES, ET AL.
(2009) AND HYDROSHEDS DATA BY BERNHARD LEHNER
FOR INFORMATION REGARDING AVAILABLE MAPS CALL
1-800-962-1643 OR WRITE TO NATIONAL GEOGRAPHIC MAPS,
PO BOX 4357, EVERGREEN, CO 80437-4357. YOU CAN FIND US
ON THE INTERNET AT NATIONALGEOGRAPHIC.COM/MAPS.
COPYRIGHT © 2010 NATIONAL GEOGRAPHIC SOCIETY,
WASHINGTON, D.C. PRINTED FEBRUARY 2010.

This map uses a modified version of a database
called HydroSHEDS, a digital compilation of the
world's river channels and basins mapped with
unprecedented precision. HydroSHEDS is based
on high-resolution elevation data gathered by
NASA's space shuttle during the 2000 Shuttle
Radar Topography Mission. It was developed by
the World Wildlife Fund Conservation Science
Program (Bernhard Lehner, Kris Verdin, Andrew
Jarvis, 2008; worldwildlife.org/hydrosheds).
A global hydrological model was integrated to
estimate where and how much water flows.

WINKEL TRIPEL PROJECTION

0 mi   1000
0 km   1000

NATIONAL GEOGRAPHIC
World of Rivers

Every river system in the world is represented in this poster, including the world's ten longest rivers, their exact length, and an estimate of how much water flows through them. The map's oceans are signified with white instead of the usual blue, creating a startling contrast between land and water by directing the viewer's attention to the abundance of water—or scarcity of it—within the continents.

Year: 2010—Designer and Map Director: William McNulty—Copywriter: Jane Vessels—Designers: Mollie Bates and Elaine Bradley—GIS and Map Production: Ted Sickley, Debbie Gibbons—Publisher: *National Geographic Magazine*

Map Legend

Perennial river
(Average discharge 1961-1990, gallons per second)
More than 130,000
7,500–130,000
1,250–7,499
250–1,249
Fewer than 250

Intermittent river
(Average discharge 1961-1990, gallons per second)
More than 7,500
1,250–7,500
250–1,249
Fewer than 250

Glaciated area or ice sheet
Lake
Permafrost
(More than 90 percent of the ground continuously frozen)
Major wetland

China's Yangtze River powers the Three Gorges Dam, unequaled in hydroelectric generating capacity. Another monumental project is now under way to divert water from the Yangtze to China's dry, populous north. There, the Yellow River, drawn down for irrigation and industry, often fails to reach the sea.

Sediment carried from the Himalaya and the Tibetan Plateau creates some of the world's largest river deltas, including the Indus, the Mekong, and the great delta where the Ganges meets the Brahmaputra River system. Worldwide, deltas are home to an estimated 500 million people.

Ten Longest Rivers

1. **Nile** (Africa) 4,400 miles
2. **Amazon** (South America) 4,150 miles
3. **Yangtze** (Asia) 3,880 miles
4. **Mississippi-Missouri** (North America) 3,780 miles
5. **Yenisey-Angara** (Asia) 3,610 miles
6. **Yellow** (Asia) 3,590 miles
7. **Ob-Irtysh** (Asia) 3,430 miles
8. **Amur** (Asia) 3,420 miles
9. **Lena** (Asia) 3,200 miles
10. **Congo** (Africa) 3,180 miles

The Murray-Darling is Australia's only major river system, rising in the mountain ranges of the southeast. Heavily tapped for irrigation, its flow has declined during a decade of drought. The continent's intermittent rivers and lakes can fill if water flows south after heavy seasonal rains in the tropical north.

The Water Below

Most of the planet's liquid fresh water is groundwater, precipitation that seeps down to fill the spaces in layers of sand, gravel, and permeable rock called aquifers. Groundwater exists almost everywhere, at varying depths. Since the mid-20th century, its extraction for human use has accelerated, often at unsustainable rates. How readily groundwater recharges depends on precipitation, geology, and topography. Groundwater can emerge as a spring, the start of many rivers and for some a major contributor. Up to 40 percent of the volume of the Mississippi River is estimated to come from groundwater.

Groundwater recharge
Very high   Moderate   Very low

EQUATOR

153

NATIONAL GEOGRAPHIC
1   Lives Still at Risk

Years after the devastation of hurricane Katrina, many people in New Orleans continue to live in harm's way. The map shows that at the time of publication, 500,000 people live at or below sea level in different neighborhoods within the city.

Year: 2008—Designer and Map Director: William McNulty—Research: Kris Goodfellow—Publisher: *National Geographic Magazine*

DIETER DUNEKA
2   Durchstich!

An infographic that accompanied an article about the completion of the tunnel that will eventually lead motorists underneath the Swiss Alps for 57.1 km. The length of the tunnel (which makes it the longest in the world) as well as other facts such as its role within the European transportation system, and an examination of the kind of rocks workers had to drill through are illustrated in the graphic.

Year: 2011—Client: *Die Zeit*—Design, Illustration: Dieter Duneka—Quellen: AlpTransit Gotthard AG, ETH Zürich, Wikipedia—Recherche: Urs Willmann

IXTRACT
3   Da ist noch Luft

Infographic of possible locations in Germany where wind farms could be built. Densely populated areas, nature preserves, or otherwise unsuitable areas are plotted on a map. The leftover areas—about eight percent of Germany's landscape—are potential locations for green energy production.

Designer: Stefan Fichtel—Agency: ixtract.de—Client: *Die Zeit*

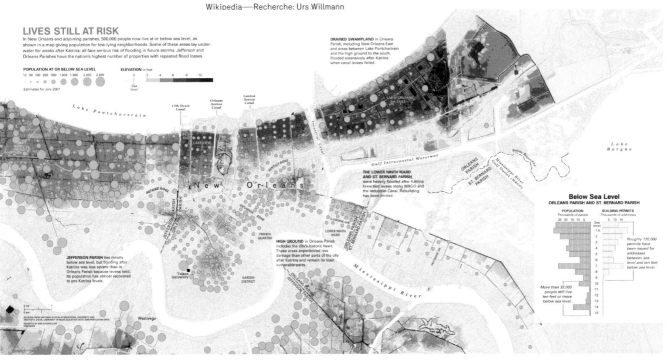

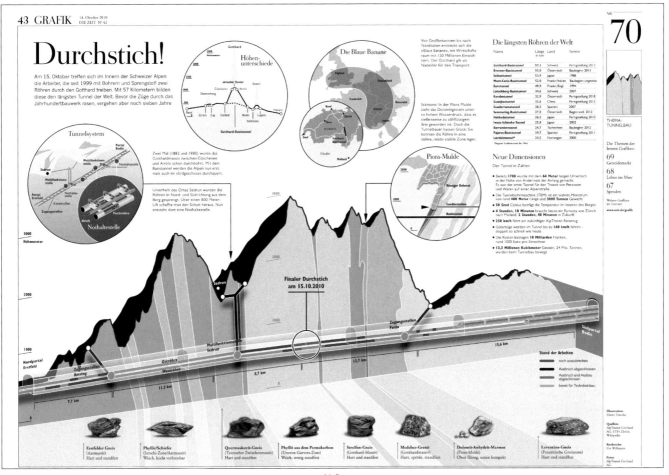

1 \ 2

N°
101

THEMA:
ENERGIE

Die Themen der
letzten Grafiken:
100
Jubiläumsgrafik
99
Eurovision Song
Contest
98
Selig und heilig

Weitere Grafiken
im Internet:
www.zeit.de/grafik

Da ist noch Luft

Eine Studie zeigt: Deutschland könnte einen großen Teil seines Strombedarfs durch Windenergie decken

Viel Wind

Durch-
schnittlich
viel Wind

Wenig Wind

1 Wo bläst der Wind?

Um die geeigneten Positionen für Windräder zu identifizieren, wurden nur Orte
berücksichtigt, an denen ein maximal 150
Meter hohes Standard-Windrad mindestens
4800 Megawattstunden pro Jahr erzeugt.

I Kilometer Mindestabstand
zur nächsten Siedlung

2 Abstand halten

In der Studie wurde ein Mindestabstand von
einem Kilometer zur nächsten Siedlung
zugrunde gelegt (einzeln stehende Gehöfte
konnten nicht berücksichtigt werden). Ein
Drittel aller heutigen Anlagen erfüllt dieses
Kriterium nicht! Würde der Puffer auf 1,5
Kilometer erhöht, würde die nutzbare
Fläche gar um zwei Drittel schrumpfen.

I. Anlage wird
bestmöglich platziert

2. Anlage folgt im
Sicherheitsabstand

3 Windräder aufstellen

Sobald eine grundsätzlich geeignete Fläche
gefunden war, wurde (gedanklich) die erste
Anlage an jener Stelle platziert, die den
höchsten Windertrag versprach. Um diese
Position blieb eine Zone von vier Rotor-
durchmessern frei. Dann wurden ringsum
wieder die verfügbaren Standorte mit dem
stärksten Wind identifiziert und besetzt.

65 %

4 Das Ergebnis

Mindestens zwei Prozent der deutschen
Landfläche sind uneingeschränkt als
Standorte für Windkraftanlagen nutzbar,
die zwei Drittel des derzeitigen deutschen
Strombedarfs erzeugen könnten.

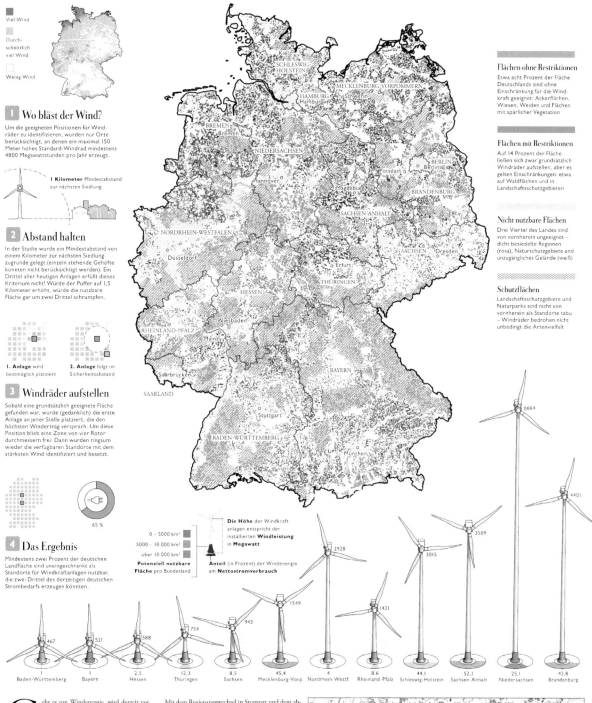

Flächen ohne Restriktionen

Etwa acht Prozent der Fläche
Deutschlands sind ohne
Einschränkung für die Wind-
kraft geeignet: Ackerflächen,
Wiesen, Weiden und Flächen
mit spärlicher Vegetation

Flächen mit Restriktionen

Auf 14 Prozent der Fläche
ließen sich zwar grundsätzlich
Windräder aufstellen, aber es
gelten Einschränkungen: etwa
auf Waldflächen und in
Landschaftsschutzgebieten

Nicht nutzbare Flächen

Drei Viertel des Landes sind
von vornherein ungeeignet –
dicht besiedelte Regionen
(rosa), Naturschutzgebiete und
unzugängliches Gelände (weiß)

Schutzflächen

Landschaftsschutzgebiete und
Naturparks sind nicht von
vornherein als Standorte tabu
– Windräder bedrohen nicht
unbedingt die Artenvielfalt

0 – 5000 km²
5000 – 10 000 km²
über 10 000 km²

**Potenziell nutzbare
Fläche** pro Bundesland

Die Höhe der Windkraftanlagen entspricht der
installierten **Windleistung**
in **Megawatt**

Anteil (in Prozent) der Windenergie
am **Nettostromverbrauch**

Windrad	Megawatt	Bundesland	Anteil
1	467	Baden-Württemberg	1
2	521	Bayern	1
3	588	Hessen	2,5
4	754	Thüringen	12,3
5	943	Sachsen	8,5
6	1549	Mecklenburg-Vorp.	45,4
7	1421	Nordrhein-Westf.	4
8	2928	Rheinland Pfalz	8,6
9	3015	Schleswig-Holstein	44,1
10	3509	Sachsen-Anhalt	52,1
11	4401	Niedersachsen	25,1
12	6664	Brandenburg	42,8

Geht es um Windenergie, wird derzeit vor
allem über Anlagen auf hoher See gespro-
chen. Die haben den Charme, dass sie
kaum jemanden stören. Allerdings liegt
ihr Beitrag zum deutschen Strommix bis-
her nahe bei null, und die nötigen Milliardeninvestitio-
nen können nur Großunternehmen stemmen.

Ganz anders die Situation an Land: Gut 21 000
Windräder erzeugen bereits sechs Prozent unserer Elek-
trizität. Betrieben werden sie häufig von Gemeinschaften
kleiner Investoren. Vor allem in der Nähe der norddeut-
schen Küsten und im ostdeutschen Flachland decken die
Anlagen bereits knapp die Hälfte des Strombedarfs.

Doch der Ausbau ist ins Stocken geraten. Im vergan-
genen Jahr wurden nur noch 754 neue Windräder aufge-
stellt, der niedrigste Wert seit 1994. Der Grund: Im
Norden werden gute Standorte knapp, im Süden haben
die Landesregierungen potenzielle Windinvestoren mit
restriktiven Auflagen vergrault. In Bayern und Baden-
Württemberg wird daher nur ein Prozent des Elektrizi-
tätsverbrauchs durch Windenergie gedeckt.

Mit dem Regierungswechsel in Stuttgart und dem ab-
sehbaren Ende der Atomkraft dürfte sich das jetzt än-
dern. Das Potenzial ist jedenfalls gewaltig. Auf 125 Tera-
wattstunden pro Jahr – das sind 20 Prozent des deutschen
Strombedarfs – schätzt eine vom Bundesverband Windenergie in Auftrag gegebene Studie des Fraunhofer-
Instituts IWES den möglichen Beitrag der beiden süd-
deutschen Flächenländer zum Strommix der Republik.

22 Prozent der Fläche Deutschlands sind laut der
Studie grundsätzlich für die Errichtung von Windparks
geeignet. Zieht man Wälder (10 Prozent) und alle ir-
gendwie geschützten Gebiete (4 Prozent) ab, bleiben
noch immer 8 Prozent der deutschen Landfläche übrig.
Würde nur ein Viertel davon für Windparks genutzt,
ließen sich damit zwei Drittel unseres Stroms erzeugen.
Insbesondere dann, wenn man auf höhere Windräder
setzt, denn in der Höhe weht der Wind stärker: Jeder zu-
sätzliche Meter bringt ein Prozent mehr Ausbeute.

Das alles klingt gut – doch schön anzuschauen wäre es
nicht. Detaillierte Karten zeigen, wie massiv so ein Wind-
kraftboom das Landschaftsbild verändern würde.

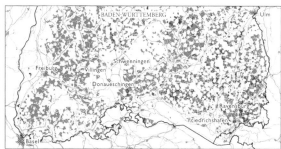

Auch im Süden (hier im Ausschnitt der Südschwarzwald mit dem Oberrheintal) gibt es geeignete Flächen mit
starkem Wind. Werden die südwestdeutschen Ökobürger eine »Verspargelung« ihrer Umgebung hinnehmen?

Illustration:
Stefan Fichtel
www.ixtract.de

Recherche:
Dirk Asendorpf

Quellen:
Fraunhofer-Institut
für Windenergie
und Energiesystem-
technik (IWES),
Bundesverband
Windenergie,
Deutscher
Wetterdienst,
openstreetmaps.org

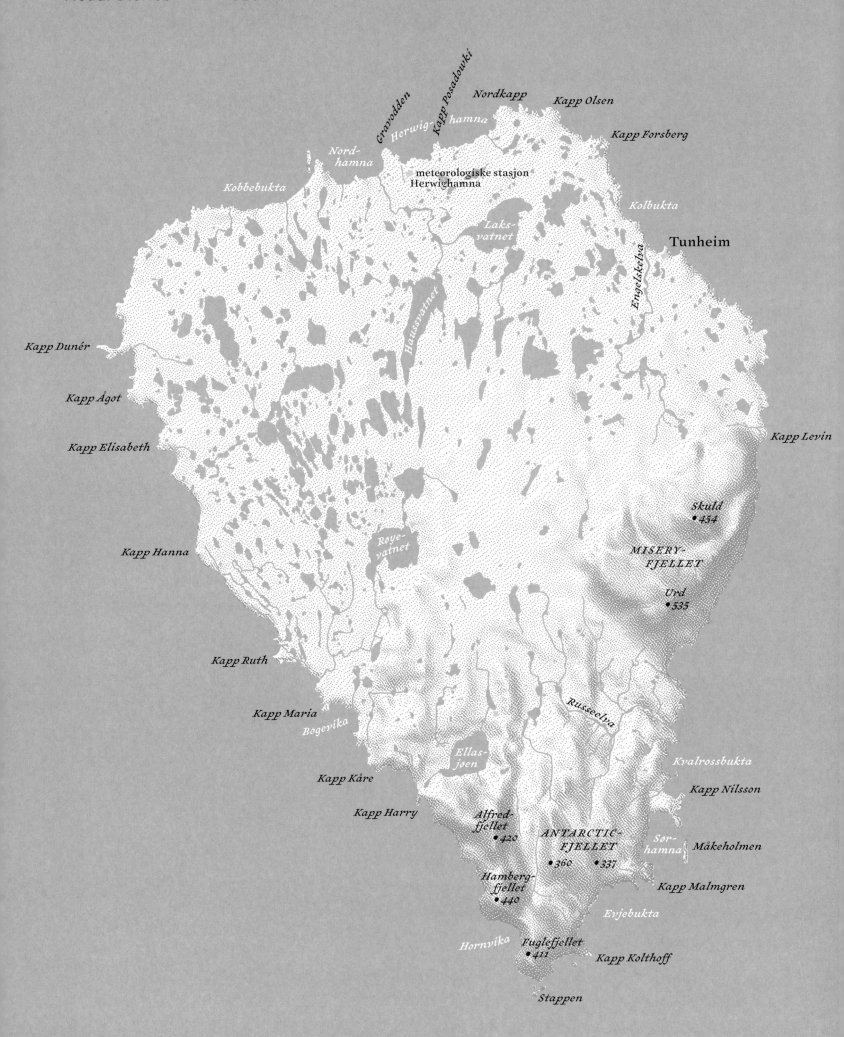

Gravodden

Kapp Posadowki

Nordkapp

Kapp Olsen

Herwig-hamna

Kapp Forsberg

Nord-
hamna

meteorologiske stasjon
Herwighamna

Kobbebukta

Kolbukta

Laks-
vatnet

Tunheim

Haussvatnet

Engelskelva

Kapp Dunér

Kapp Ågot

Kapp Elisabeth

Kapp Levin

Skuld
• 454

Kapp Hanna

Røye-
vatnet

MISERY-
FJELLET

Urd
• 535

Kapp Ruth

Russeelva

Kapp María

Bogevika

Kvalrossbukta

Ellas-
jøen

Kapp Nilsson

Kapp Kåre

Sør-
hamna

Måkeholmen

Kapp Harry

Alfred-
fjellet
• 420

ANTARCTIC-
FJELLET
• 360   • 337

Kapp Malmgren

Hamberg-
fjellet
• 440

Evjebukta

Hornvika

Fuglefjellet
• 411

Kapp Kolthoff

Stappen

Deception-Insel *Südliche Shetlandinseln* (Antarktis)

62° 57′ S
60° 38′ W

ENGLISCH *Deception Island* [›Täuschungsinsel‹] | SPANISCH *Isla Decepción*

98,5 km² | unbewohnt

20 km
⌐→ Livingston-Insel
100 km
⌐→ Antarktische Peninsula
1490 km
⌐→ Peter-I.-Insel (132)

15. November 1820 entdeckt Nathaniel Palmer die Einfahrt in die Caldera   *1967–70* Vulkanausbrüche

29. Januar 1820 vermutlich gesichtet von Edward Bransfield und William Smith   *1906–31* Betrieb der Walfangstation

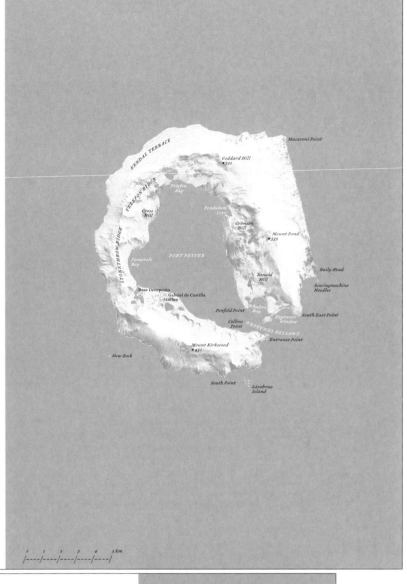

Die Einfahrt ist leicht zu verfehlen, der Eingang in die Caldera nicht mal 200 Meter breit. Hier, in Neptuns Blasebalg, der Höllenpforte, dem Drachenmaul, stürmt es ununterbrochen. Dahinter aber liegt, unter dem schlummernden Vulkan versteckt, einer der sichersten Häfen der Welt: die Bucht der Walfischfänger. Neu Sandefjord nennen die Bewohner diesen Ort, die südlichste Trankocherei der Welt, Drehscheibe des Walfangs mit eigener Flotte, zwei Dreimastern, acht kleinen und zwei großen Walfischdampfern. Abgesehen von ein paar chilenischen Heizern leben hier 200 Norweger und eine Frau: Marie Betsy Rasmussen, das erste und einzige weibliche Wesen, das bisher in die Antarktis kam, Gattin von Kaptein Adolf Amandus Andresen, dem Geschäftsführer einer der drei Gesellschaften, die hier seit zwei Jahren den Walfang betreiben.   Die Saison dauert von Ende November bis in die letzten Tage des Februars hinein. Sie jagen mit neuen Fangmethoden, die im Norden erprobt worden sind. Mit Sprengladungen versehene Harpunen kommen aus Kanonen des Vorderdecks geschossen, bohren sich in die Rücken der großen Tiere, die alle Walfänger schon von Weitem unterscheiden können: Der Buckelwal stößt einen niedrigen Wasserstrahl aus und trägt auf dem Rücken einen Höcker. Der Finnwal ist durch einen steilen Strahl zu erkennen. Den wertvollsten unter ihnen aber, den Blauwal, verraten seine Rückenflosse und ein hoher Blas. Bis zu sechs Tiere erbeutet ein Dampfer und schleppt sie abends in die Bucht. Am schwarzen Strand brechen die Walfänger die vollen Bärte aus den Mäulern, ziehen die glänzende Haut ab, trennen den Speck vom Fleisch und verkochen das weiße Gold in riesigen Bottichen zu Tran. Die Kessel werden nicht mit Kohle, sondern mit toten Pinguinen beheizt, die sie vom Baily Head fangen.   Den Rest lassen sie verkommen. Am Strand ragen die weißen Zäune der Walskelette aus dem dunklen Sand, das Wasser ist rot vom Blut und die Luft durchdrungen vom Gestank des fauligen Fleisches. Tausende geplünderte Körper verwesen im überfluteten Kraterbecken.

ATLAS
DER
ABGELEGENEN
INSELN

VON

Judith Schalansky

*Fünfzig Inseln,
auf denen ich nie war und
niemals sein werde*

mare

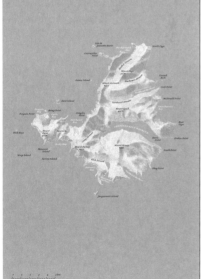

JUDITH SCHALANSKY

Atlas der abgelegenen Inseln: Fünfzig Inseln, auf denen ich nie war und niemals sein werde (Atlas of Remote Islands: Fifty Islands I Have Never Set Foot On and Never Will)

A book that attempts to show atlases as works of poetry, interpretations of reality, attempts to see the world as a whole, and as a way to locate oneself. Humans have made their mark on the world with maps by giving the natural world names that tell of human hopes and disappointments. This book is not a travel guide; it is a book for the armchair explorer, describing places that exist in reality but only come to life in the imagination.

Year: 2009—Client: mareverlag—Medium: Book, 144 pp.—5 spot colors, orange colored edge

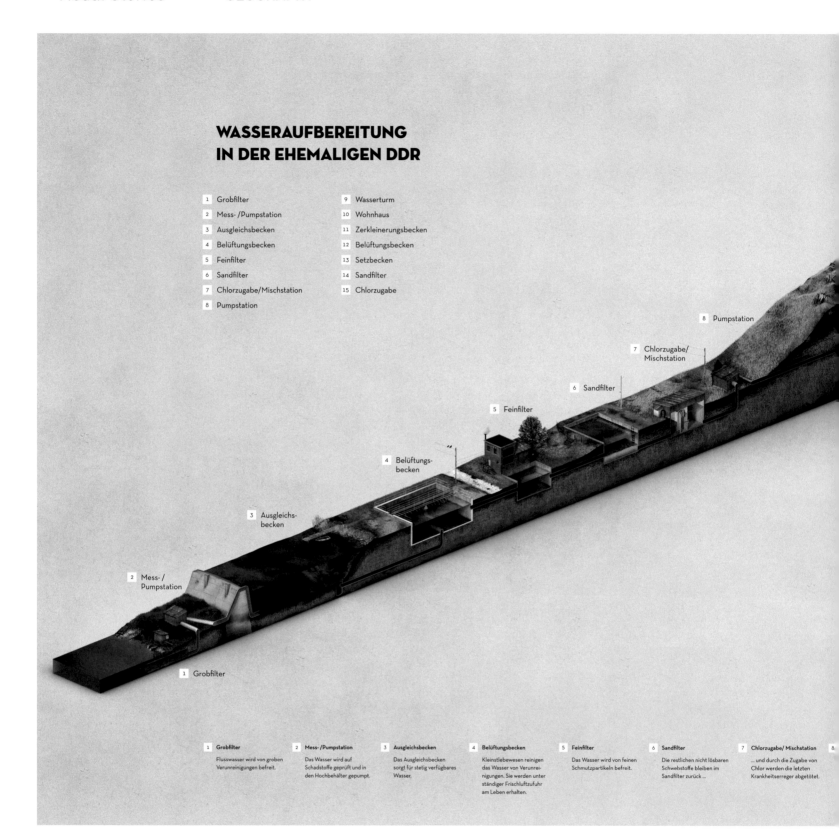

WASSERAUFBEREITUNG IN DER EHEMALIGEN DDR

1	Grobfilter	9	Wasserturm
2	Mess- /Pumpstation	10	Wohnhaus
3	Ausgleichsbecken	11	Zerkleinerungsbecken
4	Belüftungsbecken	12	Belüftungsbecken
5	Feinfilter	13	Setzbecken
6	Sandfilter	14	Sandfilter
7	Chlorzugabe/Mischstation	15	Chlorzugabe
8	Pumpstation		

8 Pumpstation

7 Chlorzugabe/ Mischstation

6 Sandfilter

5 Feinfilter

4 Belüftungs- becken

3 Ausgleichs- becken

2 Mess-/ Pumpstation

1 Grobfilter

1 Grobfilter
Flusswasser wird von groben Verunreinigungen befreit.

2 Mess-/Pumpstation
Das Wasser wird auf Schadstoffe geprüft und in den Hochbehälter gepumpt.

3 Ausgleichsbecken
Das Ausgleichsbecken sorgt für stetig verfügbares Wasser.

4 Belüftungsbecken
Kleinstlebewesen reinigen das Wasser von Verunreinigungen. Sie werden unter ständiger Frischluftzufuhr am Leben erhalten.

5 Feinfilter
Das Wasser wird von feinen Schmutzpartikeln befreit.

6 Sandfilter
Die restlichen nicht lösbaren Schwebstoffe bleiben im Sandfilter zurück ...

7 Chlorzugabe/ Mischstation
... und durch die Zugabe von Chlor werden die letzten Krankheitserreger abgetötet.

8

KONSTANTIN DATZ
○ with Philipp Datz,
Moritz von Volkmann
Wasseraufbereitung in der
ehemaligen DDR
This infographic shows the basic water processing system in the former German Democratic Republic. It begins with river water that is purified into drinking water and follows that water as it is consumed and passed back through the system.
Year: 2010—Student work

Wasserturm

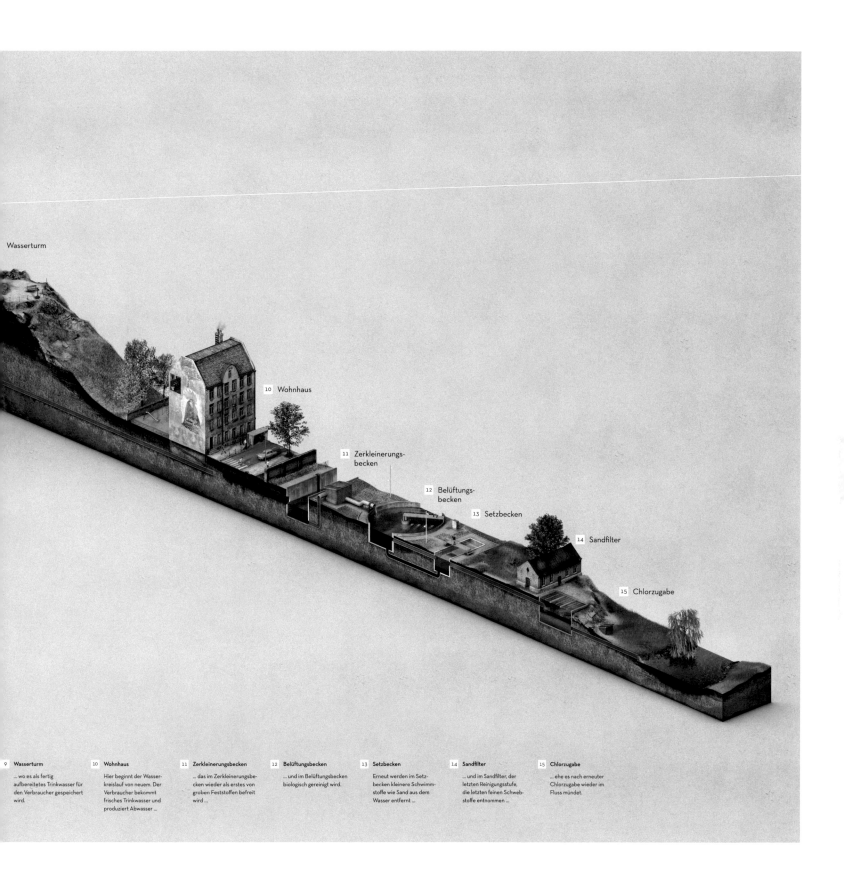

10 Wohnhaus

11 Zerkleinerungs-
becken

12 Belüftungs-
becken

13 Setzbecken

14 Sandfilter

15 Chlorzugabe

9 Wasserturm

... wo es als fertig
aufbereitetes Trinkwasser für
den Verbraucher gespeichert
wird.

10 Wohnhaus

Hier beginnt der Wasser-
kreislauf von neuem. Der
Verbraucher bekommt
frisches Trinkwasser und
produziert Abwasser ...

11 Zerkleinerungsbecken

... das im Zerkleinerungsbecken wieder als erstes von
groben Feststoffen befreit
wird ...

12 Belüftungsbecken

... und im Belüftungsbecken
biologisch gereinigt wird.

13 Setzbecken

Erneut werden im Setz-
becken kleinere Schwimm-
stoffe wie Sand aus dem
Wasser entfernt ...

14 Sandfilter

... und im Sandfilter, der
letzten Reinigungsstufe,
die letzten feinen Schwebstoffe entnommen ...

15 Chlorzugabe

... ehe es nach erneuter
Chlorzugabe wieder im
Fluss mündet.

Visual Stories

GEOGRAPHY

SERIAL CUT™

1 Bravia 3D

Vivid colors and a three-dimensional landscape pop up and out of a 3D television, showcasing its powerful 3D graphic capabilities.

Year: 2011—Client: Sony Spain

2 Plug into the Smart Grid

A 3D data visualization poster showcasing innovative technologies used by General Electric to implement the Smart Grid, a renewable energy system. It also highlights the impact of its website across paid and unpaid media.

Year: 2010—Client: General Electric USA

1

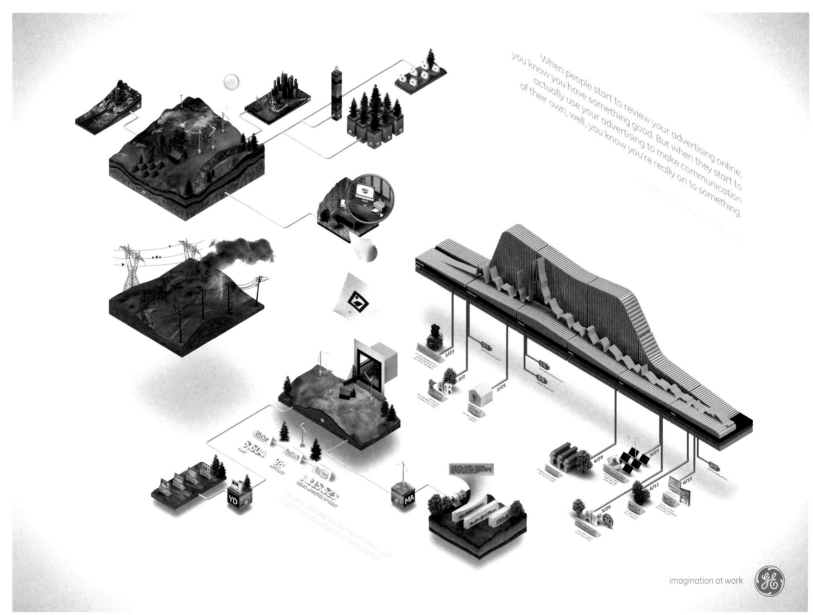

When people start to review your advertising online, you know you have something good. But when they start to actually use your advertising to make communication of their own, well, you know you're really on to something.

imagination at work

2

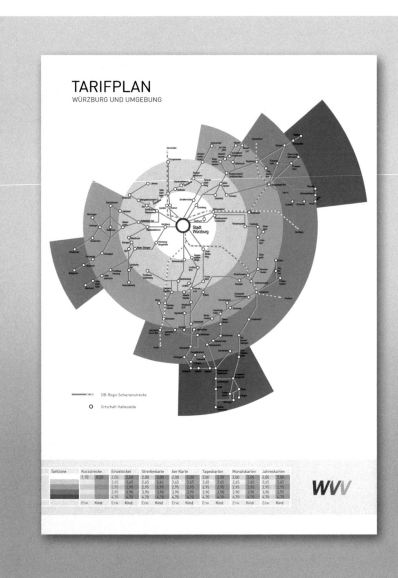

TARIFPLAN
WÜRZBURG UND UMGEBUNG

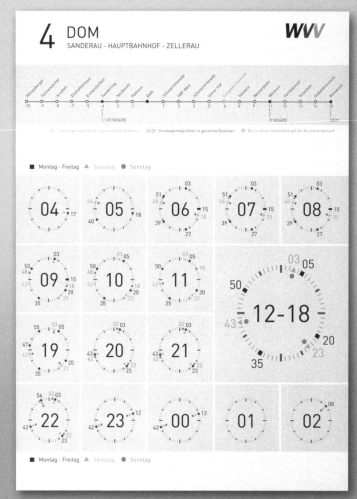

4 DOM
SANDERAU - HAUPTBAHNHOF - ZELLERAU

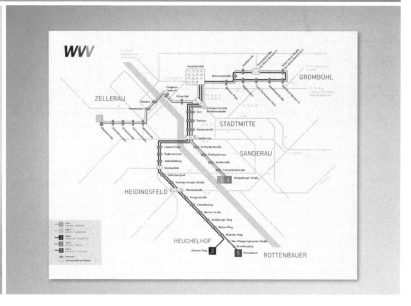

MARTIN OBERHÄUSER
Public Transportation Timetable Concept

The public transportation services in Würzburg, Germany, have used the same old-fashioned (and confusing) time tables for years. This prompted Martin Oberhäuser to create a conceptual redesign of these materials in which he developed a new system for the composition of the timetables based on an analog clock instead of the usual tabular presentation. This clock is also the central element of the homepage, which shows the current time and upcoming connections.

Year: 2008—Student project at University of applied science Würzburg, Germany

161

MARTIN OBERHÄUSER
Stadtistik
Year: 2009—Diploma Thesis at University of applied science Würzburg, Germany

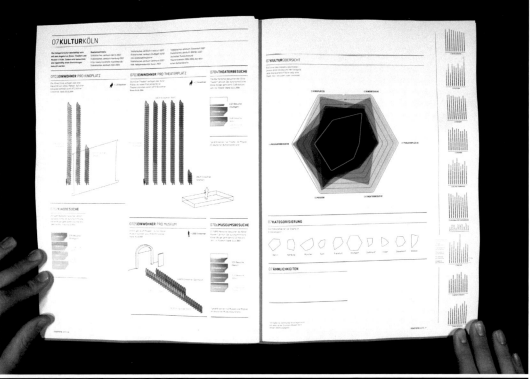

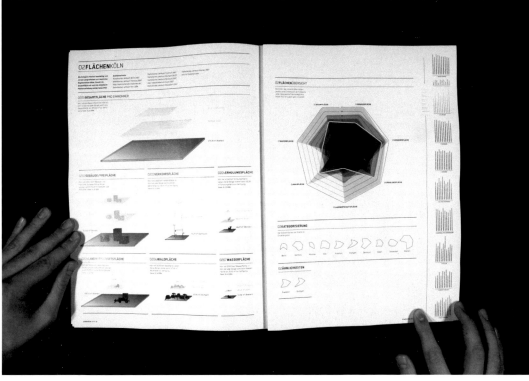

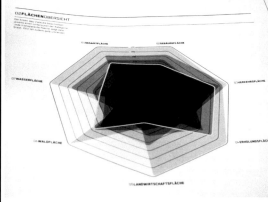

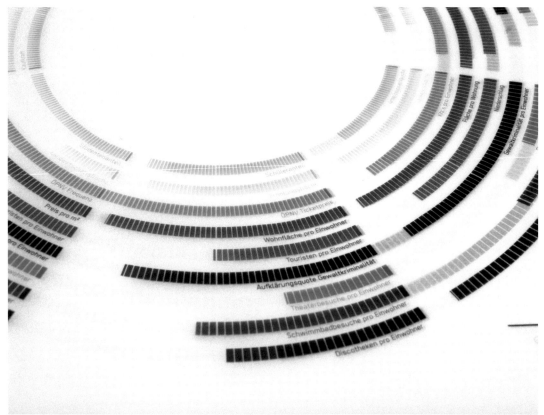

Stadtistik deals with miscella-neous statistics in various areas of ur-ban life in the ten largest German cit-ies. For each city, a newspaper with nine statistical categories is available. The intention of this work is to enable the viewer to objectively evaluate and characterize the cities for themselves. The graphic shown on the front page is printed on an additional piece of trans-lucent paper. By changing the front page between the different issues, a quick comparison between the differ-ent cities is provided.

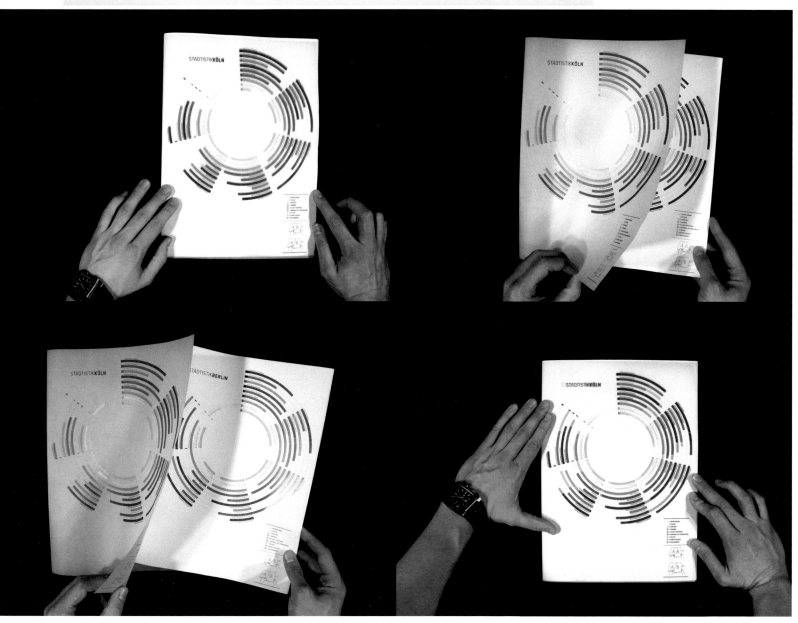

1

VAHRAM MURATYAN
1   Paris vs New York: L'obsession
2   Paris vs New York: Le pain
3   Paris vs New York: Le réalisateur
    A set of side-by-side images that
compares and contrasts New York and
Paris. Using a combination of images
with titles and captions, Vahram Muratyan points out surprising similarities and a fresh take on well-known
stereotypes.
    Year: 2010—Personal work

FERNANDO VOLKEN TOGNI
○   for Agency Fish
4   24 Hours in Cape Town
     Series of illustrations for Qa-
tar Airway's magazine, *Oryx*. The series, which also included pieces about
Shanghai, Melbourne, New York, Mos-
cow, and Phuket, focused on 24 hours
in each city
     Year: 2010—Client: *Oryx* Magazine,
Qatar Airways

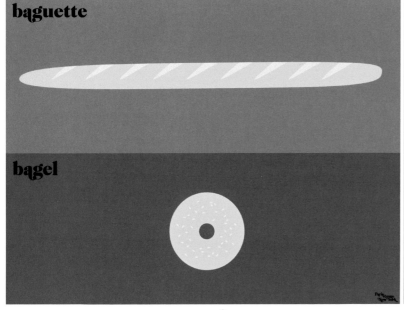

2

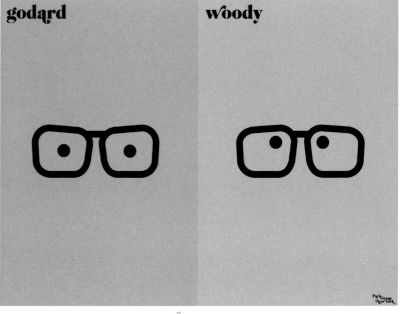

3

24 HOURS IN **CAPE TOWN**

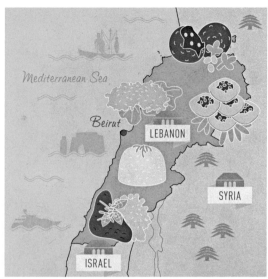

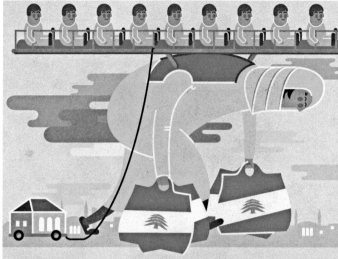

VESA SAMMALISTO
1   Monocle Lebanon Survey
2   Monocle Finland Survey
Vesa Sammalisto created the cover and additional illustrations for the *Monocle Lebanon Survey* and *Monocle Finland Survey*. Each survey created by Monocle collects information about a country's economy, transportation, culture, design, and tourism and then compiles this information to create a portrait of that country.
Year: 2010—Client: *Monocle*

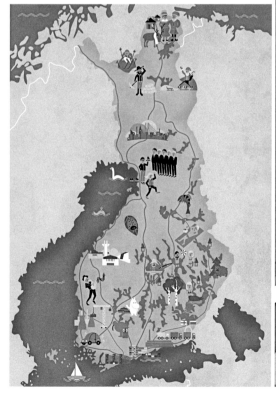

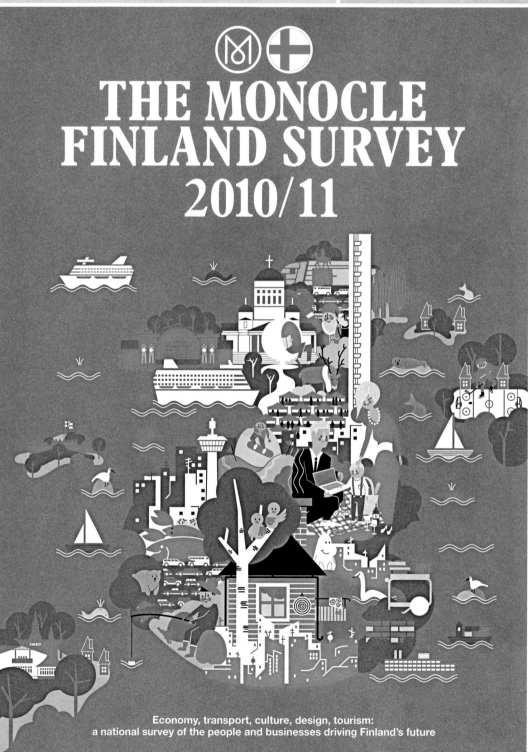

THE MONOCLE
FINLAND SURVEY
2010/11

Economy, transport, culture, design, tourism:
a national survey of the people and businesses driving Finland's future

1 \ 2

3

4

5

3   Living in 2050
     Editorial illustration imagining life
in Finland in the year 2050.
     Year: 2010—Client: Helsingin Sanomat
     TEEMA

4   Lifecycle of Cheese
     This infographic shows the lifecy-
cle of cheese
     Year: 2010—Client: HSY (Hel-
     sinki Region Environmental Services
     Authority)—Poster

5   Mallorca Map
     An editorial illustration for an arti-
cle about Mallorca.
     Year: 2011—Client: *Die Weltwoche* Stil

VESA SAMMALISTO
Cities
One in a series of urban survey posters for the cities of Helsinki, London, and New York. The posters and accompanying small prints were exhibited for the first time at Kaapeli (Cable Factory) Helsinki during the Factory Superstars group exhibition in October 2010.
Year: 2010—Personal work

1 \ 2 \ 3

TILL HAFENBRAK

1   Forest Clearance 1
   An illustration featured in Édition Biografiktion's latest issue of *HUMAN NEWS*.
   Year: 2010—Client: Édition Biografiktion

2   Day
   Illustration for the fourth issue of *Nobrow* magazine, an independent publication featuring illustration and graphic arts.
   Year: 2010—Client: *Nobrow* magazine

BEN THE ILLUSTRATOR

3   Great Britain Strip Illustration
5   Great Britain Map
   Two illustrations—one in a panoramic strip format and the other in a standard map view—were commissioned by *Monocle* to accompany a feature article about the current state of Great Britain.
   Year: 2010—Client: *Monocle* magazine

LOTTA NIEMINEN

4   Map of Europe
   An editorial illustration for a customer magazine published by Kela. The map shows the average number of years spent at work in different EU countries.
   Year: 2010—Client: Finnish Social Insurance Institution Kela—Art director: Katju Aro, BOTH

ALBERTO ANTONIAZZI

6   Italia
   An infographic map about the characteristics of the various regions of Italy.
   Year: 2009—Personal work

4

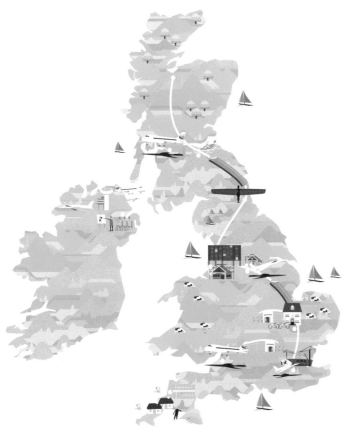

5

6

171

3

HUMAN EMPIRE
1   Lower Bavaria Map
3   Lower Bavaria
     A map of cities and special plac-
es in Lower Bavaria for *Neuland*
magazine.
     Year: 2009—Client: *Neuland* magazine

2   Sustainability
     An article about sustainability
standards at the Deutsche Bahn AG.
     Year: 2009—Client: *Mobil* (DB maga-
zine)

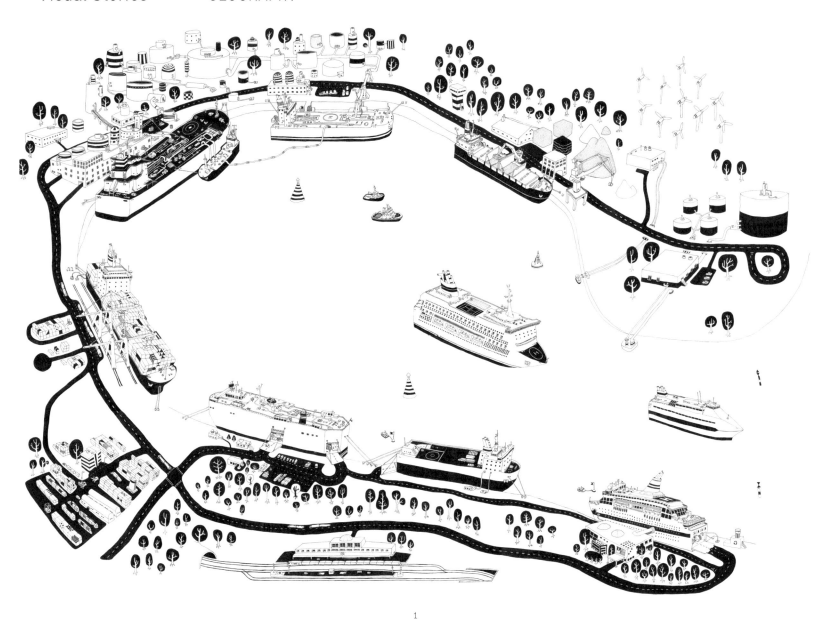

1

2

5

KLAS ERNFLO
1   Harbour
     This drawing for the Baltic Sea Position was commissioned by the Sjöfartstidningen in Gothenburg, Sweden, for use in a mural and other materials.
     Year: 2010 —Client: Baltic Sea Position & Sjöfartsbyrån

ANTOINE CORBINEAU
2   Aéroport de Paris—Orly,
     Friendly, colorful graphics orient visitors in this illustration for a mural installed in the Paris-Orly Airport. Airport services such as the currency exchange, duty free shopping area, baggage claim, and cafes are shown as a hand drawn map.
     Year: 2010—Client: Aéroport de Paris/W&Cie

FILIPE JARDIM
3   Barcelona Map
4   Sao Paulo Map
     Cidade Magazine, a luxury magazine from Sao Paulo, Brazil, commissioned maps for two separate articles about Barcelona and Sao Paulo. Each map is hand drawn with a slightly different style in order to reflect the personality of each city.
     Year: 2009—Client: *Cidade* Magazine

YTJE VEENSTRA
5   London
     Hide and Chic magazine commissioned this map to accompany an editorial about sightseeing in London. The sketchy quality of the drawing gives a personal feeling to the travel tips in the article.
     Year: 2008—Client: Hemels Publishers—Ytje, represented by Unit CMA, Amsterdam

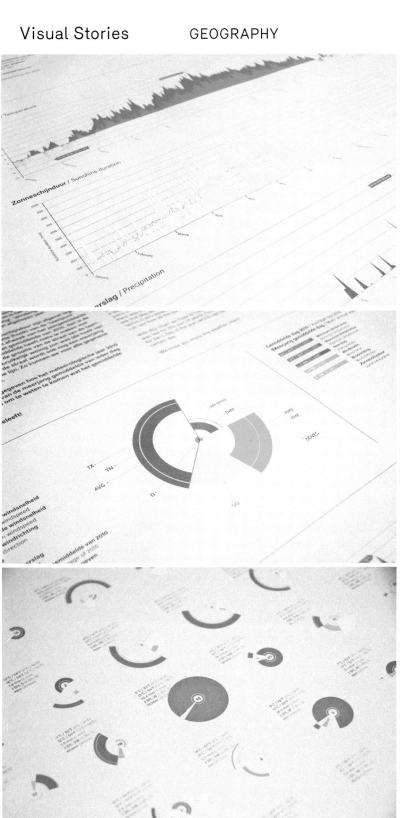

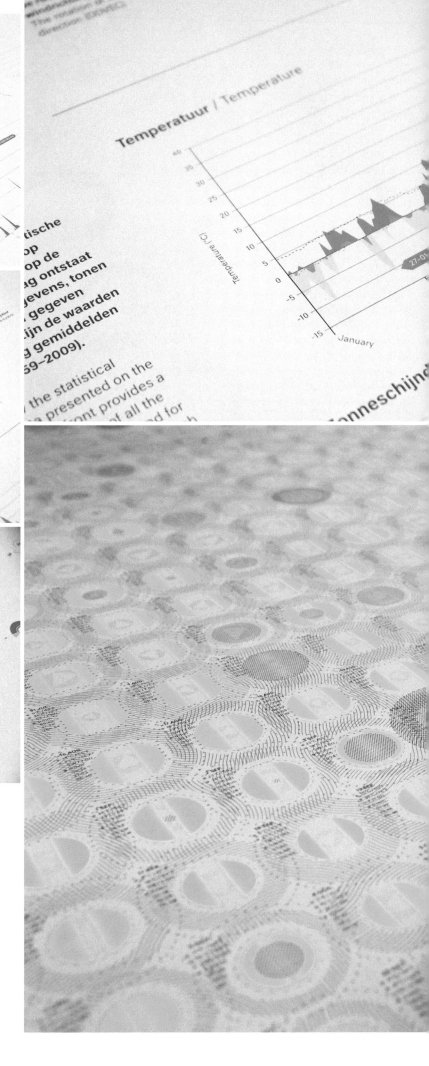

CLEVER°FRANKE
1   Weather Chart
The visual identity of design agency CLEVER°FRANKE combines the first letters of the co-founders' last names with a degree symbol in between, referencing the temperature measurements of Celsius and Fahrenheit. In keeping with the theme of weather, each year they design a weather chart with an overview of the previous year's weather. The chart shows the following data per day: the minimum and maximum temperatures, sunshine, sunrise, sunset, wind speed and direction, precipitation, as well as multi-year averages of all data for the period 2000–2010.

Year: 2010—Self-initiated poster

WEATHER CHART BY
CLEVER°FRANKE

Visual Stories

GEOGRAPHY

NOBUHIRO NAKANISHI
Nobuhiro Nakanishi's *Layer Drawing* series uses laser prints mounted on plexiglass or film. These are then either suspended from the ceiling or mounted to the wall in precise alignment, creating a sense of blurred movement in their repetition.

1   Layer Drawing 28 × 28 — Aomori Sunrise
    Year: 2008—Location: Toyota Municipal Museum of Art, Toyota, Japan—Material: Laser print mounted with plexiglass, acrylic—Size 28 × 29 × 87.1 cm—For the group exhibition *The Doors of Perception*

2   Layer Drawing — Tokyo Sunrise
    Year: 2010—Location: Gallarie Kashya Hildebrand, Zurich, Switzerland—Material: Inkjet print on film—Size 100 × 100 × 600 cm (30 sheets)—For the solo exhibition *Time Space*—Photography: Gallery Kashya Hildebrand

3   Layer Drawing — Cloud/Fog
    Year: 2006—Location: Osaka Contemporary Art Center, Osaka, Japan—Material: Inkjet print on film—Size: 100 × 100 × 2000 cm (100 sheets each)—For the solo exhibition *Saturation*—Photography: Seiji Toyonaga

4   Layer Drawing — Cloud/Fog
    Year: 2005—Location: Contemporary Art Center, Aomori, Japan—Material: Inkjet print on film—Size: 100 × 100 × 2000 cm (100 sheets each)—For the exhibition *The Exhibition of Artists in Residence Program 2005/Autumn, transformation/ metamorphosis*

1

2

178

3

4

TOILET PAPER MAGAZINE
○ Maurizio Cattelan,Pierpaolo
Ferrari, Micol Talso
Untitled—Image from TP2

Toilet Paper, conceived and edited by the artist Maurizio Cattelan and photographer Pierpaolo Ferrari, is a new generation magazine that combines commercial photography, twisted narratives, and surrealistic imaginary. The result is a visual tableaux of appropriated and found images collected from or inspired by the information highway.

Year: 2011—Editors: Maurizio Cattelan, Pierpaolo Ferrari—Design: Maurizio Cattelan, Pierpaolo Ferrari, and Micol Talso—Publisher: DESTE Foundation for Contemporary Art

Visualizing the
Modern World

Chapter

4

Visualizing the
MODERN WORLD

*Simplicity is about subtracting the obvi-
ous, and adding the meaningful.*

○ John MAEDA

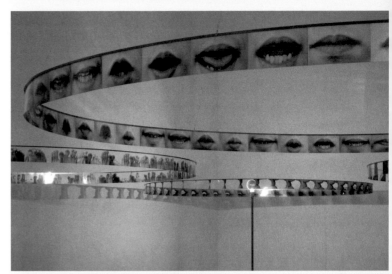

3

1

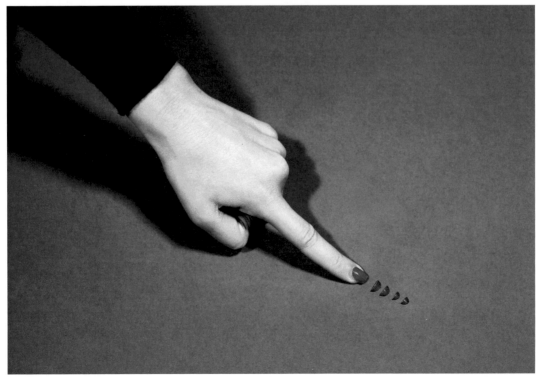

2

SARAH ILLENBERGER
1 Misunderstandings of Love
(Missverständnisse der Liebe)
Speech bubble made from objects
to represent the thoughts of a man op-
posed to the wishes of a woman.
 Year: 2008—Client: Neon magazine—
 Photography: Ragnar Schmuck

**MAURIZIO CATTELAN,
PIERPAOLO FERRARI,
MICOL TALSO**
2 Untitled—Image from TP2
Year: 2011

NOBUHIRO NAKANISHI
3 Interference
Body parts, including eyes and
mouths, are printed on film, which is
made into a lantern-like object. The images are projected onto the wall with a
light that is placed in the middle of the
piece, becoming the installation Interference at Gallery Nomart in Osa-
ka, Japan.
 Year: 2010—Material: Inkjet print
on film, size 500×700 cm exhibition
Interference (solo show)—Photography:
Haruo Kaneko

The world is an eternally confusing place. Filled with new ideas, new devices, new ways of connecting, new ways of communicating... as everything moves forward around us, it can be a struggle even to remain in one place.

Visualizations are both a part of the changes in our culture, and also an attempt to explain them. Adopted by political activists and politicians, advertisers and musicians, they are used to inspire people, to promote ideas, and to explore concepts.

As we try to invent new categories for each cultural movement, visual storytelling aims to soothe us into realizing that there's nothing new under the sun—or at least, if there is, that it too can be explained in clear and elegant ways.

In this chapter, you'll find a wide variety of subjects and approaches. Lamosca and Francesco Franchi →58 both reveal the data behind fundamental and frivolous societal issues through the use of a restricted set of bold icons and connective symbols. Mattson Creative's *Dexter* advertising poster and Brandon Schaefer's book covers attempt the opposite trick, abstracting familiar tales to the point where the puzzle becomes how to connect our prior knowledge of the cultural experience to the simplified imagery on show.

Challenge and limitation is at the heart of most art. Esteve Padilla gave himself an exacting brief with his new year's greeting: how many different stories could he tell through the use of four digits? In his piece shown in this chapter, Gareth Holt also explored restriction, straining the visual vocabulary of electronic circuitry in order to represent famous figures.

Music has always been an area for experimentation and expression. Stefanie Posavec and Greg McInerny have worked with the bands Inch-Time and OK Go to reinterpret their music through different visual abstractions, discovering new patterns and ideas, fomenting graphic equalizers of a handmade variety; whereas We Ain't Plastic chose a more overall approach to the subject with their piece, demonstrating the pure physicality of music reproduction.

One of the benefits of using more conventional infographic language is that it can have the effect of removing some of the emotive language around certain subjects, leaving the data itself to create an impact in the viewer. Gregoraisch's simple visualization of the dissertation of the (now former) German minister of defense highlights the levels of his plagiarism in ways that an enraged editorial would not; with such a clear narrative, we are left to add the emotion ourselves.

Emotional connection is a feature of reading of the sublime 2010 edition of *The Feltron Report*. Nicholas Felton's annual infographic publication of the minutiae in his life has become a favorite among designers, in part for the care with which the irrelevant aspects of his life have been so precisely documented. This issue, however, has a simple and poignant twist: it's a report of the life of his now-deceased father, reconstructed through the calendars, slides, and other ephemera that he found among his papers. A life abstracted, by what appears to be nothing but pure data—right up to the weather report on the time and date of his death. The reader fills in the human life that was the context to each pure statistic.

The real world features quite literally in Garret Johnston's itemizations of objects, turning so many constituent elements of machines and more into symmetrical patterns. Maria Fischer also used a real-world visualization to create an internet-like linking system, using needles and thread to sew connections between words and pages in her dreamlike book *Traumgedanken* (Thoughs on Dreams). And the design studio Superfertile combined the real world, the iconography of infographics and modern bling to literally hang the combined global economic debt around the necks of future generations.

But the last word on this subject is reserved for Jose Duarte, whose handmade visualization toolkit contains small wooden blocks, balloons, thread, chalk, and a series of different sized circles—everything we need to have a hands-on attempt at making sense of our world by physicalising approximations of the data that define it.

FRANCESCO MUZZI
La Fabbrica del Sapere
This illustration for Italian *Wired* portrays Italian schools as a kind of Victorian steampunk factory, in which students are dropped in or fall away. Data shows information such as the total hours spent in school by students and teachers, the student dropout rate, the values of Italian instruction in various fields, and the number of graduates searching for work abroad.
Year: 2009—Client: *Wired Italia,* Condè Nast

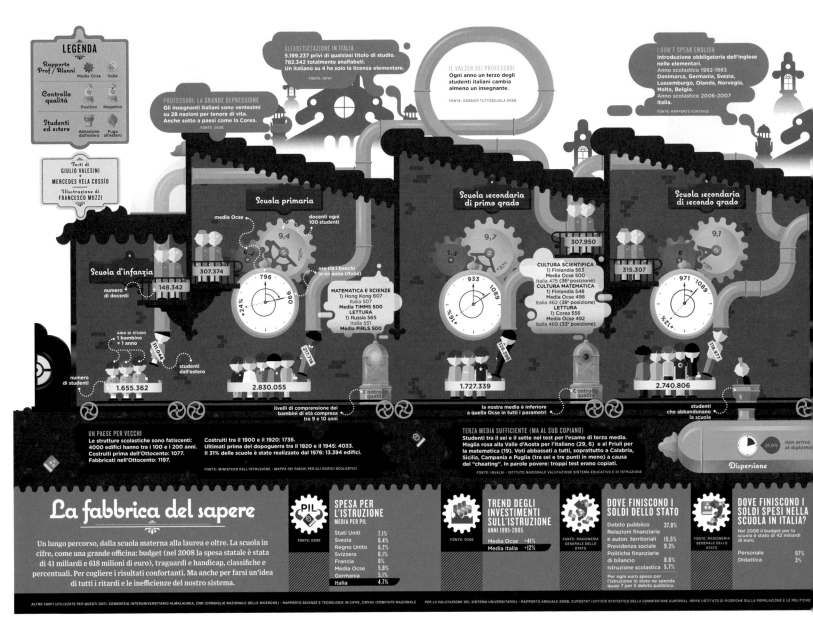

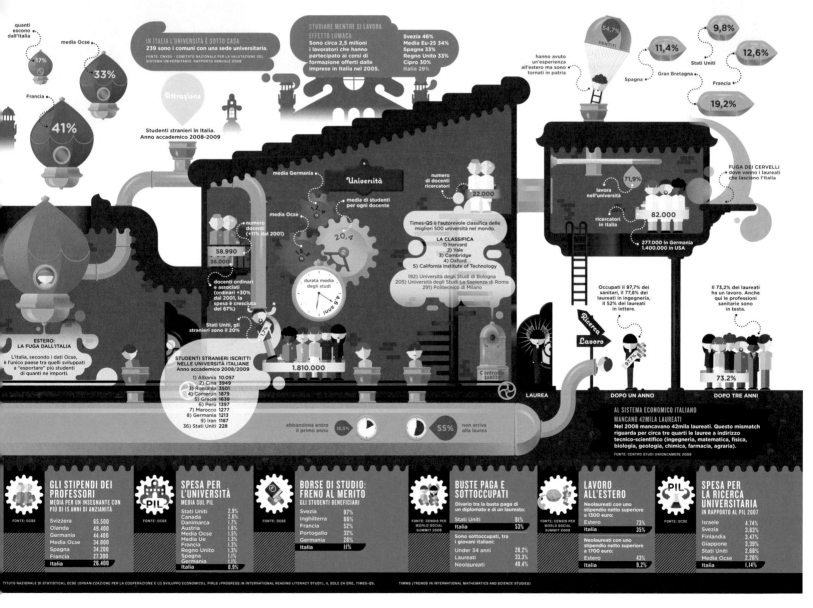

IL | ISTRUZIONI PER L'USO – NOZZE PER PRINCIPIANTI

SCETTICI SULLE BOMBONIERE?
I consigli di IL

CONFETTI A VOLONTÀ
— Durante il banchetto, non lesinate sulla quantità di confetti (rigorosamente con la mandorla). Se qualche ospite vuole portarne un po' anche a casa mettete a disposizione mini sacchetti bianchi di carta. Soluzione casalinga, ma l'effetto è garantito.

BUON BERE
— Si tratta di un'opzione non esattamente economica, soprattutto se volete fare le cose per bene. Una bottiglia di vino, magari della vostra regione, è sempre ben accetta. Gli ospiti, una volta a casa, potranno brindare a voi.

NEL PALLONE — Adatto per matrimoni primaverili ed estivi, un pallone risveglierà l'*homo ludens* degli invitati. Anche un Super Tele va bene, certo sarà un problema trasportarne cento. Un'alternativa pieghevole può essere un aquilone.

FIORI E PIANTE — Un dono destinato a crescere. Ma attenzione alla stagione. I bulbi di tulipani e giacinti si piantano in autunno; quelli di dalie e gladioli in primavera. Le semine varie sono a Pasqua. Date un occhio ai giardini tascabili di Eugea (*eugeastore.com*).

GIOCHI PORTATILI
— Oltre alle varie carte da gioco (anche qui potete sbizzarrirvi con la vostra origine geografica) rispolverate piccoli classici come domino, shangai e tangram, o avviatevi all'esplorazione di giochi africani, come quelli del gruppo dei mancala.

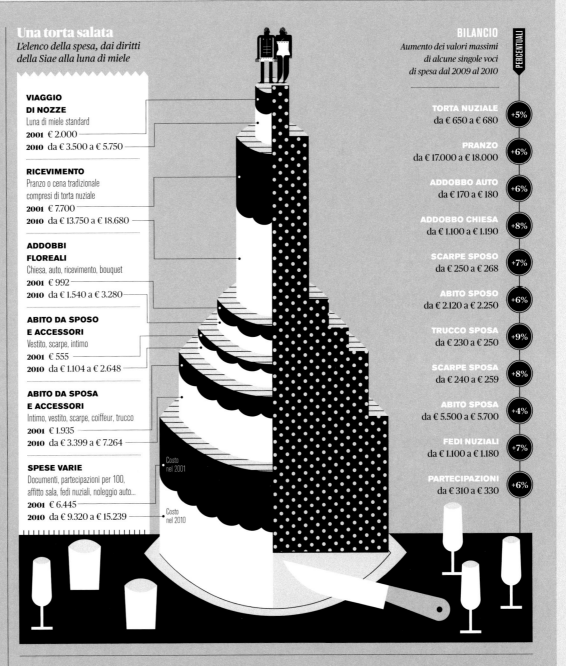

Una torta salata
L'elenco della spesa, dai diritti della Siae alla luna di miele

VIAGGIO DI NOZZE
Luna di miele standard
2001 € 2.000
2010 da € 3.500 a € 5.750

RICEVIMENTO
Pranzo o cena tradizionale compresi di torta nuziale
2001 € 7.700
2010 da € 13.750 a € 18.680

ADDOBBI FLOREALI
Chiesa, auto, ricevimento, bouquet
2001 € 992
2010 da € 1.540 a € 3.280

ABITO DA SPOSO E ACCESSORI
Vestito, scarpe, intimo
2001 € 555
2010 da € 1.104 a € 2.648

ABITO DA SPOSA E ACCESSORI
Intimo, vestito, scarpe, coiffeur, trucco
2001 € 1.935
2010 da € 3.399 a € 7.264

SPESE VARIE
Documenti, partecipazioni per 100, affitto sala, fedi nuziali, noleggio auto...
2001 € 6.445
2010 da € 9.320 a € 15.239

Costo nel 2001

Costo nel 2010

BILANCIO
Aumento dei valori massimi di alcune singole voci di spesa dal 2009 al 2010

PERCENTUALI

TORTA NUZIALE da € 650 a € 680 — +5%
PRANZO da € 17.000 a € 18.000 — +6%
ADDOBBO AUTO da € 170 a € 180 — +6%
ADDOBBO CHIESA da € 1.100 a € 1.190 — +8%
SCARPE SPOSO da € 250 a € 268 — +7%
ABITO SPOSO da € 2.120 a € 2.250 — +6%
TRUCCO SPOSA da € 230 a € 250 — +9%
SCARPE SPOSA da € 240 a € 259 — +8%
ABITO SPOSA da € 5.500 a € 5.700 — +4%
FEDI NUZIALI da € 1.100 a € 1.180 — +7%
PARTECIPAZIONI da € 310 a € 330 — +6%

---

dove si nascondono i colpi di scena? «Nell'arrivo della sposa. Addio dalla vecchia auto di famiglia, adesso è tutto accuratamente studiato per **stupire**: c'è chi arriva a dorso di un asino, come nel film *Mamma Mia!*, e chi sceglie una più comoda 500. Ci sono spose che planano a bordo di un idrovolante sul lago e ce ne sono altre che arrivano in **tandem**. L'unico consiglio che do sempre è: occhio all'acconciatura», ammonisce Parabiago.

Che – oltre a (tentare) di contenere i costi – i futuri marito e moglie si ispirino a piccolo e grande schermo lo confermano altre due tendenze che stanno prendendo

piede nel Bel Paese: quella delle *bridesmaid* e del discorso degli amici degli sposi. «La nostra abitudine era quella di far accompagnare la sposa da damigelle bambine. Ora vedo comparire sempre più spesso accanto alla sposa le **amiche**, che si vestono uniformandosi alle sue indicazioni. È un modo per distinguerle, tenerle più vicine e riconoscere loro un grado quasi parentale». Discorso a parte, è il caso di dirlo, è quello degli amici che si preparano una serie di racconti e **aneddoti**, dal sapore scherzoso e dal tono ufficiale. Un'altra novità nel matrimonio made in Italy è quella delle *wed-*

ding planner, osserva Banzi: «Un fenomeno in forte crescita. Propone preventivi e soluzioni diverse, si prende carico dell'organizzazione, in qualche caso fa persino da psicologa e dà **consigli** per evitare vestiti improponibili».

Tra i tanti innesti esterofili, cosa resta della nostra tradizione? «Durante i preparativi – risponde Banzi – meglio tenere lontane sposa e **futura suocera**. Secondo i nostri sondaggi, questo resta sicuramente un *evergreen*». Inoltre ricordate: se non vi sentite a vostro agio con kolossal degni di Tom Cruise, tanto vale limitarsi. E fare un po' quel che più piace. **IL**

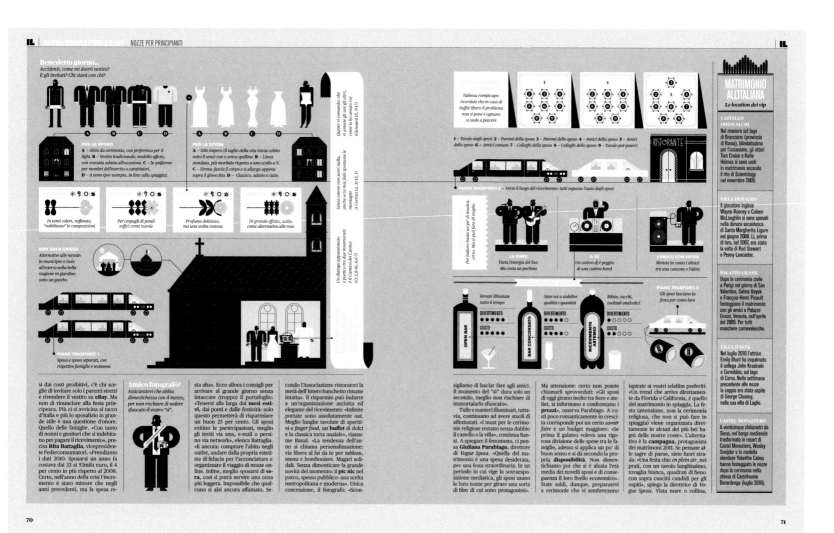

Preghiera per principianti

— Come districarsi tra genuflessioni, antropologia e rosari

Sono tutte richieste di precari

Dall'incertezza della condizione umana si alza una voce verso l'alto

TESTO — **Andrea Tagliapietra**
SCHEDE A CURA DI — **Cristina Piotti**
ILLUSTRAZIONI — **Francesco Muzzi**

L a preghiera è l'intenzione dell'uomo, la sua devozione e il suo raccoglimento, il suo dolore e la sua gioia, la sua paura e la sua speranza, le sue parole e i suoi gesti. La preghiera è spesso **poesia** e canto, quasi a sottolineare il prevalere dei significanti, della musica e della immagine simbolica, sulla povertà assoluta del significato, ovvero di quell'inconoscibile su cui essa sporge. Pregare è un gesto metaforico, un fare "come se" qualcuno o qualcosa potesse **ascoltare**. È quindi un atteggiamento che si può studiare antropologicamente, cioè in termini esclusivamente linguistici e psicologici, senza impiegare nessun concetto teologico, né presuppore alcun simbolismo religioso particolare.

La preghiera, come già facevano intendere le parole di **Hegel** — «la lettura del giornale, la mattina presto, è una sorta di realistica preghiera mattutina». Uno orientà il proprio comportamento nei confronti della realtà: secondo Dio, oppure secondo ciò che il mondo — può muovere da un bisogno di **sicurezza**. La stessa etimologia della parola "preghiera" rinvia all'aggettivo latino *precarius*, "che si ottiene con la preghiera", ma che traslatamente evoca quell'ambito dell'esperienza in cui, non avendo alcuna certezza di

Attenzione all'ingresso
Come entrare nei luoghi di culto

EBREI
In sinagoga gli uomini sono tenuti a entrare sempre con il capo coperto. Basta la kippah.

MUSULMANI
Si entra in moschea a piedi nudi e dopo aver fatto le abluzioni. Le donne devono coprirsi.

BUDDISTI
Si tolgono le mani, si tolgono le scarpe, poi si prostrano con ginocchi, mani e fronte fino a terra.

CATTOLICI
In chiesa i fedeli si genuflettono e si fanno il segno della croce con acqua benedetta.

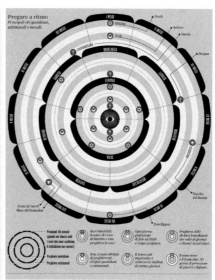

FRANCESCO MUZZI
1   Finchè Conto non vi Separi—P. 3
The increment in pricing for all wedding expenditure categories such as clothes, rings, and honey moon. Each level of the pie is proportional to the total expenditure of each category. The black topping represents the cost in 2001; the white part represents the cost in 2010.

2   Finchè Conto non vi Separi—P. 2
Information about planning a wedding day from the choosing of the dress (top left) to what to drink at the party (bottom right).
Year: 2011—Client: IL - Intelligence in lifestyle—Art direction: Francesco Franchi

3   Preghiera per Principianti—P. 1
Infographic accompanying an article about the practice of praying in the world's four most widespread religions: Catholicism, Islam, Buddhism, and Judaism. This first page shows what to do, whether it is making the sign of the cross or taking off one's shoes before entering the different places of worship.

4   Preghiera per Principianti—P. 3
A calendar that indicates the most important moments for praying in each religion. It is divided in concentric circles representing months of the year, days of the week, and moments during the day.
Year: 2010—Client: IL - Intelligence in lifestyle—Art direction: Francesco Franchi

LAMOSCA
Data Series
Over the course of 250 weeks, Lamosca produced an infographic for the Spanish newspaper *La Vanguardia*. Each infographic was based on the week's cover theme, ranging in topics from gas burning in the Niger Delta to popular culture.
Year: 2007/2010—Client: La Vanguardia/Culturas

Data 125
LAMOSCA

Delta del Niger / A todo gas

Nigeria es el primer quemador mundial de gas asociado al petróleo. El 70% del gas natural asociado se quema sin más expulsando toneladas de CO$_2$ a la atmósfera.

● Gas asociado al petróleo   3.500.000.000m^3
● Porción quemada   2.500.000.000m^3

Fuente: www.foe.co.uk/

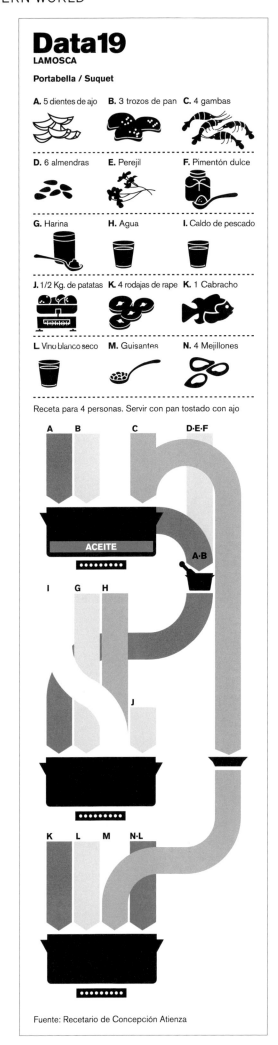

Data19
LAMOSCA

Portabella / Suquet

A. 5 dientes de ajo   **B.** 3 trozos de pan   **C.** 4 gambas

D. 6 almendras   **E.** Perejil   **F.** Pimentón dulce

G. Harina   **H.** Agua   **I.** Caldo de pescado

J. 1/2 Kg. de patatas   **K.** 4 rodajas de rape   **K.** 1 Cabracho

L. Vino blanco seco   **M.** Guisantes   **N.** 4 Mejillones

Receta para 4 personas. Servir con pan tostado con ajo

ACEITE

Fuente: Recetario de Concepción Atienza

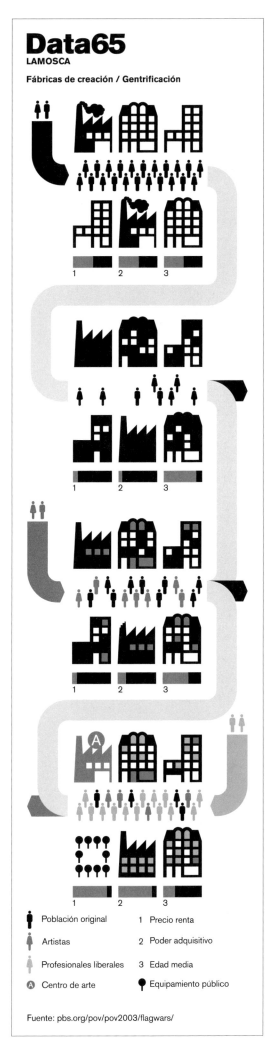

Data65
LAMOSCA

Fábricas de creación / Gentrificación

👤 Población original   1 Precio renta

👤 Artistas   2 Poder adquisitivo

👤 Profesionales liberales   3 Edad media

🅐 Centro de arte   🌳 Equipamiento público

Fuente: pbs.org/pov/pov2003/flagwars/

Data81
LAMOSCA

Geopolítica española / El increíble imperio menguante

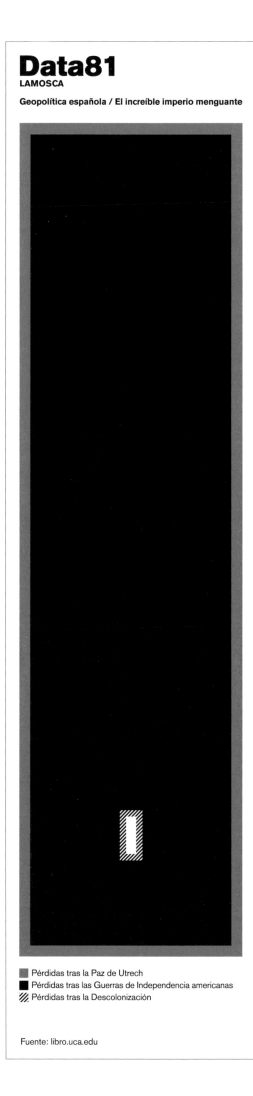

- Pérdidas tras la Paz de Utrech
- Pérdidas tras las Guerras de Independencia americanas
- Pérdidas tras la Descolonización

Fuente: libro.uca.edu

Data21
LAMOSCA

Leonardo / Miedo a volar

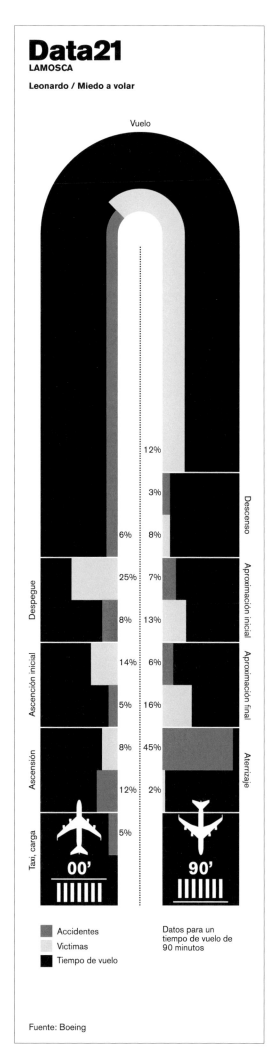

- Accidentes
- Víctimas
- Tiempo de vuelo

Datos para un tiempo de vuelo de 90 minutos

Fuente: Boeing

Data97
LAMOSCA

Ajedrez / Valor relativo

Valor relativo de las piezas de ajedrez

El rey carece de valor relativo

- 9
- 3
- 1
- 5
- 3

Fuente: Lasker's Chess Primer

Visual Stories

THE MODERN WORLD

DRIVEN BY DATA
o Gregor Aisch
1 Visualizing Plagiarism of Karl-Theodor zu Guttenberg

When the story broke in the German press that the current Minister of Defense, Karl-Theodor zu Guttenberg, had plagiarized portions of his PhD dissertation, the result was his eventual resignation. This graphic powerfully illustrates the extent of the plagiarism by highlighting plagiarized lines in red and dark red.

Year: 2011—Client: driven-by-data.net

KLAS ERNFLO
2 Short Story Poster

This typographic poster took the words from the short story *Sheep May Safely Graze* by Jess Row to create an illustration for the story.

Year: 2011—Personal Project

Schafe können sicher weiden,
Wo ein guter Hirte wacht.
Wo Regenten wohl regieren,
Kann man Ruh und Friede spüren
Und was Länder glücklich macht.

Sheep can safely graze,
where a good shepherd watches over them.
Where rulers are ruling well,
we may feel peace and rest
and what makes countries happy.

Short story *Sheep May Safely Graze* by Jess Row and design by Klas Ernflo.

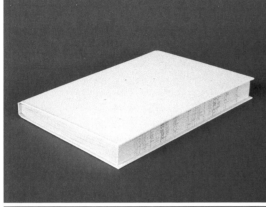

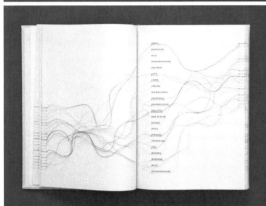

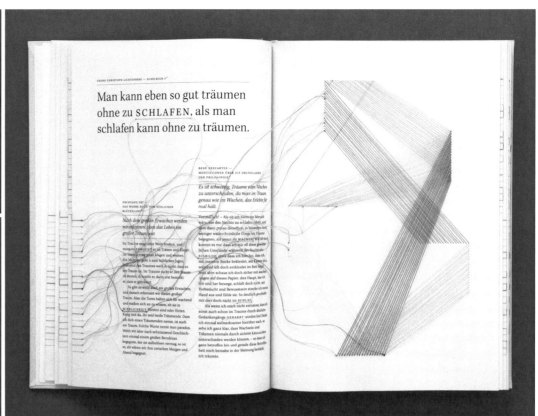

MARIA FISCHER
Traumgedanken
The book *Traumgedanken* (Thoughts on Dreams) contains a collection of literary, philosophical, psychological, and scientific texts which provide insights into dream theories. Similar to a dream, in which pieces of reality are assembled to build a story, the book brings different text excerpts together and connects them by threads that tie into key words, creating an abstract image of the dream about dreaming.

Year: 2010—Final Year Project at University of Applied Sciences Augsburg—200×280 mm, 76 PP.

BEATE BARBARA
BLASCHCZOK
Schöpfung

Schöpfung (Creation) visualizes the various myths and stories of creation along one timeline that stretches out over 600 pages. It starts with the Big Bang, covers the Hindu saga of creation, as well as the history of evolution. The message of this book is that all stories about evolution are too short to be visible at all, offering a perspective that shows human evolution from its beginnings to the present day on only a few centimeters.

Year: 2008—Photography: Debbie Runkel

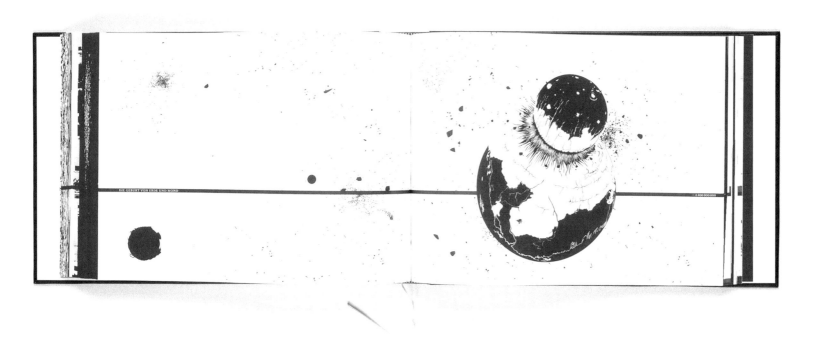

Visual Stories

THE MODERN WORLD

NICHOLAS FELTON
Feltron 2010 Annual Report
Nicholas Felton is known for his annual reports, which gather and display detailed data from his personal life. In 2010, he switched things up by creating a report of the life of his father, who escaped Nazi Germany as a child and went on to live in the UK, Canada, and finally the United States. Felton used data from his father's calendars, slides, and other assorted artifacts to document his life from 1931 until his death in 2010.
Year: 2011—Personal work

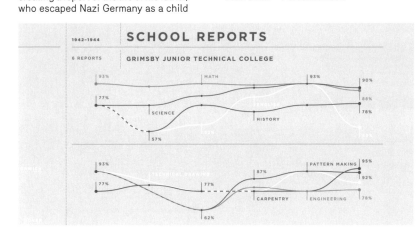

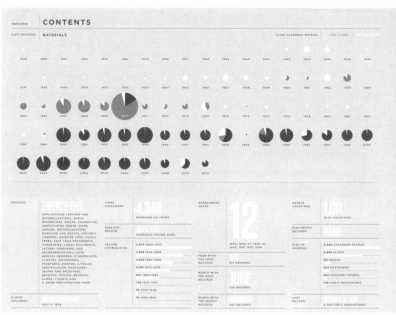

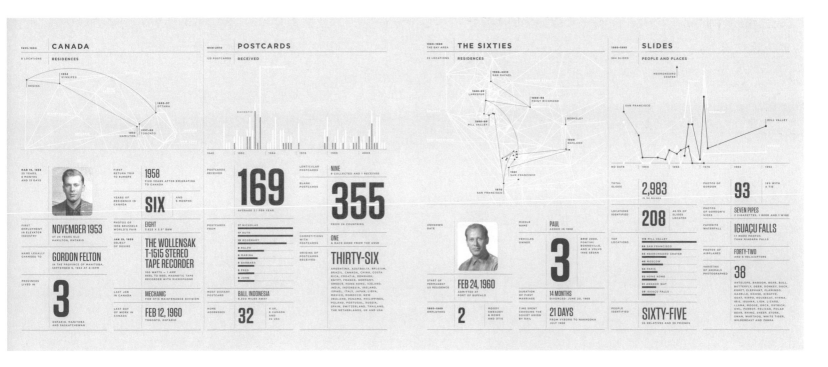

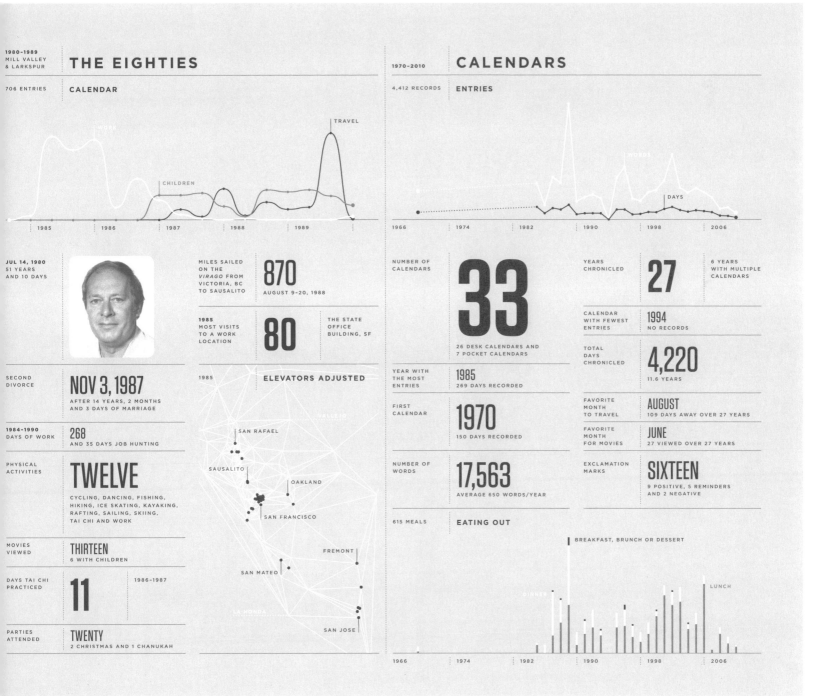

Visual Stories

THE MODERN WORLD

ONE YEAR STUDY
TEDxAustin NOW

In early 2010, TEDx Austin asked *One Year Study* and *Public School* to create an opening video for their 2011 conference. They wanted a visual representation of their written manifesto, which explains why Austin is an appropriate venue for the TED conference. The TED motto, "Ideas Worth Spreading," served as the foundation of the concept. Six of the largest industries in Austin—music, education, fitness, tech, art, and film—showed how ideas overlap and inspire progress; each industry not only promotes itself, but keeps Austin relevant. Throughout the video, characters interact with a tightly constructed grid of objects, illustrating how each industry cross-pollenates and evolves. In the end, the objects form an X, representing not only the TEDx brand, but the idea that Austin is the place to be.

Year: 2011—Client: TEDx

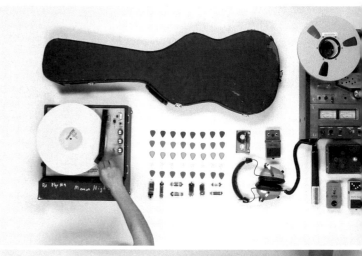

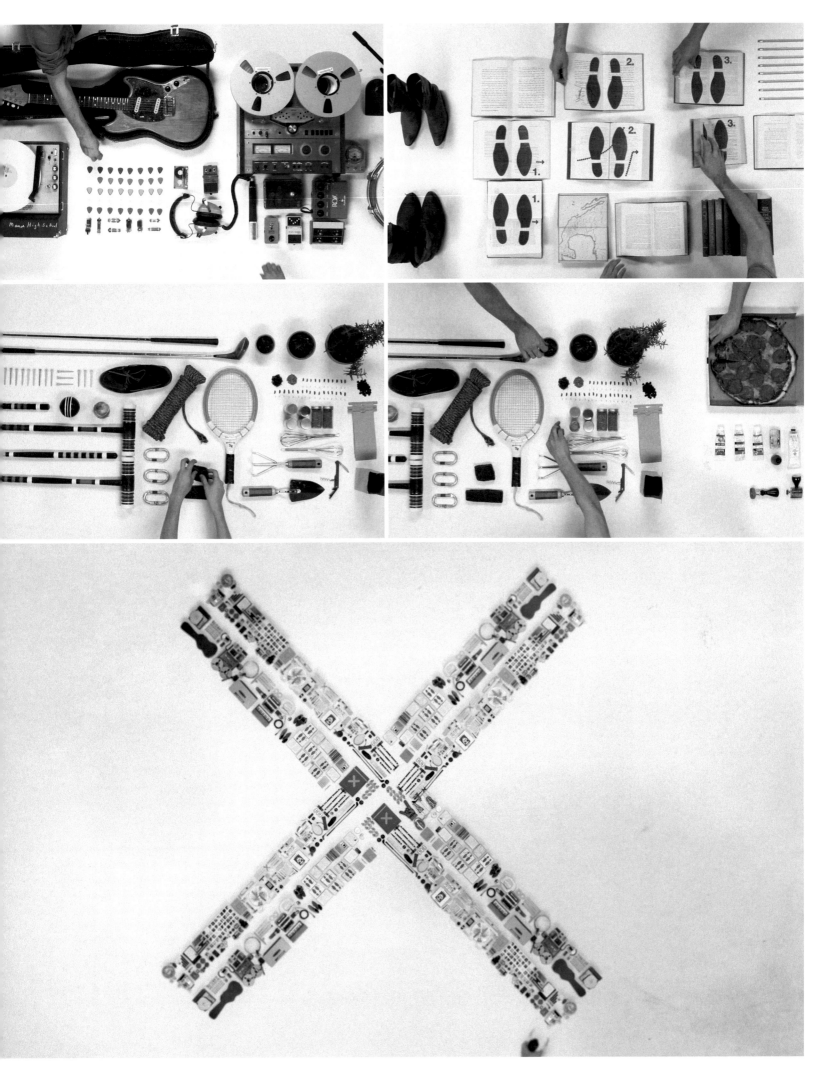

HUNTERGATHERER
REDU
The 2-minute stop-motion animation explaining what REDU, an education reform destination, is all about. It was created almost entirely in-camera and with thousands of individually cut blocks.

Year: 2010—Client: REDU/CAA—Collaboration between bing, CAA, Task Force and Good Magazine, among others

2 Prius Goes Plural Intro Video
An animated commercial asking viewers to take part in deciding how the plural form of "Prius" should be spelled.
Year: 2011—Client:Toyota/Saatchi & Saatchi LA

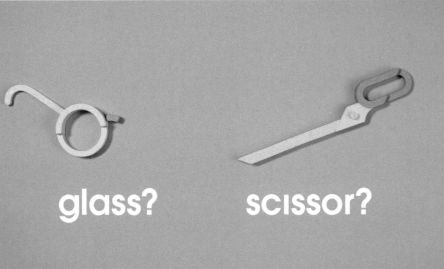

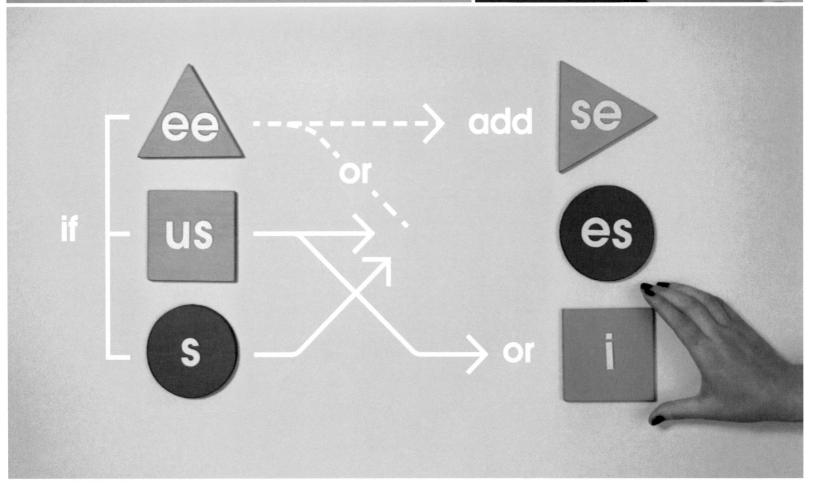

SALOTTOBUONO
Instructions and Manuals

Salottobuono redraws the plans, sections, diagrams, distribution charts, and construction details of the projects published inside *Abitare* magazine, providing readers with an immediately understandable visual tool. In addition

THE MODERN WORLD

to offering a selection of technical and design information about how projects were designed, built, and organized, they also show which technologies were used and offer a context for their form, function, and environment.

Year: 2008—Client: *Abitare* magazine

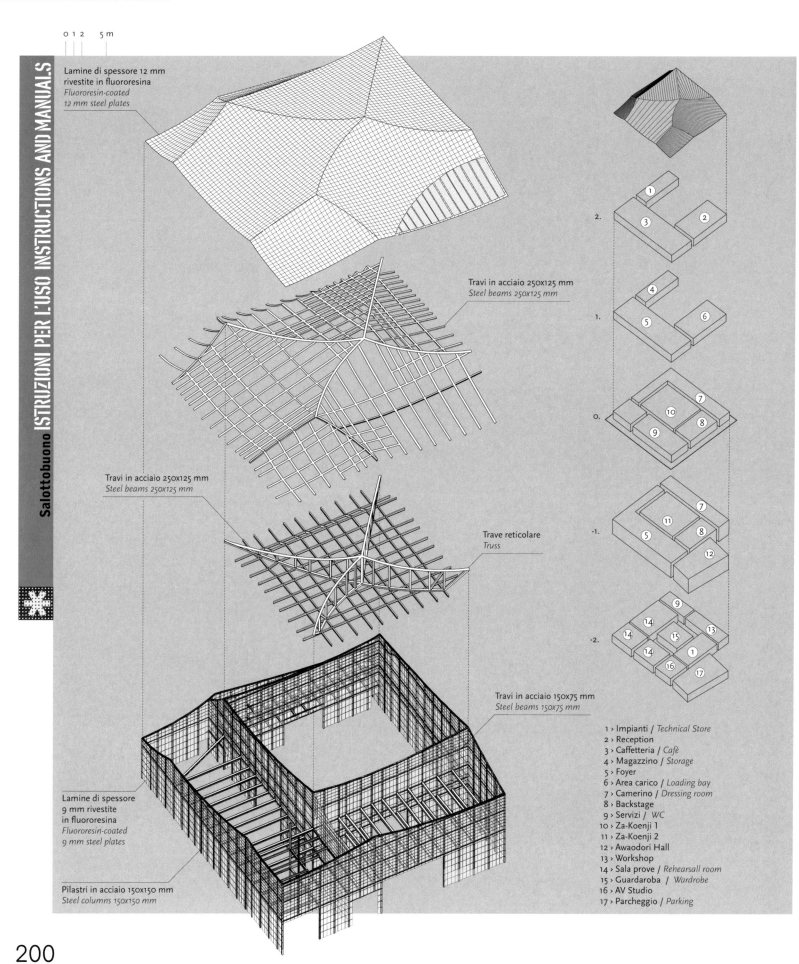

Salottobuono ISTRUZIONI PER L'USO INSTRUCTIONS AND MANUALS

0 1 2   5 m

Lamine di spessore 12 mm rivestite in fluororesina
Fluororesin-coated 12 mm steel plates

Travi in acciaio 250x125 mm
Steel beams 250x125 mm

Travi in acciaio 250x125 mm
Steel beams 250x125 mm

Trave reticolare
Truss

Travi in acciaio 150x75 mm
Steel beams 150x75 mm

Lamine di spessore 9 mm rivestite in fluororesina
Fluororesin-coated 9 mm steel plates

Pilastri in acciaio 150x150 mm
Steel columns 150x150 mm

1 › Impianti / *Technical Store*
2 › Reception
3 › Caffetteria / *Cafè*
4 › Magazzino / *Storage*
5 › Foyer
6 › Area carico / *Loading bay*
7 › Camerino / *Dressing room*
8 › Backstage
9 › Servizi / *WC*
10 › Za-Koenji 1
11 › Za-Koenji 2
12 › Awaodori Hall
13 › Workshop
14 › Sala prove / *Rehearsall room*
15 › Guardaroba / *Wardrobe*
16 › AV Studio
17 › Parcheggio / *Parking*

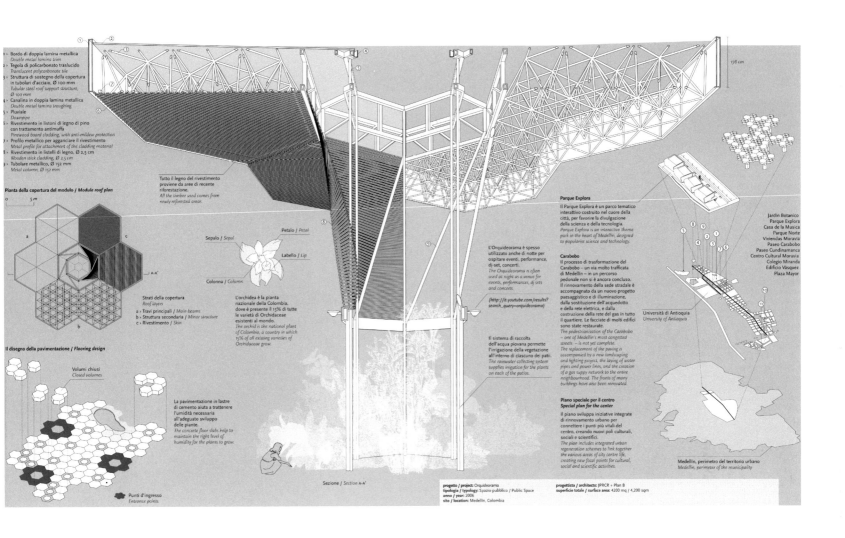

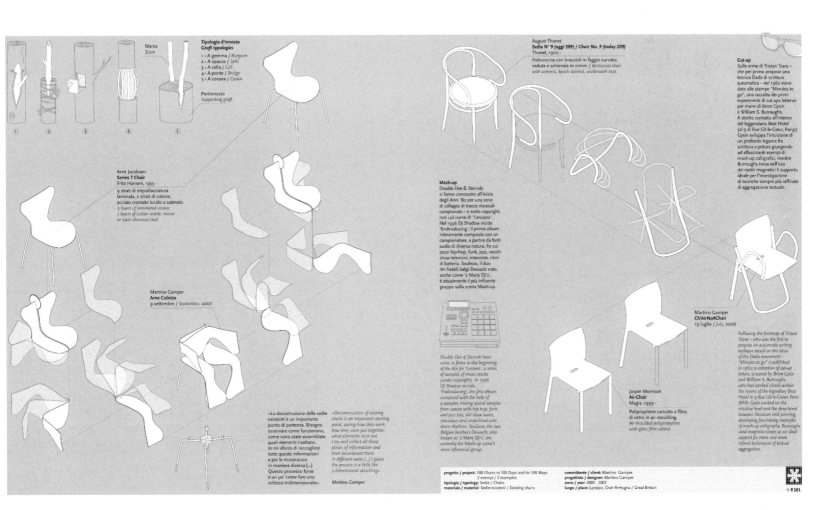

201

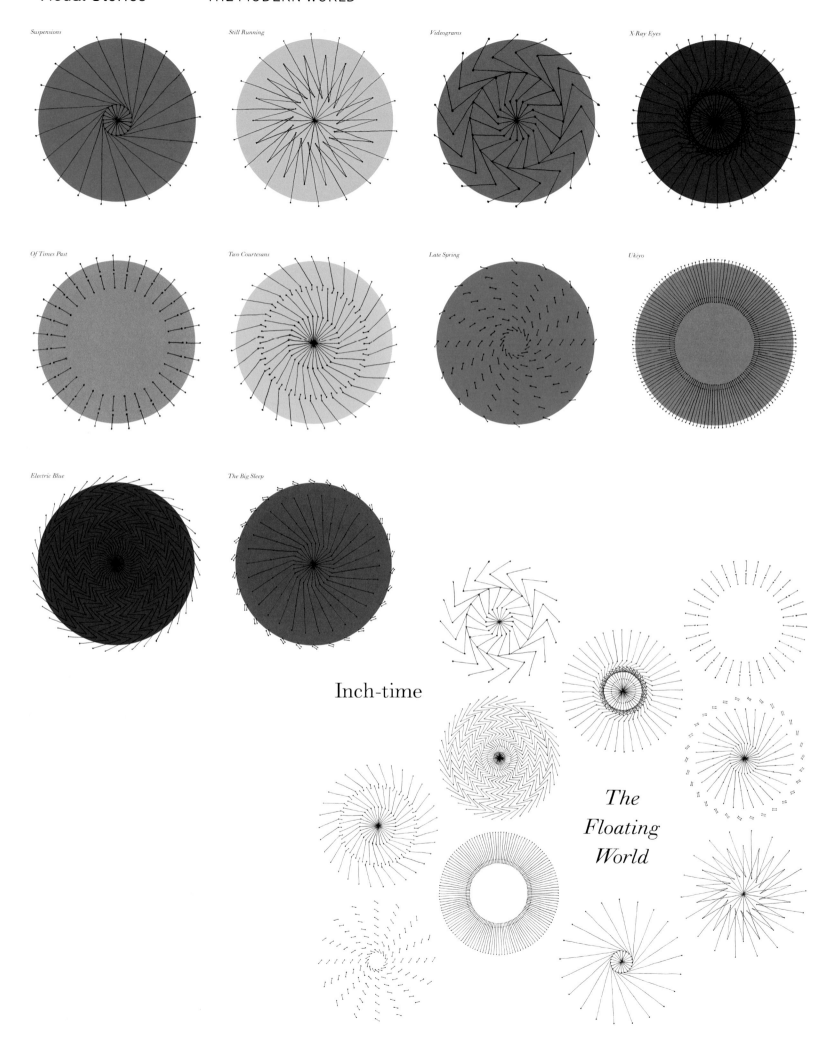

Suspensions

Still Running

Videograms

X-Ray Eyes

Of Times Past

Two Courtesans

Late Spring

Ukiyo

Electric Blue

The Big Sleep

Inch-time

The Floating World

STEFANIE POSAVEC &
GREG MCINERNY

1   Album Artwork for The Floating
World, by Inch-time
This album artwork is composed of
a pencil song mandala for each track
that was created by listening to the
songs and drawing their journey up
and down the musical scale.
Year: 2010—Client: Mystery Plays
Records

2   Album Artwork for Of the Blue
Colour of the Sky, by OK Go
The album artwork for OK Go's *Of
the Blue Colour of the Sky* album uses computer programs to gather data
from the album's lyrics as well as the
book *The Influence of the Blue Ray of
the Sunlight and of the Blue Colour of
the Sky,* by General A.J. Pleasonton.
The programs find patterns in stressed
and unstressed syllables, sentence
length, and similar words between the
two texts. Simple, graphic visuals represent these patterns. Rainbow colors,
which are referenced in Pleasonton's
book, represent *OK Go* songs while
white graphics represent data from
Pleasanton's book.
Client: Capitol Records.

OK GO
OF THE
BLUE
COLOUR
OF THE
SKY

The diagrams on pages 2-7 compare the album's
lyrics to an excerpt of the book it is named after,
General A.J. Pleasonton's *The Influence of the Blue
Ray of the Sunlight and of the Blue Colour of the Sky,*
published in 1876 by Claxton, Remsen & Haffelfinger,
Philadelphia. The graphs on page 8 compare the
lyrics with the entirety of Pleasonton's text.

The diagrams are color coded as shown below.

**The Influence of the Blue Ray of the
Sunlight and of the Blue Colour of
the Sky**

WTF?
This Too Shall Pass
All Is Not Lost
Needing/Getting
Skyscrapers
White Knuckles
I Want You So Bad I Can't Breathe
End Love
Before the Earth Was Round
Last Leaf
Back From Kathmandu
While You Were Asleep
In the Glass

**Pages 2-3
Sentence Length**

Each bar represents one sentence. They are arranged
by word count.

1 word = .3 millimeter

0   25   50   75   100
words per sentence

**Pages 6-7
Parts of Speech**

Each line represents a word, and they are grouped
in rings by their function.

Pronoun
Noun
Verb
Adverb
Adjective
Preposition
Article
Conjunction
Infinitive
Interjection

One
occurrence

**Pages 4-5
Syllables**

The texts are represented linearly. Each line segment
corresponds to a syllable.

Stressed Syllable   Two Stressed Syllables

Unstressed Syllable   Two Unstressed Syllables

**Page 8
Words Common to Both Texts**

Each line graphs a song. Every unique word in
the book is represented as a point on the x-axis,
arranged alphabetically. Y values show the number
of times that word occurs in the song.

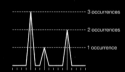

3 occurrences

2 occurrences

1 occurrence

Front Cover

The front cover displays themes common to the book
and the album. Each line represents a sentence,
with the album's lyrics fanning to the left and the
text of the book fanning to the right. Each theme is
represented by a color. For sentences dealing with
multiple themes, the colors are added together as
light is (see below), such that each theme's color
both lightens and tints the resultant line.

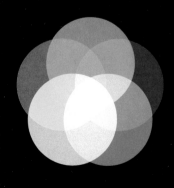

Themes

1   Unfounded or Wildly Broad Claims
2   Wonderment
3   Causality/Unavoidable Consequences/
Compelled Behavior
4   Reference to an Individual, or Direct
Address to/from One
5   Anecdotal or Expository Context
6   Figuring It All Out
7   Unanswerable/Impossible/
Rhetorical Questions
8   Light/Optics/Color
9   Fire/Combustion/Chemical/
Physical Reactions
10 Atmospheric Properties
11 Things That, in Retrospect, Proved to
be Wrong
12 Plants and Animals/Animal Behavior
13 The Sky or Things Falling From It
14 Women
15 Optimism/Hope
16 Dissatisfaction
17 Bodies/Body Parts/Bodily Function
18 God/Faith
19 Corruscation
20 Death
21 Magic
22 Global Mechanics
23 Confusion/Curiosity
24 Pride
25 Prescriptions for a Better World

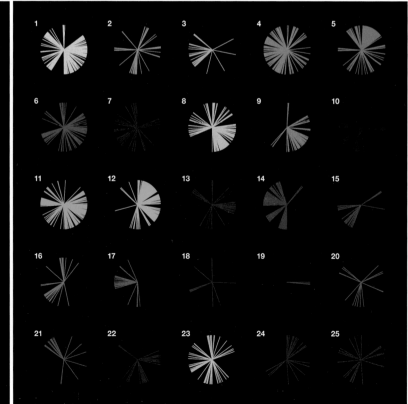

2

203

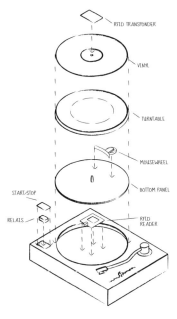

Digging in the Crates is an interactive installation that aims to describe all aspects of the sampling culture and offer the possibility for the user to explore sampling as a production technology of contemporary music. Modified turntables are used to navigate dynamic data visualizations, while information graphics and auditory contributions help the user understand complex contents and relations. Besides the history of sampling, visitors can obtain information on the dissociation of sample-based productions and other musicological phenomena such as remixes, mashups, or covers.

Year: 2010——Diploma thesis at the University of Applied Sciences in Augsburg, Germany

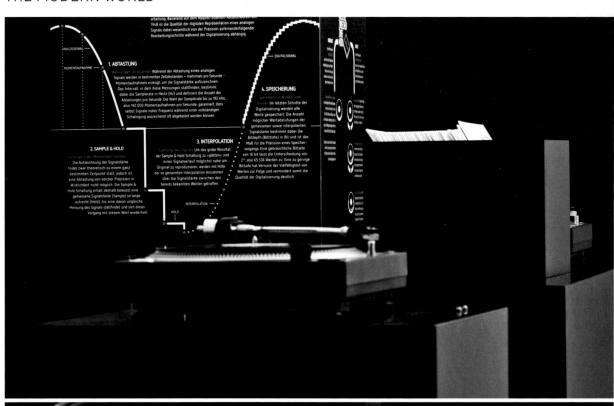

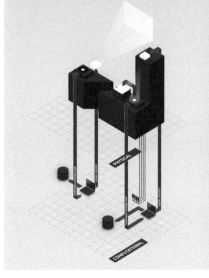

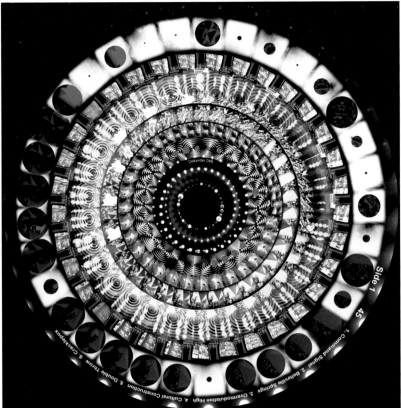

DAN HAYHURST,
REUBEN SUTHERLAND
Rotary Signal Emitter

Rotary Signal Emitter is a zoetropic animation on a vinyl picture disc LP. This LP can be played normally or as a self-contained film. To see the video content, a bright light must be directed at the record as it plays at 45 rpm. The film will then play on the surface of the record as it spins

Year: 2011—Client: Vinyl Picture Disc LP by Sculpture (Dekorder Records)

1

KENZO MINAMI
Digitizer

Digitizer is a collaboration between Kenzo Minami and Affinity Cycles, and was produced by Cinecycle. For this project, colorful graphics are applied to the bicycle and become animated when in motion. Within the chaos of visual information found on city streets, the design makes the bicycle stand out and be noticeable by pedestrians and cars.

Year: 2010—Daniel Leeb courtesy of Cinecycle "Kissena" track frame by Affinity Cycles—Project produced by Cinecycle

AGENCY RUSH
○ Jonny Wan
DDB Head

This was a large scale, back-lit poster illustration commissioned by DDB London for display in the reception area of Gutenberg Paperhat. The image celebrates the partnership of the two production companies, Gutenberg and Paperhat; close inspection reveals that all the wording within the illustration is relevant to their business.

Year: 2010—Client: DDB London

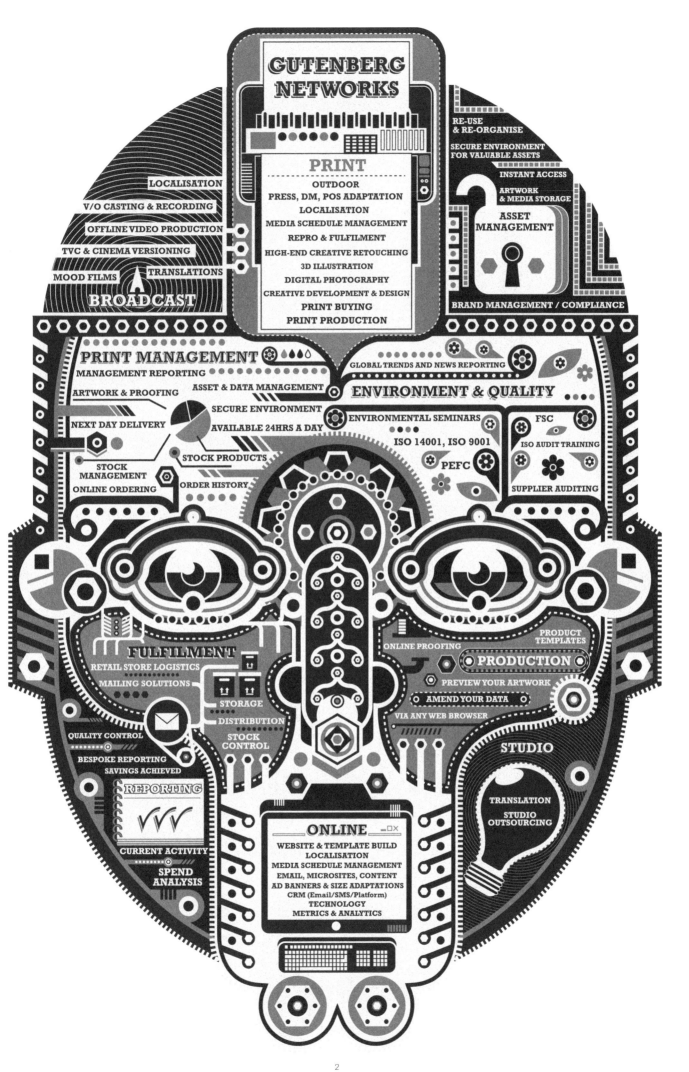

SUPER FERTILE
o Kali Arulpragasam

1 CRA$H

Jewelry designer Kali Arulpragasam's Summer 2010 collection turns phrases referencing current issues of the economy, unemployment, and debt into oversized, glittering medallions.

Year: 2010—Creative director/Art Director: Kali Arulpragasam—Client: *Vice* magazine—Photography: Dan Wilton

2 TOURISM

Iraq, Afghanistan, Sri Lanka, and other countries in conflict were the subject of Super Fertile's 2008 collection, *Tourism*. Each piece is bronze with 22 ct gold and silver plating. A montage of images associated with the country are linked together, showing the countries in a positive light, preserving their identities for the future.

Year: 2010—Creative director: Kali Arulpragasam—Client: *Time* magazine—Photography: Joachim

1

2

HYPERAKT

1 How You Will Get Hurt At Burning
Man Infographic

Spending a few nights in the desert with tens of thousands of people
can have its downfalls: dehydration,
mental breakdowns, cuts and blisters,
and drug-related mishaps, to name a
few. This infographic provides a look
at the festival's injury reports over the
past three years so that future festival
attendees can prevent becoming part
of the statistics.

Year: 2010—Client: *Good* magazine—
Creative Direction: Deroy Peraza, Julia
Vakser—Design: Jason Lynch

I INFOGRAFIA

o Carlos Monteiro
2 The Guide To Find Your Way In
Lost

This graphic shows the main story
events over the course of the television
series *Lost*. It was publish just before
the premiere of the final season.

Year: 2010—Client: *JORNAL i*

MATTSON CREATIVE

o Ty Mattson
3 Dexter Season Three Print
4 Dexter Season Five Print

Limited edition silk-screen prints
that celebrate Showtime's hit series,
Dexter.

Year: 2010—Client: Showtime Networks

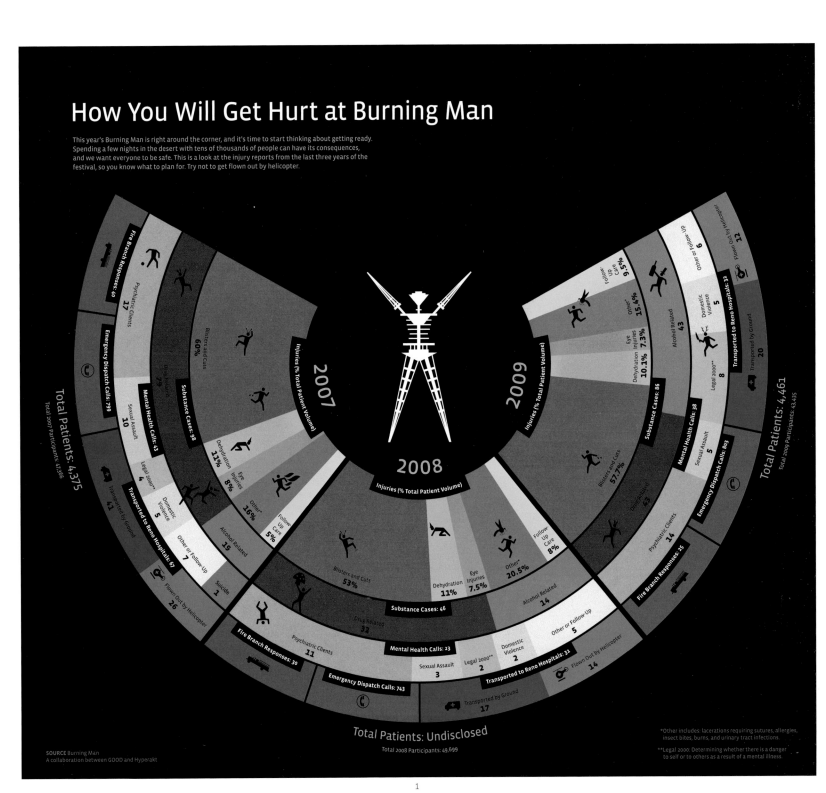

1

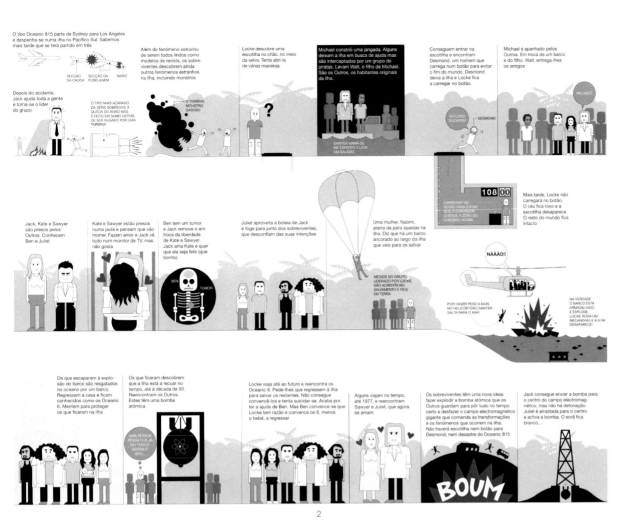

I WANT TO MAKE A MOVIE

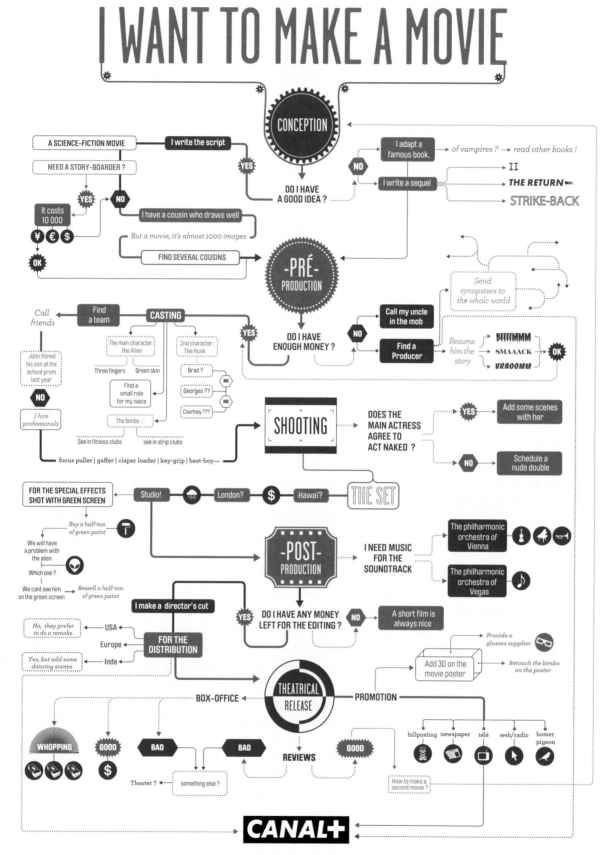

SHOOTING A FILM ISN'T THAT SIMPLE
CANAL+ SUPPORTS THOSE WHO MAKE MOVIES

GREGORY FEREMBACH
The Movies Flowcharts
Want to make a movie? These flow-chart lay out everything that goes into a film project: tight budgets, hungover cameramen, no-show actors, and grumpy directors.

Year: 2011—Client: Canal+—Copywriters: David Troquier, Gregory Ferembach——Art Directors: Gregory Ferembach, David Troquier——Illustrators: Les Graphiquants——Agency: BETC Paris

I WANT TO MAKE AN ANIMATED MOVIE

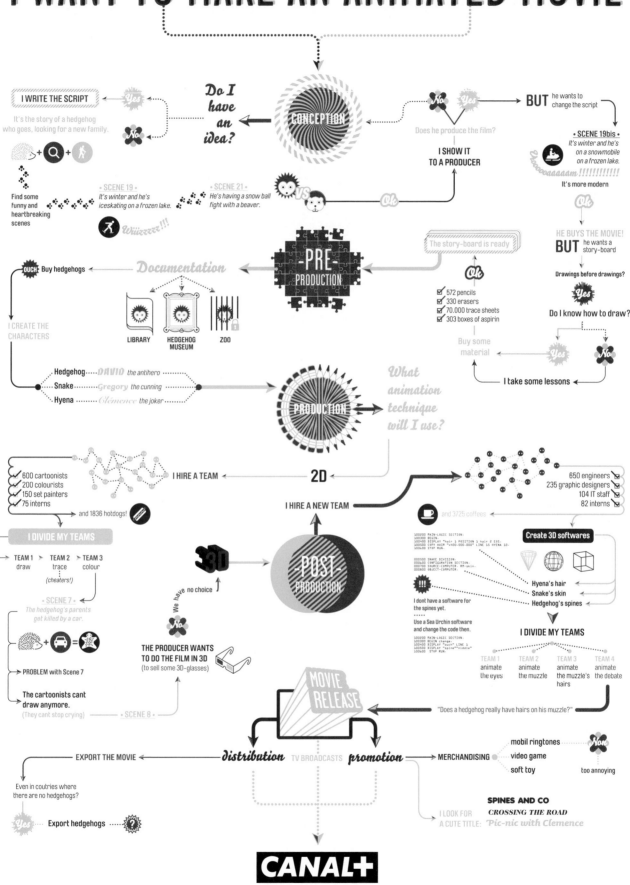

CONCEPTION

Do I have an idea?

I WRITE THE SCRIPT
It's the story of a hedgehog who goes, looking for a new family.

Yes / No

Find some funny and heartbreaking scenes

• SCENE 19 •
It's winter and he's iceskating on a frozen lake.

• SCENE 21 •
He's having a snow ball fight with a beaver.

Wiiizzzzz !!!

VS — Ok

I SHOW IT TO A PRODUCER

Does he produce the film?

No / Yes

BUT he wants to change the script

• SCENE 19bis •
It's winter and he's on a snowmobile on a frozen lake.
Vrooooaaaaam !!!!!!!!!!!!!
It's more modern

Ok

HE BUYS THE MOVIE!

BUT he wants a story-board

Drawings before drawings?

Yes

Do I know how to draw?

Yes / No

I take some lessons

Buy some material

☑ 572 pencils
☑ 330 erasers
☑ 70.000 trace sheets
☑ 303 boxes of aspirin

Ok

The story-board is ready

-PRE- PRODUCTION

Documentation

LIBRARY   HEDGEHOG MUSEUM   ZOO

OUCH: Buy hedgehogs

I CREATE THE CHARACTERS

Hedgehog ...... DAVID the antihero
Snake ...... Gregory the cunning
Hyena ...... Clémence the joker

PRODUCTION

What animation technique will I use?

2D

I HIRE A TEAM

✓ 600 cartoonists
✓ 200 colourists
✓ 150 set painters
✓ 75 interns

and 1836 hotdogs!

I DIVIDE MY TEAMS

TEAM 1 draw → TEAM 2 trace (cheaters!) → TEAM 3 colour

• SCENE 7 •
The hedgehog's parents get killed by a car.

+ 🚗 =

PROBLEM with Scene 7

The cartoonists cant draw anymore.
(They cant stop crying) • SCENE 8 •

3D

We have no choice

No

THE PRODUCER WANTS TO DO THE FILM IN 3D
(to sell some 3D-glasses)

-POST- PRODUCTION

I HIRE A NEW TEAM

650 engineers
235 graphic designers
104 IT staff
82 interns

and 3726 coffees

```
100200 MAIN-LOGIC SECTION.
100300 BEGIN.
100400 DISPLAY "hair 1 POSITION 1 hair 2 EXS.
100500 COPY HAIR "x000-000-000" LINE 15 HYENA 10.
100600 STOP RUN.

000600 SNAKE DIVISION.
000600 CONFIGURATION SECTION.
000700 SOURCE-COMPUTER. RM-win-
000800 OBJECT-COMPUTER.
```

!!!

I dont have a software for the spines yet.
•••••
Use a Sea Urchin software and change the code then.

```
100200 MAIN-LOGIC SECTION.
100300 BEGIN change.
100400 DISPLAY "duck" LINE 1
100600 DISPLAY "spine""nimble"
100600    STOP RUN.
```

Create 3D softwares

Hyena's hair
Snake's skin
Hedgehog's spines

I DIVIDE MY TEAMS

TEAM 1 animate the eyes
TEAM 2 animate the muzzle
TEAM 3 animate the muzzle's hairs
TEAM 4 animate the debate

"Does a hedgehog really have hairs on his muzzle?"

MOVIE RELEASE

distribution   TV BROADCASTS   promotion

EXPORT THE MOVIE

Even in coutries where there are no hedgehogs?

Yes → Export hedgehogs ⋯ ?

MERCHANDISING
mobil ringtones
video game
soft toy

None
too annoying

SPINES AND CO
CROSSING THE ROAD
I LOOK FOR A CUTE TITLE: *Pic-nic with Clemence*

CANAL+

SHOOTING A FILM ISN'T THAT SIMPLE
CANAL+ SUPPORTS THOSE WHO MAKE MOVIES

213

SECTION DESIGN

o Paul Butt

1 Meet iPad's Competition

This infographic is based on the article *The iPad Changes Everything*, originally published by *Fortune* magazine. It illustrates the introduction of the iPad and how many devices in different markets are now finding themselves in direction competition with the popularity of the iPad and the App Store.

Year: 2010—Client: *Courrier Japon*

2 Digital Nostalgia—Life Online

Digital Nostalgia began as a series of posters documenting recent changes in technology and the social changes they have influenced. *Wired Italia* converted them into a magazine spread illustrating the key technological milestones of the internet layered with related cultural and legal events on top. This layout shows how technology has directly influenced social events.

3 Digital Nostalgia—Media and Storage

This spread documents the advances in media and computer storage. The first page shows the different eras of audio and video formats, comparing their physical size and recording capacity while documenting the social milestones influenced by this technology. The other image illustrates the exponential growth of computer storage capacity.

Year: 2010—Client: *Wired Italia*

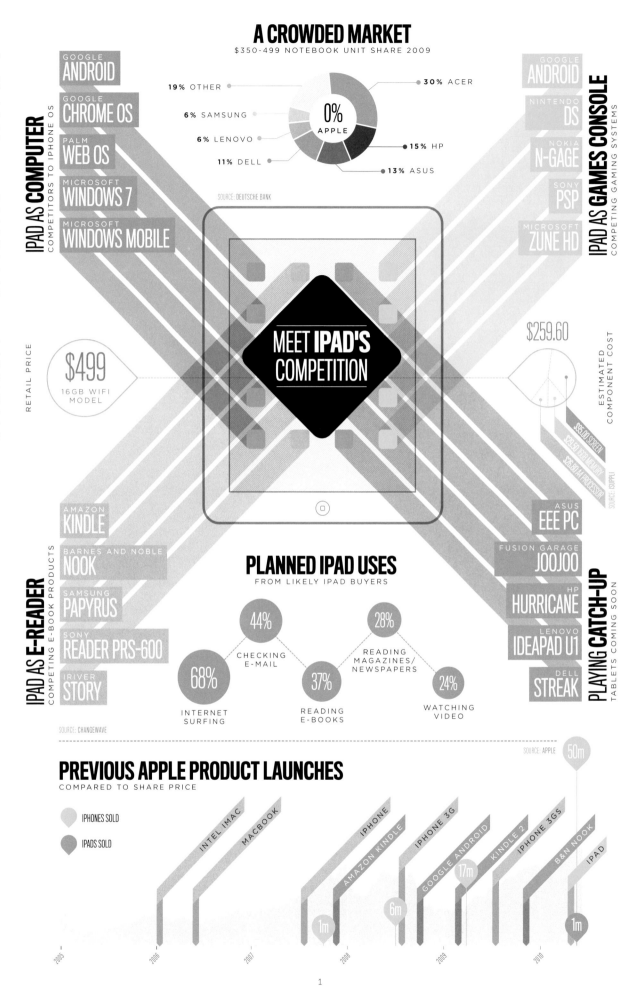

A CROWDED MARKET
$350-499 NOTEBOOK UNIT SHARE 2009

- 19% OTHER
- 6% SAMSUNG
- 6% LENOVO
- 11% DELL
- 0% APPLE
- 30% ACER
- 15% HP
- 13% ASUS

SOURCE: DEUTSCHE BANK

IPAD AS COMPUTER COMPETITORS TO IPHONE OS

GOOGLE **ANDROID**
GOOGLE **CHROME OS**
PALM **WEB OS**
MICROSOFT **WINDOWS 7**
MICROSOFT **WINDOWS MOBILE**

IPAD AS GAMES CONSOLE COMPETING GAMING SYSTEMS

GOOGLE **ANDROID**
NINTENDO **DS**
NOKIA **N-GAGE**
SONY **PSP**
MICROSOFT **ZUNE HD**

MEET IPAD'S COMPETITION

RETAIL PRICE
$499
16GB WIFI MODEL

$259.60

ESTIMATED COMPONENT COST

$65.00 SCREEN
$29.50 NAND MEMORY
$26.80 A4 PROCESSOR

SOURCE: ISUPPLI

IPAD AS E-READER COMPETING E-BOOK PRODUCTS

AMAZON **KINDLE**
BARNES AND NOBLE **NOOK**
SAMSUNG **PAPYRUS**
SONY **READER PRS-600**
IRIVER **STORY**

PLAYING CATCH-UP TABLETS COMING SOON

ASUS **EEE PC**
FUSION GARAGE **JOOJOO**
HP **HURRICANE**
LENOVO **IDEAPAD U1**
DELL **STREAK**

PLANNED IPAD USES
FROM LIKELY IPAD BUYERS

- 44% CHECKING E-MAIL
- 28% READING MAGAZINES/NEWSPAPERS
- 68% INTERNET SURFING
- 37% READING E-BOOKS
- 24% WATCHING VIDEO

SOURCE: CHANGEWAVE

PREVIOUS APPLE PRODUCT LAUNCHES
COMPARED TO SHARE PRICE

SOURCE: APPLE

IPHONES SOLD
IPADS SOLD

- INTEL IMAC
- MACBOOK
- IPHONE
- AMAZON KINDLE — 1m
- IPHONE 3G
- GOOGLE ANDROID — 6m
- KINDLE 2 — 17m
- IPHONE 3GS
- B&N NOOK
- IPAD — 1m
- 50m

2005 · 2006 · 2007 · 2008 · 2009 · 2010

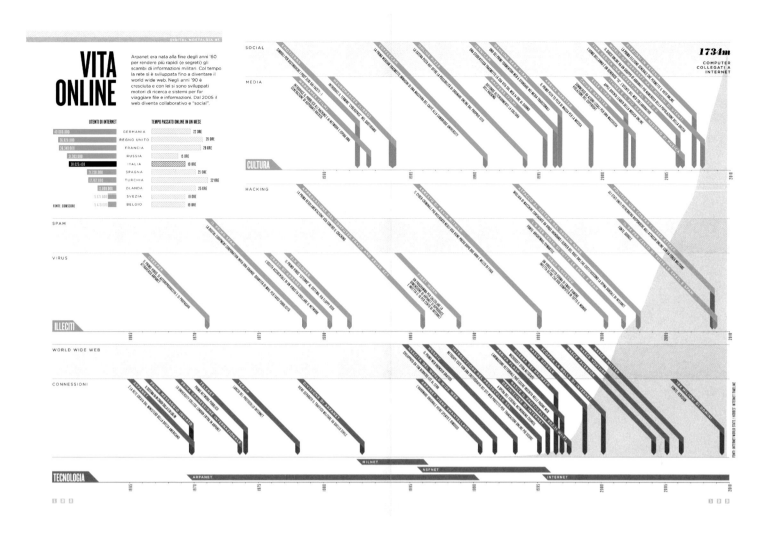

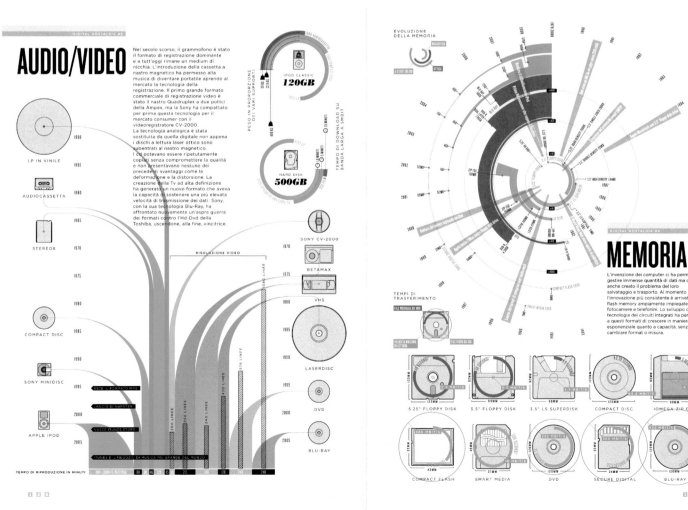

Visual Stories

BRANDON SCHAEFER

1   War of the Worlds
A poster for one of the most famous works by Orson Wells in which the inhabitants of Earth clash with invaders from Mars.
Year: 2009——Personal work

2   Nineteen Eighty-Four
A poster pulled from the shutter of a camera for Orwell's masterpiece, *1984*.
Year: 2010——Personal work

3   2001
One in a series of posters based on the films of director Stanley Kubrick.
Year: 2010——Personal work

THE MODERN WORLD

ALBERT EXERGIAN

4   Iconic TV
A series of self-initiated posters inspired by modernism and television.
Year: 2009–2010——Personal work

2

1

3

CALIFORNICATION

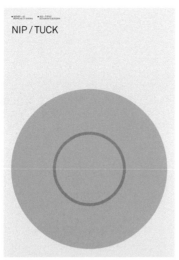

NIP / TUCK

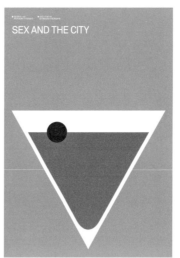

SEX AND THE CITY

TWIN PEAKS

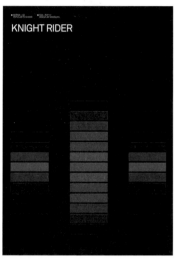

KNIGHT RIDER

MAGNUM

DEXTER

KOJAK

SIX FEET UNDER

DEADWOOD

THE SOPRANOS

THE WIRE

MIAMI VICE

WEEDS

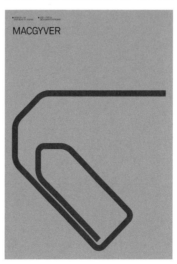

MACGYVER

THE X FILES

4

THE MODERN WORLD

OHHH
○ Esteve Padilla
1 2011 The Year...
A poster that imagines all the things that could happen in the year 2011.
Year: 2010—Self promotion (Esteve Padilla | OHHH)——Photography: OHHH

GARETH HOLT
2 Satellites & Spectrums
An ongoing series of posters that record and define famous and legendary people and events in one graphic.
Year: 2010—Personal work

2011
The second year of the decade.

201111111
The year that unemployment goes down?

2011.1
The International Year of Forests.

201.
The year that ten years ago changed the world.

2011
The year that Wikileaks will help to make the world a little bit more transparent.

2011
The year that the stock exchange will still go up and down?

2011111111
The year that American troops are scheduled to leave Iraq.

2011
The year that Palestine and Israel will want to talk?

Bon nadal   Merry Christmas
i feliç Any Nou!   and happy New Year!   **2011**

estevepadilla.info

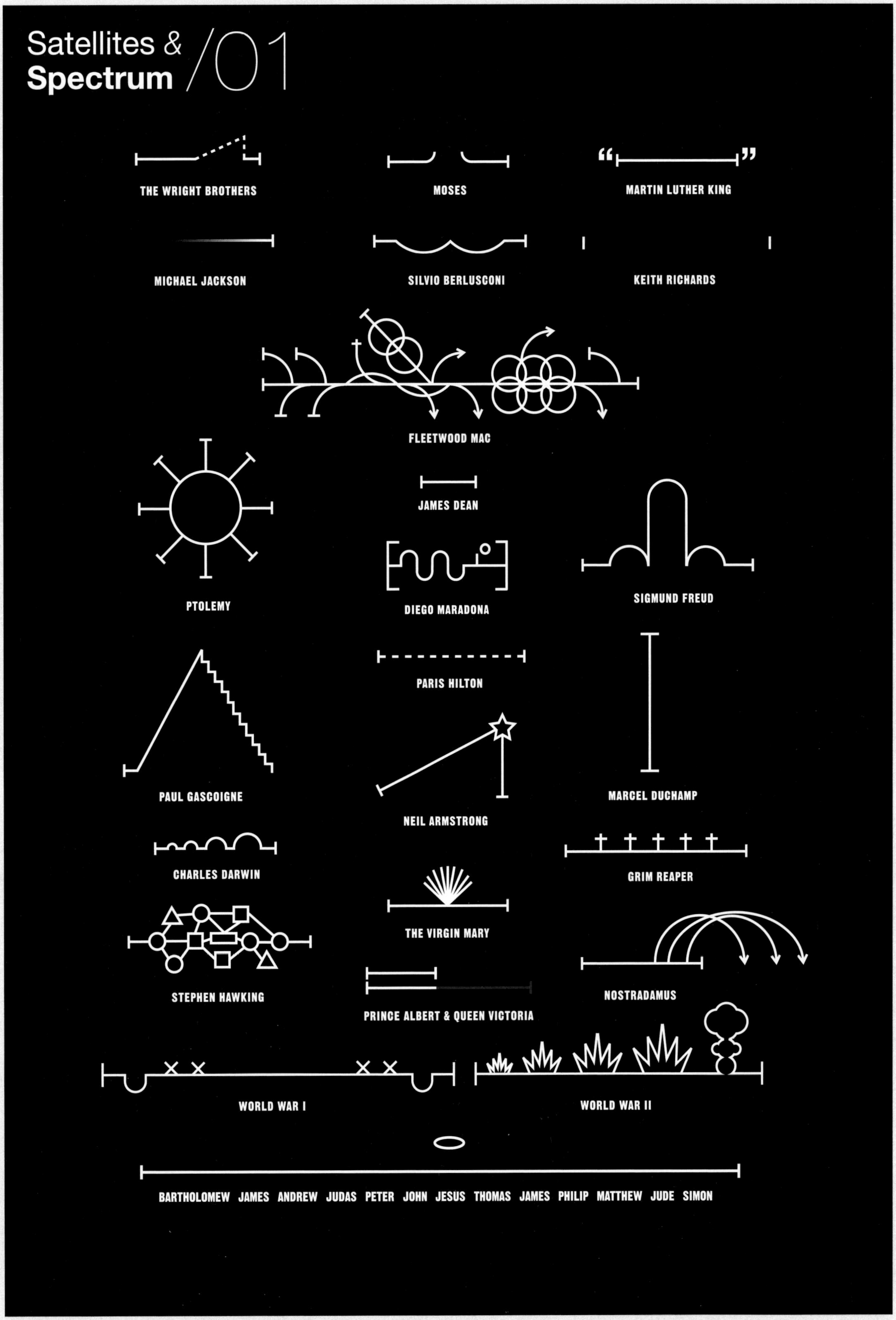

THE WRIGHT BROTHERS

MOSES

MARTIN LUTHER KING

MICHAEL JACKSON

SILVIO BERLUSCONI

KEITH RICHARDS

FLEETWOOD MAC

PTOLEMY

JAMES DEAN

SIGMUND FREUD

DIEGO MARADONA

PAUL GASCOIGNE

PARIS HILTON

MARCEL DUCHAMP

NEIL ARMSTRONG

CHARLES DARWIN

GRIM REAPER

THE VIRGIN MARY

STEPHEN HAWKING

NOSTRADAMUS

PRINCE ALBERT & QUEEN VICTORIA

WORLD WAR I

WORLD WAR II

BARTHOLOMEW   JAMES   ANDREW   JUDAS   PETER   JOHN   JESUS   THOMAS   JAMES   PHILIP   MATTHEW   JUDE   SIMON

2

SARAH ILLENBERGER
Cut Art
Several illustrations for *Neon*
magazine dealing with esthetic
surgery.
Year: 2005—Client: *Neon* magazine

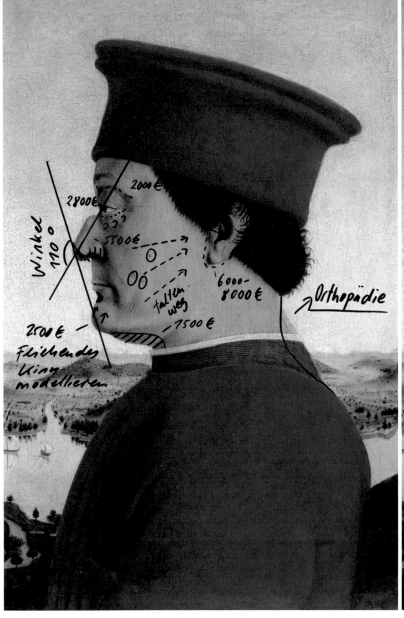

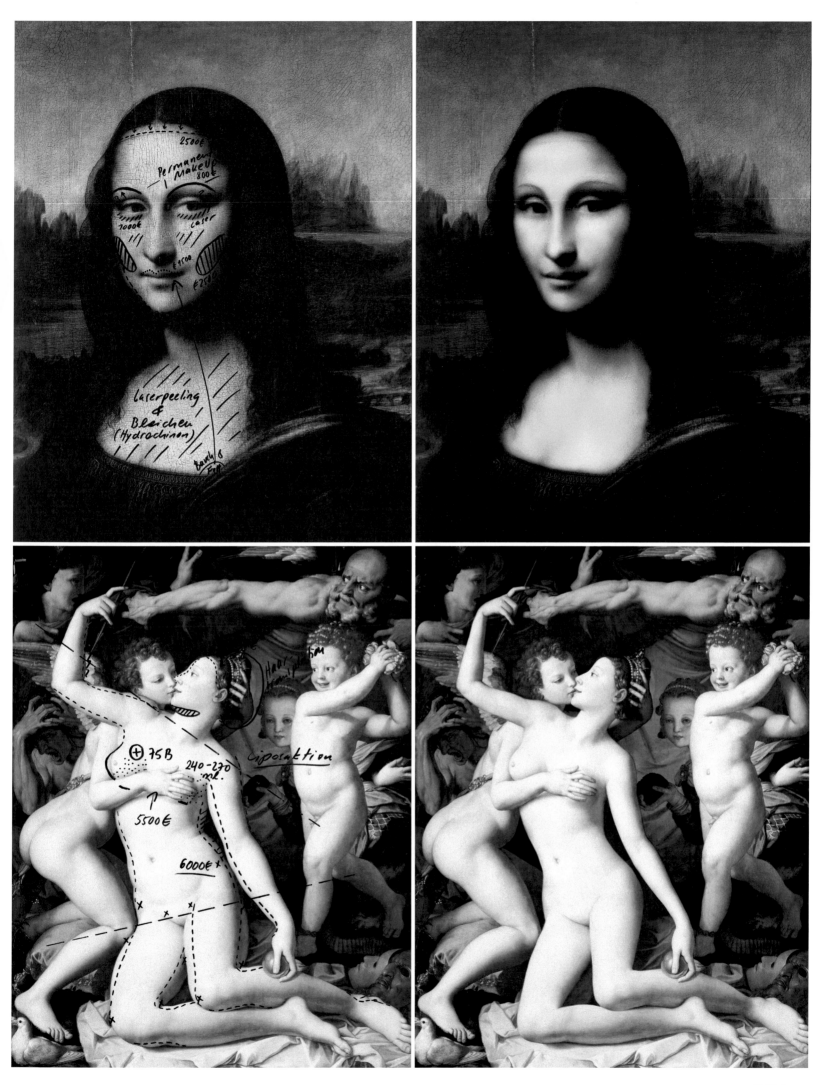

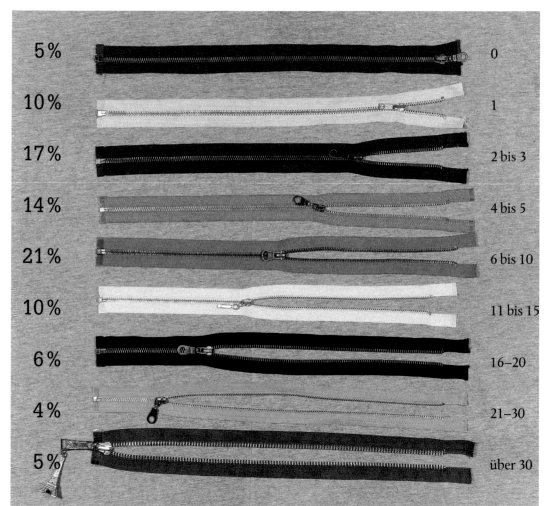

5 %	0
10 %	1
17 %	2 bis 3
14 %	4 bis 5
21 %	6 bis 10
10 %	11 bis 15
6 %	16–20
4 %	21–30
5 %	über 30

SARAH ILLENBERGER

1   10 Years of Viagra
Phallic Cacti used to represent the
Birthday of the Viagra pill.
Year: 2008—Client: Vanity Fair
magazine Arts—Photography: Andreas
Achmann

2   The Truth About Sex
Visual statistics used in a survey
about sex for the *Neon* magazine.
Year: 2008—Client: *Neon* magazine

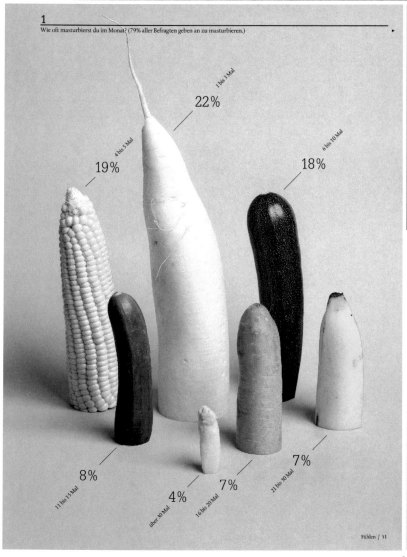

1
Wie oft masturbierst du im Monat? (79% aller Befragten geben an zu masturbieren.)

22 % 1 bis 3 Mal
19 % 4 bis 5 Mal
18 % 6 bis 10 Mal
8 % 11 bis 15 Mal
4 % über 30 Mal
7 % 16 bis 20 Mal
7 % 21 bis 30 Mal

Fühlen / 51

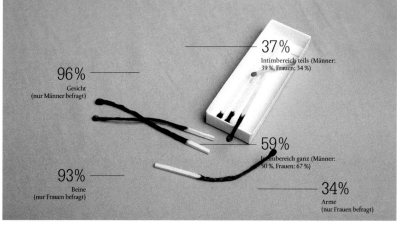

96 %
Gesicht
(nur Männer befragt)

37 %
Intimbereich teils (Männer:
39 %, Frauen: 34 %)

93 %
Beine
(nur Frauen befragt)

59 %
Intimbereich ganz (Männer:
50 %, Frauen: 67 %)

34 %
Arme
(nur Frauen befragt)

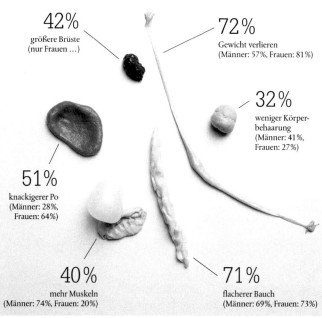

42 %
größere Brüste
(nur Frauen …)

72 %
Gewicht verlieren
(Männer: 57 %, Frauen: 81 %)

32 %
weniger Körper-
behaarung
(Männer: 41 %,
Frauen: 27 %)

51 %
knackigerer Po
(Männer: 28 %,
Frauen: 64 %)

40 %
mehr Muskeln
(Männer: 74 %, Frauen: 20 %)

71 %
flacherer Bauch
(Männer: 69 %, Frauen: 73 %)

2

SARAH ILLENBERGER
How Are We Doing—
The Big Survey
Year: 2005—Client: *Neon* magazine

sehr zufrieden **17 %**

63 %
eher zufrieden

16 %
eher unzufrieden

1 %
weiß nicht

2 % sehr unzufrieden

1. Mit wem würden Sie lieber zu Abend essen gehen – Gerhard Schröder oder Angela Merkel?

mit Gerhard Schröder
29%

mit keinem von beiden
50%

20%
mit Angela Merkel

1%
weiß nicht

225

8.6 million
.org world domains

3
.

88.8 million
.com world domains

illion
ld domains

420 million
China Internet users

337 million
European Union

110 million
India

76 million
Brazil

32 million
Mexico

5 million
Portugal

@ladygaga
9062883 twitter followers

@BarackObama
7183716 followers

@katyperry
6430594 followers

@algore
2226181 followers

1 \ 2

1966 million
2010

1802 million
2009

1574 million
2008

1319 million
2007

1093 million
2006

1018 million
2005

817 million
2004

719 million
2003

587 million
2002

313 million
Internet users 2001

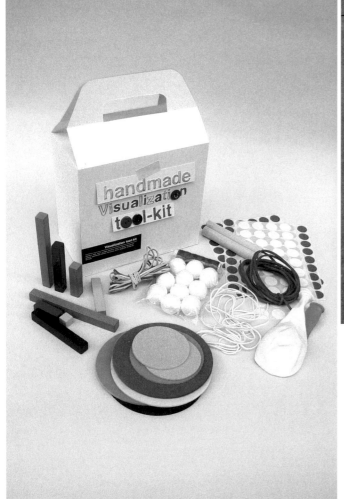

3 \ 4

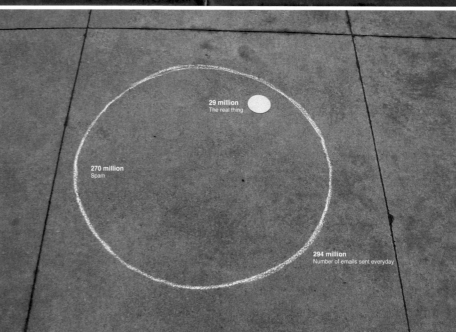

29 million
The real thing

270 million
Spam

294 million
Number of emails sent everyday

5

JOSE DUARTE

The *Handmade Visualization Tool-kit* explores new and simple ways to represent information. The box includes balloons, tape, markers, post-its, nylon, wire, wood sticks, colored paper, plasticine, circle stickers, and spheres. The kit enables users to make any kind of graphic including: abstracts maps and diagrams, area graphs and charts, arrow diagrams, bar graphs, venn diagrams, time line charts, bubble graphs, circle diagrams, proportional charts, organization charts, etc.

Year: 2011—Personal work

CHÂTEAU-VACANT
Tout Est Irradié
(Everything Is Irradiated)
Chemical reactions are microscopic and therefore invisible. *Tout Est Irradié* (Everything Is Irradiated) visualizes these phenomena by exploring notions of release and absorption of energy, explosions, the epicenter, and the suspension of time and motion. Radiation, like light, passes through matter, changing its form and physiology. The key words examined were: cosmic, meteor, atoms, and molecules.
Year: 2010——Client: L'Incident——Material: Tennis racket, wood, plastic ball, wool——Photography: Émilie The Voice

Chapter

5

Observing
SPORTS

I always turn to the sports section first. The sports page records people's accomplishments; the front page has nothing but man's failures.

○ Earl WARREN

1

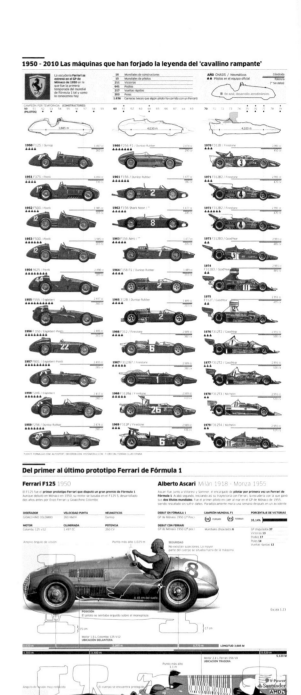

2

JAN VON HOLLEBEN
1   Gameboys and -girls
Homo ludens is the playing man who defines strong and advanced personal and social development through play. In his 1938 book, *Homo Ludens,* Johan Huizinga suggested that play is a necessary (though not sufficient) component to the development of culture. He characterized play as embodying freedom, being separate from ordinary life, demanding order, and having no material interests because no profit can be gained from it.
Year: 2010—Client: *GDI* magazine

PÚBLICO
○ Samuel Granados
2   The Grandfathers of Alonso
The history of Ferrari in Formula One was told over a three-page spread, using the first page to compare the first Formula One Ferrari, driven by Alberto Ascari in 1950, with the last one driven by Fernando Alonso in 2010. The double spread provides detailed information about each model from the decades in between.
Year: 2010—Client: *Público*

From a certain angle, one could view sport as perhaps the ultimate activity in visual abstraction.

All sport is, at its heart, about the celebration of human achievement. It involves an arbitrary series of limited actions, designed to highlight a slightly different aspect of the physical potential of our species. These abilities are framed within a widely understood method of comparison, giving a generally agreed framework within which to acknowledge human accomplishment in physical effort, engineering, applied science, intelligence, and skill.

Perhaps this is an abstraction too far. However, there is no doubting that sports have a unique relationship to data. Statistics are a matter of obsession both for spectators and coaches. Fantasy leagues exist, consisting of nothing but number crunching and abstraction. Television coverage now consists as much of graphs, on-the-spot animations and computer overlays as it does of footage of the sportsmen and women themselves. Because they are more predictable than most major news events, large newspapers can dedicate significant resources to making complex, detailed infographics based on sporting events, sometimes for special themed supplements. And of course, the remarkable detail and breadth of imagery available from the television coverage also allows for the development of extensive recreations of great moments during an event.

Sports are like life, but easier. There are clear rules that we understand, there are arbitrators whose job it is to uphold them, and at the end of a game, once all the effort, skill, beauty and brutality has concluded, what emerges is a simple set of numbers: the result.

Many of the infographics showcased in this chapter are exemplary for the clarity with which they explain the rules and the equipment of different sports. Infomen's *America's Cup* diagram, for instance, explains the basics of a competitive activity that is very hard to make sense of, even on television. *Clarín* explained how a soccer ball is not just a soccer ball with their World Cup infographic, while Ricardo Santos lifted the hood on motor racing, showing many of the details that are lost in the blur of the live event.

Together with Carlos Monteiro, Santos also created, for the Portuguese newspaper *i,* an infographic poster explaining everything from cricket to bullfighting—a remarkable achievement in efficient design, as was the Spanish newspaper *Público's* series on winter sports.

The *New York Times* uses a variety of media, and visualization methods, to describe sporting technique and achievement. Animation of a style more often seen in videogames is aptly applied to a video explaining the skills and physics involved in snowboarding, while a more clearly analytical form is used to demonstrate different female skiers' techniques. The paper edition, meanwhile, uses color and illustration to make clear what a single photograph never could.

Golden Section Graphics, however, took an entirely different approach with their *Transfer Calligraphy.* Football transfers are simple enough to understand, however their piece made abstract, zen-like beauty out of the commerce, removing the personalities and instead allowing the numbers to paint a very un-football-like series of balletic visuals.

This graphic was itself a winner, of a gold medal at the Malofiej infographics awards in 2011. Whether or not they took a lap of honor afterwards is unrecorded.

TRANSFER CALLIGRAPHY

Soccer Transfer // Transfermarkt Fußball

Soccer is by far the sport in which the highest transfer fees are paid. Current record holder is Cristiano Ronaldo with € 94 million. In the graph below, the width of the strokes symbolize the fees paid for the player in question. The numbered dots indicate the club to which they transferred. // Im Fußball gibt es die höchsten Transfer-Ablösen in der Sportwelt. Den Rekord hält Ronaldo mit 94 Millionen Euro. Die Strichstärken beziehen sich auf die gezahlte Ablösesumme, die nummerierten Punkte visualisieren den örtlichen Wechsel beim Transfer eines Fußballpielers.

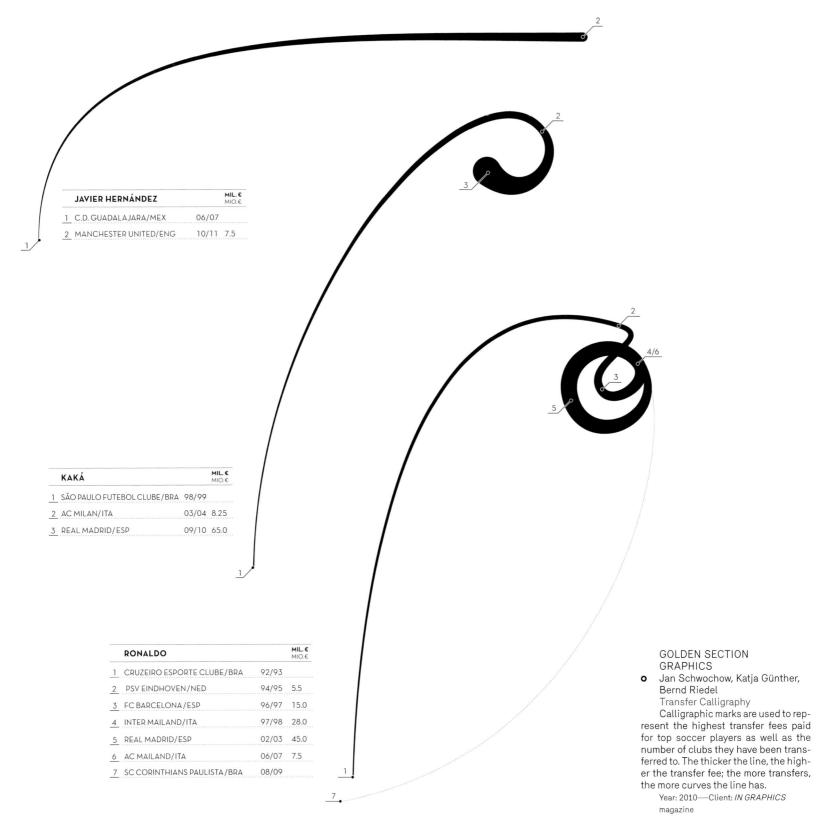

JAVIER HERNÁNDEZ

			MIL. € MIO.€
1	C.D. GUADALAJARA/MEX	06/07	
2	MANCHESTER UNITED/ENG	10/11	7.5

KAKÁ

			MIL. € MIO.€
1	SÃO PAULO FUTEBOL CLUBE/BRA	98/99	
2	AC MILAN/ITA	03/04	8.25
3	REAL MADRID/ESP	09/10	65.0

RONALDO

			MIL. € MIO.€
1	CRUZEIRO ESPORTE CLUBE/BRA	92/93	
2	PSV EINDHOVEN/NED	94/95	5.5
3	FC BARCELONA/ESP	96/97	15.0
4	INTER MAILAND/ITA	97/98	28.0
5	REAL MADRID/ESP	02/03	45.0
6	AC MAILAND/ITA	06/07	7.5
7	SC CORINTHIANS PAULISTA/BRA	08/09	

GOLDEN SECTION
GRAPHICS
o Jan Schwochow, Katja Günther,
Bernd Riedel
Transfer Calligraphy
Calligraphic marks are used to represent the highest transfer fees paid for top soccer players as well as the number of clubs they have been transferred to. The thicker the line, the higher the transfer fee; the more transfers, the more curves the line has.
Year: 2010—Client: *IN GRAPHICS*
magazine

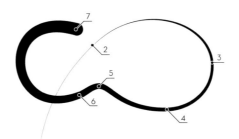

ZINEDINE ZIDANE		MIL. € MIO.€
1 AS CANNES/FRA	88/89	
2 FC GIRONDINS BORDEAUX/FRA	92/93	7.0
3 JUVENTUS FOOTBALL CLUB/ITA	96/97	3.5
4 REAL MADRID/ESP	01/02	73.5

YAYA TOURÉ		MIL. € MIO.€
1 ASEC MIMOSAS/CIV	00/01	
2 K.S.K. BEVEREN/BEL	01/02	
3 FC METALLURG DONETSK/UKR	03/04	2.0
4 OLYMPIACOS PIRÄUS/GRE	05/06	2.7
5 AS MONACO/MON	06/07	5.5
6 FC BARCELONA/ESP	07/08	9.0
7 MANCHESTER CITY/ENG	10/11	30.0

ZLATAN IBRAHIMOVIC		MIL. € MIO.€
1 MALMÖ FF/SWE	98/99	
2 AJAX AMSTERDAM/NED	01/02	7.8
3 JUVENTUS FOOTBALL CLUB/ITA	04/05	25.0
4 INTER MAILAND/ITA	06/07	24.8
5 FC BARCELONA/ESP	09/10	69.5
6 AC MAILAND/ITA	10/11*	6.0
7 FC BARCELONA/ESP	11/12	

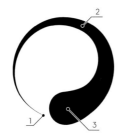

CRISTIANO RONALDO		MIL. € MIO.€
1 SPORTING CP/POR	01/02	
2 MANCHESTER UNITED/ENG	03/04	17.5
3 REAL MADRID/ESP	09/10	94.0

DAVID SILVA		MIL. € MIO.€
1 VALENCIA CF/ESP	03/04	
2 SD EIBAR/ESP	04/05*	
3 VALENCIA CF/ESP	04/05	
4 CELTA DE VIGO/ESP	05/06*	
5 VALENCIA CF/ESP	06/07	
6 MANCHESTER CITY/ENG	10/11	28.75

DAVID VILLA		MIL. € MIO.€
1 SPORTING DE GIJÓN/ESP	00/01	
2 REAL ZARAGOZA/ESP	02/03	1.5
3 VALENCIA CF/ESP	05/06	12.0
4 FC BARCELONA/ESP	10/11	40.0

SAMI KHEDIRA		MIL. € MIO.€
1 VFB STUTTGART/GER	06/07	
2 REAL MADRID C.F./ESP	10/11	14.0

JÉRÔME BOATENG		MIL. € MIO.€
1 HERTHA BSC/GER	06/07	
2 HAMBURGER SV/GER	07/08	1.10
3 MANCHESTER CITY/ENG	10/11	12.5

MICHAEL BALLACK		MIL. € MIO.€
1 CHEMNITZER FC/GER	95/96	
2 1. FC KAISERSLAUTERN/GER	97/98	0.075
3 BAYER 04 LEVERKUSEN/GER	99/00	3.9
4 FC BAYERN MÜNCHEN/GER	02/03	6.0
5 CHELSEA FC/ENG	06/07	
6 BAYER 04 LEVERKUSEN/GER	10/11	

*lent // ausgeliehen

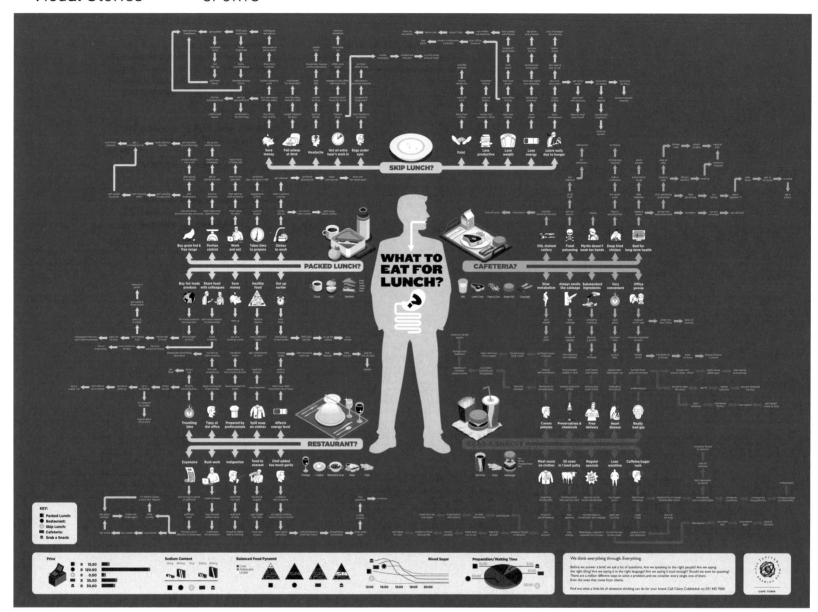

1

LUCAS VAN VUUREN

1 Lunch

This self-promotional mailer tackles the question of what to eat for lunch with a thoroughness that reflects the agency's own meticulous method of problem solving when it comes to their clients' brands.

Year: 2011—Client: The Jupiter Drawing Room Print Mailer —Creative Director: Joanne Thomas—Art Director: Lucas van Vuuren—Illustrator: Andrew Donaldson, Bernice Lizamore

INFONAUTS

2 Core Obstacle

The story is about the obstacles men encounter when trying to lose weight including stress, fast food, long work hours, shrinking food budgets, and bad habits.

Year: 2010—Client: *Mens Health Magazine*

HUMAN EMPIRE

3 Marathon

An illustration that shows what happens to the body when running a marathon.

Year: 2010—Client: *Die Zeit* magazine

2

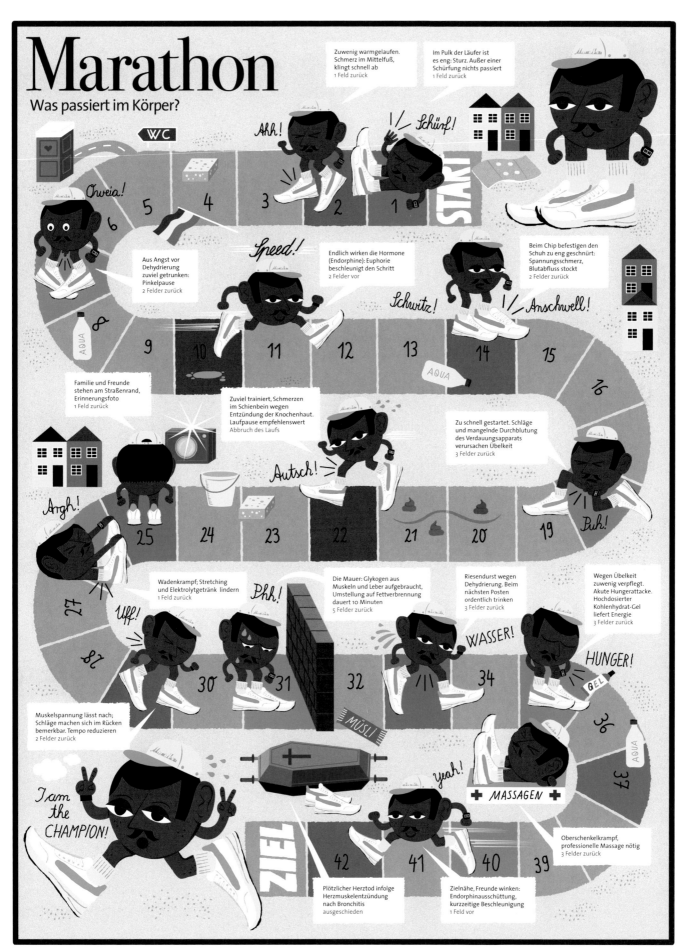

SPORT & FREIZEIT

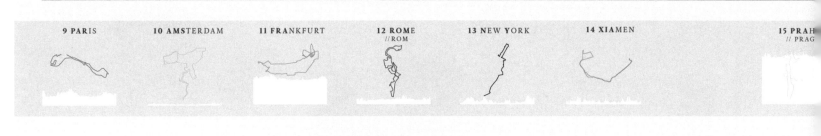

| 9 PARIS | 10 AMSTERDAM | 11 FRANKFURT | 12 ROME // ROM | 13 NEW YORK | 14 XIAMEN | 15 PRAH // PRAG |

DIE LAUFBEDINGUNGEN // THE RACE CONDITIONS

Monat und Durchschnittstemperatur des Rennens
// month and average temperature of the race

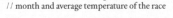

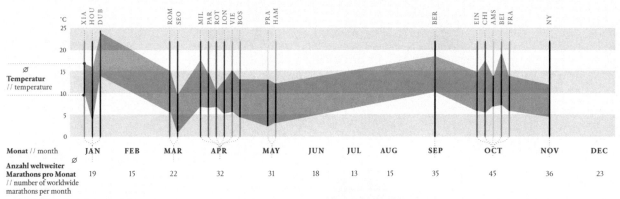

°C

XIA HOU DUB   ROM SEO   MIL PAR ROT LON VIE BOS   PRA HAM   BER   EIN CHI AMS BEI FRA   NY

25
20
15   **Temperatur** // temperature
10
5
0

Teilnehmer in Mio. // participants in mil. 40

Starter 30

Finisher (im Ziel angekommen) 20

10

Monat // month

	JAN	FEB	MAR	APR	MAY	JUN	JUL	AUG	SEP	OCT	NOV	DEC
Anzahl weltweiter Marathons pro Monat // number of worldwide marathons per month	19	15	22	32	31	18	13	15	35	45	36	23

Startgeld in € // Fee in € ∅

DIE ENTWICKLUNG // THE DEVELOPMENT

4h

Olympischer Marathon (Männer) // Olympics (men)

Entwicklung der Weltrekorde (Frauen) //Development of World Records (women)

1964, RYD
Mit ihrem brach Dal 30 Minute
Marathon ∈
to break th

Entwicklung der Weltrekorde (Männer) //Development of World Records (men)

3h

1926, CHISWICK (ENG)
Violet Piercy (ENG) war, laut dem Internationalen Leichtathletikverband (IAAF) die erste Frau die einen Marathon-Weltrekord aufstellte. // Violet Piercy (ENG) was according to the International Association of Athletics Federations (IAAF) the first woman to set a marathon world record.

2h

| 1897 | 1900 | | '10 | | '20 | | '30 | | '40 | | '50 | |

1897, ATHEN (GRE)
Erste Olympische Spiele der Neuzeit mit einem Langstreckenlauf von ca. 40 Kilometern. Die Distanz beruht auf der Legende von einem Boten, der die Strecke von Marathon nach Athen zurücklegte. // The first modern Olympic Games had an approx. distance of 40 km. The distance is based on the legend of a messenger who ran all the way from Marathon to Athens.

1900, PARIS (FRA)
Der Gewinner Michel Theato (FRA) wurde beschuldigt, Abkürzungen durch Paris gelaufen zu sein. Er gewann trotzdem. // The winner Michel Theato (FRA) was accused of taking short cuts through to Paris. He still won the race.

1908, LONDON (GBR)
Der erste klassische Marathon über 42,195 Kilometern findet statt. Der Grund für die ungerade Zahl: Das Rennen sollte an der Ostterrasse von Schloss Windsor beginnen und vor der königlichen Loge im Wembley Stadion enden. Später sollten die Läufer John Hayes (USA) und Dorando Pietri (ITA) erneut gegeneinander antreten und als relevante Distanz wählte man wieder die 42,195 Kilometer. // The first classic marathon with a distance of 26 miles and 385 yards. The race started at the east terrace of Windsor Castle and finished at the Royal Lodge in the Wembley Stadium. The duel between John Hayes (USA) and Dorando Pietri (ITA) should be repeated and therefore the exact distance had to be known.

1921
Festlegung der Strecke auf 42,195 Kilometer durch den Internationalen Leichtathletikverband (IAAF). // The definition of the marathon distance of 26 miles and 385 yards was set by the International Association of Athletics Federations (IAAF).

1932, LOS ANGELES (USA)
Juan Carlos Zabala (ARG) wurde mit 20 Jahren der bis dahin jüngste Gewinner eines Marathons bei den Olympischen Spielen. // At age 20 Juan Carlos Zabala (ARG) was, until then, the youngest winner of an olympic marathon.

1952, SHEPERD'S BUSH (ENG)
James Peters (GBR) brach seinen eigenen Weltrekord in den Folgejahren noch dreimal hintereinander (1953, 1954). // James Peters (GBR) was to break his own world record another three times (1953, 1954).

1960, RO
1964, TO
Abebe B
barfuß w
Schwarz
eine oly
gewann
abermal
Bikila (E
and was
African
gold med
in 1964.

BEGINN DER MARATHON-VERANSTALTUNG // BEGIN OF MARATHON EVENT

BOS

SEO

⊛ aufgrund zu ku
// disputed

60

GOLDEN SECTION
GRAPHICS
o Jan Schwochow, Katja Günther
   Marathon—the fastest 524,375
   miles in the world
   The 20 fastest marathon events in
the world (with the exception of cham-
pionships) were determined by com-
piling rack records of both men and
women. The graphic shows data for
marathons around the world and a
timeline of world records.
   Year: 2011—Design: Jan Schwochow,
   Katja Günther—Client: *IN GRAPHICS*
   Vol. 02 magazine by Golden Section
   Graphics GmbH

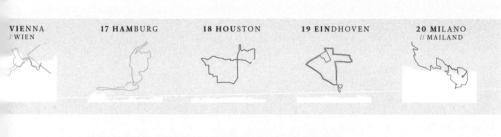

VIENNA / WIEN   17 HAMBURG   18 HOUSTON   19 EINDHOVEN   20 MILANO // MAILAND

DIE TEILNAHME // THE PARTICIPATION

Teilnehmer und Startgelder 2010/11 (Starter werden nur gezeigt, wenn bekannt)
// participants and fees 2010/11 (starters only shown when known)

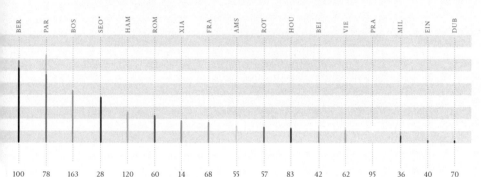

BER	PAR	BOS	SEO*	HAM	ROM	XIA	FRA	AMS	ROT	HOU	BEI	VIE	PRA	MIL	EIN	DUB
100	78	163	28	120	60	14	68	55	57	83	42	62	95	36	40	70

...rzahl, keine genauen Werte vorhanden // average number of runners, no exact data available

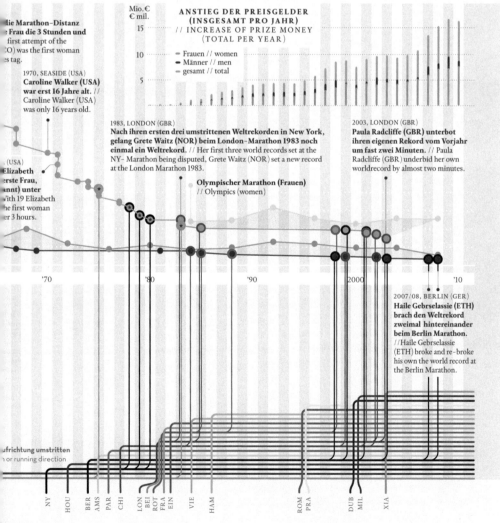

Mio.€
€ mil.

ANSTIEG DER PREISGELDER (INSGESAMT PRO JAHR)
// INCREASE OF PRIZE MONEY (TOTAL PER YEAR)

15
10
5

- Frauen // women
- Männer // men
- gesamt // total

...lie Marathon-Distanz
...e Frau die 3 Stunden und
first attempt of the
...CO) was the first woman
...es tag.

1970, SEASIDE (USA)
Caroline Walker (USA)
war erst 16 Jahre alt. //
Caroline Walker (USA)
was only 16 years old.

...(USA)
...Elizabeth
...erste Frau,
...annt) unter
...vith 19 Elizabeth
...he first woman
...er 3 hours.

1983, LONDON (GBR)
Nach ihren ersten drei umstrittenen Weltrekorden in New York,
gelang Grete Waitz (NOR) beim London-Marathon 1983 noch
einmal ein Weltrekord. // Her first three world records set at the
NY- Marathon being disputed, Grete Waitz (NOR) set a new record
at the London Marathon 1983.

Olympischer Marathon (Frauen)
// Olympics (women)

2003, LONDON (GBR)
Paula Radcliffe (GBR) unterbot
ihren eigenen Rekord vom Vorjahr
um fast zwei Minuten. // Paula
Radcliffe (GBR) underbid her own
worldrecord by almost two minutes.

'70   '80   '90   2000   '10

2007/08, BERLIN (GER)
Haile Gebrselassie (ETH)
brach den Weltrekord
zweimal hintereinander
beim Berlin Marathon.
//Haile Gebrselassie
(ETH) broke and re-broke
his own the world record at
the Berlin Marathon.

...ufrichtung umstritten
...n or running direction

NY HOU BER AMS PAR CHI LON BEI ROT FRA EIN VIE HAM ROM PRA DUB MIL XIA

2

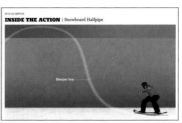

THE NEW YORK TIMES

o Gabriel Dance, Xaquín G. V.,
   Jigar Mehta and Bedel Saget

1 Snowboard

Using a combination of video, graphics, and 3D, United States half-pipe coach Mike Jankowski explains the different components of an Olympic half-pipe run. Presenting the information in this way allows the viewer to see real snowboarders in action with video, which then cuts to the slower and clearer qualities of 3D imagery combined with graphics for explanations of snaps, grabs, and big air.

Year: 2010—Client: The *New York Times*

1

THE NEW YORK TIMES

o Joe Ward, Shan Carter, Graham
   Roberts, Mika Gröndahl, Sergio
   Peçanha, Amanda Cox, Archie
   Tse, and Bill Pennington

2 Women's Skiing

Julia Mancuso skied an almost perfect run at the Women's Downhill during the Vancouver Olympics. However, it was her main rival, Lindsey Vonn, who would go on to win the gold. In this video, a series of graphics compares the positioning of Vonn and Mancuso on the course, explaining how—despite skiing a further distance than Mancuso—Vonn's speed ultimately put her in first place.

Year: 2010—Client: The *New York Times*

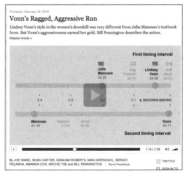

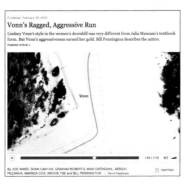

2

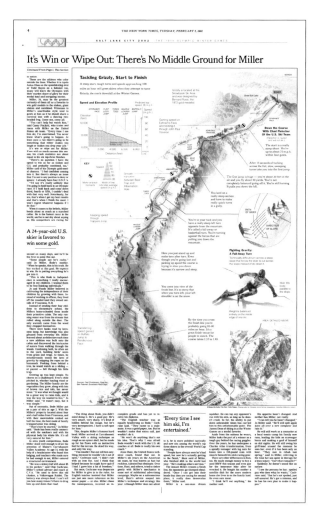

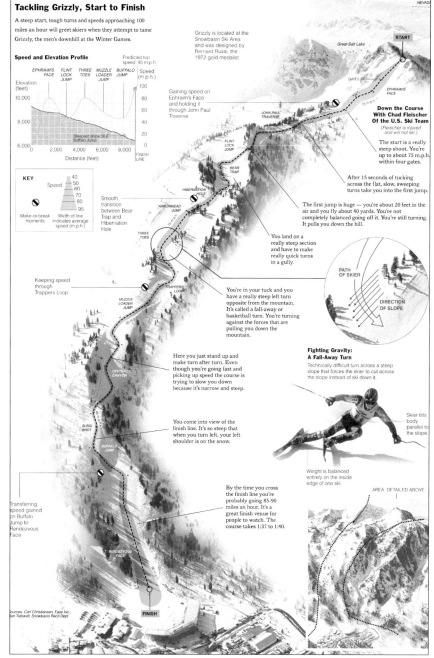

THE NEW YORK TIMES
○ William McNulty
3 Tackling Grizzly: The Men's Downhill Course at Salt Lake City

A flow line chart measures the speed of skiers on Grizzly, the men's downhill course during the Salt Lake City Olympics. The graphic is inspired by the famous chart made by Charles Joseph Minard, which showed the devastating effects of time and weather conditions on Napoleon's dwindling army during its 1812 march to Russia.

Year: 2002—Client: The *New York Times*

THE NEW YORK TIMES
○ By Joe Ward and Bedel Saget
4 Coaches See Gold, And Room for Improvement

A frame-by-frame analysis of Dwight Phillips's form in the long jump. His personal coach, Greg Kraft, and Randy Huntington, who coached the long jump world record holder Mike Powell, look at what Phillips could do to secure a gold medal.

Year: 2004—Client: The *New York Times*

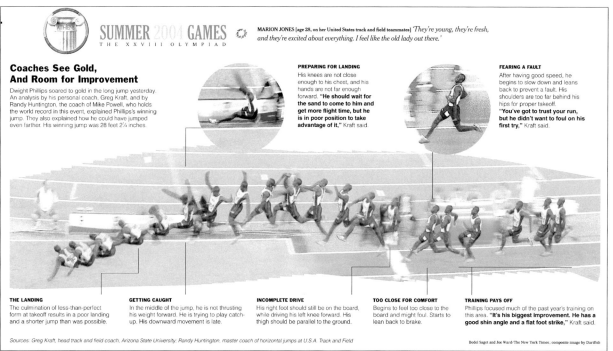

DEPORTES Olimpismo

Juegos Olímpicos de invierno» VANCOUVER 2010

Un coreano baja por la pista de luge en obras para mejorar la seguridad. REUTERS

» La seguridad se incrementa tras la muerte del atleta de luge

Pista más corta, muro más alto

«Hay que sacudirse el hielo y seguir», asegura Hackl

Público en VANCOUVER
CANADÁ

PACO GRANDE

La muerte del piloto georgiano de luge Nodar Kumaritashvili ha cambiado el guión de los Juegos. Ayer, el entrenamiento de la mañana fue cancelado. La Federación Internacional quiso exhibir seguridad –"la pista no causó el accidente del atleta, sino que fue Kumaritashvili quien entró tarde en la última curva, perdió el control del trineo y tuvo el trágico accidente"–, pero poco después los técnicos oficiales decidían acortar el recorrido del tobogán masculino (1.374 metros) igualándolo con el femenino (1.198) metros que, a su vez, también se reduce (953). Los técnicos, eso sí, justificaron su decisión más por "motivos emocionales" que de otra índole y reiteraron que la pista, considerada de las más rápidas del mundo, es segura para la competición.

"Nunca dijimos que la pista fuera demasiado rápida", insistió el presidente de la Federación Internacional, Josef Fendt, quien, no obstante, se confesó desolado: "El viernes fue el peor día de mi vida".

«Los pilotos exóticos corren más riesgos»

"No es una cuestión de cómo es la pista. Lo del viernes fue al cien por cien un error de pilotaje. Hemos tenido problemas como estos anteriormente. Sucede cuando en la pista están los llamados pilotos 'exóticos'. Todos ellos deben saber que esto es un asunto serio, no una broma", declaró el alemán Wolfgang Staudinger, entrenador del equipo canadiense de luge. Staudinger considera que "la Federación Internacional tiene que poner unas normas mucho más estrictas".

Durante la noche se realizaron otros cambios aún más significativos. Los técnicos de mantenimiento del tobogán elevaron el muro de la curva 16, última del trazado y donde chocó Kumaritashvili, e incluso se ha modificado la superficie del hielo. El primer atleta en bajar con las nuevas condiciones fue el norteamericano Tony Benshoof, que no sufrió ningún tipo de percance. Levan Gureshidze, atleta georgiano compañero de Kumaritashvili, no tomó la salida sin que se explicara oficialmente si se ha retirado. Quienes sí renunciaron a bajar fueron el argentino Rubén González y Chih-Hung Ma, de China Taipei.

Una de las estrellas del luge, el alemán George Hackl, tres veces campeón olímpico, asegura que "no hay que culpar a la velocidad del accidente. A 60 km/h también se podría haber matado". El ex piloto señaló que el georgiano cometió un "pequeño error". Hackl critica la decisión de adelantar el punto de salida de la prueba masculinas: "Sólo es una forma de complacer a aquellos que no saben nada sobre nuestro deporte. Los accidentes en el luge son parte de la rutina diaria. Les ha pasado a los mejores del mundo. Eso es normal. Hay que levantarse, sacudirte el hielo y seguir". "Lo que sí es cierto es que a veces no tenemos en cuenta lo que hay fuera de la pista", añadió refiriéndose al pilar de cemento contra el que impactó Kumaritashvili.

El esloveno Domen Pociecha, más cauto, reconoció que "es realmente difícil competir, todo el mundo está pensando en lo mismo. Se puede ver en sus caras". ▪

Deportes de invierno

I. Luge

Los participantes se lanzan **tumbados sobre un trineo** a través de una pendiente empinada. Se compite **individualmente o por parejas**

Modalidades

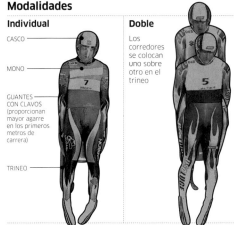

Individual

CASCO

MONO

GUANTES CON CLAVOS (proporcionan mayor agarre en los primeros metros de carrera)

TRINEO

Doble

Los corredores se colocan uno sobre otro en el trineo

El trineo

El armazón es de fibra de vidrio. Los patines (la única parte en contacto con el hielo) son de acero, y está prohibido calentarlos antes de la competición (proporcionaría ventaja sobre los competidores)

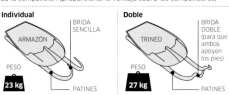

Individual — ARMAZÓN — BRIDA SENCILLA — PESO **23 kg** — PATINES

Doble — TRINEO — BRIDA DOBLE (para que ambos apoyen los pies) — PESO **27 kg** — PATINES

La carrera

Se corren dos o cuatro rondas, y se suman todos los tiempos

Individual Cuatro rondas

1ª + 2ª + 3ª + 4ª = TOTAL
46.126 46.729 47.002 46.351 3.06.208

Doble Dos rondas

1ª + 2ª = TOTAL
46.126 46.729 1.32.855

El circuito

La carrera se celebra en el Whistler Slidding Center de Vancouver

ANTIGUA SALIDA MASCULINA

META

SALIDA MASCULINA Y ANTIGUA FEMENINA
Las salidas se han adelantado, para que, al acortar el recorrido, los corredores alcancen menores velocidades. La masculina ha pasado de 1.374 m a 1.198 y la femenina de 1.198 a 953

CURVA 13
Se han elevado las paredes laterales para evitar salidas de la pista

La salida

Muy importante en la competición. Un gran impulso en la salida facilita que los corredores alcancen mayores velocidades

1. En la salida, el corredor **se balancea adelante y atrás para tomar impulso** durante 30 segundos (45 en dobles), con ayuda de dos asideros situados en los laterales de la pista

2. Al salir, **avanza los primeros tres metros empujándose con las manos** para ganar algo más de velocidad

3. **Se tumba en el trineo y continúa deslizándose**. La cabeza sólo se levanta lo imprescindible para ver mínimamente el circuito

NOTA: Debido a los sucesos acaecidos el pasado viernes, se ha variado el calendario de publicación de los gráficos. Mañana se reanudará el orden anunciado con la infografía correspondiente al **biatlón**

FUENTE: VANCOUVER2010.COM Y AFP   GRÁFICO Y DOCUMENTACIÓN: MIRIAM BAÑA

agenda

DOMINGO 14 DE FEBRERO
LA 2 Y TELEDEPORTE

19.00	Combinada. Saltos	
20.15	Biatlón. Sprint 10 kms.	Hombres
21.00	Hockey. USA-CHN.	Mujeres
22.00	Luge	Hombres
22.00	Patinaje 3.000 m.	Mujeres
22.45	Combinada 10 km.	
23.30	Esquí estilo libre	Hombres
01.30	Patinaje artístico. Parejas	
01.30	Hockey. FIN-RUS	Mujeres
02.30	Esquí artístico	Mujeres

Resultados

: Saltos trampolín normal: .1. Simon Ammann (SUI), 276,5 puntos. 2. Adam Malysz (POL), 269,5. 3. Gregor Schlierenzauer (AUT), 268,0. 4. Janne Ahonen (FIN), 263,0. 5. Michael Uhrmann (GER), 262,5. 6. Robert Kranjec (SLO), 259,5

: Biatlón 7 km: 1. Anastasia Kuzima, 2. Magdalena Neuner, 3. Marie Dorin.

Medallero

			●	○	○
1.	Suiza	1			
1	Eslovaquia	1			
2.	Polonia		1		
2.	Alemania		1		
3.	Austria			1	
3.	Francia			1	

El protagonista

Simmon Ammann

'Harry Potter', primer oro

VANCOUVER // Simmon Ammann, apodado *Harry Potter* desde los juegos de Salt Lake City, se llevó la primera medalla de oro de estos juegos olímpicos de Vancouver, al conseguir la mejor nota en la prueba de saltos de trampolín de 100 metros disputada ayer en el Whistler Olimpic Park. Ammann, líder de la Copa del Mundo, reedita el triunfo de hace ocho años en los juegos de Salt Lake City, en los que consiguió además el oro en el trampolín largo, el de 142 metros. Ammann con tres medallas olímpicas en su carrera es también favorito para ganar en el trampolín largo.

I INFOGRAFIA
o Artur Galocha, Miriam Baña,
Mónica Serrano, Samuel
Granados
Winter Sports
Because Spanish readers are not
familiar with winter sports, this series of infographics explained the main
characteristics, categories, and rules
of the different disciplines during the
2010 Winter Olympics in Vancouver.

Year: 2010—Client: *Público*

Deportes de invierno (VI)

Saltos de esquí

En esta disciplina los jueces califican según la distancia y el estilo del salto en tres categorías distintas: 90 metros, 120 y por equipos, todas ellas masculinas.

La pista

La pista de salto está situada en al segunda sede principal de los Juegos, en el Parque Olímpico de Whistler.

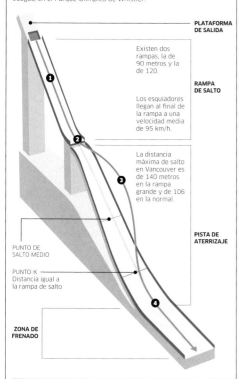

PLATAFORMA
DE SALIDA

Existen dos rampas, la de 90 metros y la de 120.

RAMPA
DE SALTO

Los esquiadores llegan al final de la rampa a una velocidad media de 95 km/h.

La distancia máxima de salto en Vancouver es de 140 metros en la rampa grande y de 106 en la normal.

PISTA DE
ATERRIZAJE

PUNTO DE
SALTO MEDIO

PUNTO·K
Distancia igual a la rampa de salto

ZONA DE
FRENADO

El salto

❶ El deslizamiento

POSICIÓN DE
LOS ESQUÍS

Los esquís discurren de forma **paralela** y el esquiador se acuclilla buscando una **menor resistencia con el viento**.

❷ El despegue

POSICIÓN DE
LOS ESQUÍS

Al llegar al **final de la rampa** el esquiador se impulsa y en apenas un segundo se levanta para colocarse en posición de vuelo.

❸ El vuelo

30°

POSICIÓN DE
LOS ESQUÍS

La **posición en V** fue creada por el sueco Jan Boklöv en 1985 en búsqueda de una mayor aerodinámica. **Aumenta la distancia de salto** en un 10%.

❹ Aterrizaje

POSICIÓN DE
LOS ESQUÍS

De forma paralela pero **con el esquí izquierdo más adelantado** el esquiador aterriza amortiguando su propio peso.

FUENTE: VANCOUVER2010.COM   GRÁFICO Y DOCUMENTACIÓN: ARTUR GV

Deportes de invierno

IV. Esquí alpino

La equipación

Los esquís varían según la modalidad y el tamaño del bastón depende de la altura del esquiador.

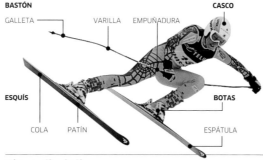

BASTÓN

GALLETA — VARILLA   EMPUÑADURA

CASCO

ESQUÍS

COLA   PATÍN

BOTAS

ESPÁTULA

Cinco disciplinas

Existen cuatro disciplinas más una quinta, la supercombinada, que consta de una prueba de descenso y otra de eslalon. Los tiempos de las dos pruebas se suman, siendo el ganador el más rápido.

Eslalon
MASCULINO — 610
FEMENINO — 610

Eslalon gigante
MASCULINO — 1.509
FEMENINO — 1.309

Super-G
MASCULINO — 2.224
FEMENINO — 2.139

Descenso
MASCULINO — 3.158
FEMENINO — 2.879

▸ Medidas en metros

Eslalon

Es la modalidad **más técnica**. La prueba consta de dos mangas. El ganador es aquel que suma el mejor tiempo **sin haberse saltado ninguna de las puertas** (entre 45 y 75 por recorrido).

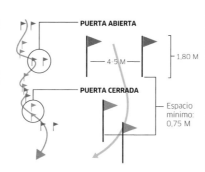

PUERTA ABIERTA

4·5 M

1,80 M

PUERTA CERRADA

Espacio mínimo:
0,75 M

Super G y Eslalon gigante

El ganador en estas dos modalidades será el que complete antes el recorrido **sin saltarse ninguna puerta**. El supergigante consta de una manga y el eslalon gigante, de dos.

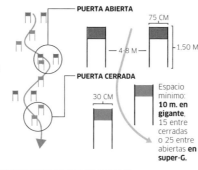

PUERTA ABIERTA

75 CM

4·8 M

1,50 M

PUERTA CERRADA

30 CM

Espacio mínimo:
10 m. en gigante, 15 entre cerradas o 25 entre abiertas **en super-G**.

Descenso

Los corredores tienen tan sólo **una manga**, siendo el ganador el que completa el recorrido en el **menor tiempo posible**.

Mínimo
8 M

En esta modalidad, la más rápida, los esquiadores alcanzan **una velocidad de hasta 150 km/h.**

FUENTE: VANCOUVER2010.COM   GRÁFICO Y DOCUMENTACIÓN: ARTUR GV

Deportes de invierno

V. Skeleton

Los participantes se lanzan **tumbados boca abajo sobre un trineo** por una pendiente empinada, hasta alcanzar velocidades de 130km/h

La salida

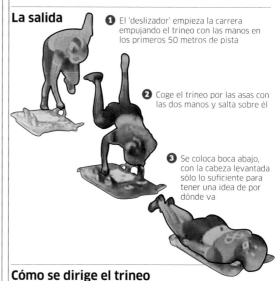

❶ El 'deslizador' empieza la carrera empujando el trineo con las manos en los primeros 50 metros de pista

❷ Coge el trineo por las asas con las dos manos y salta sobre él

❸ Se coloca boca abajo, con la cabeza levantada sólo lo suficiente para tener una idea de por dónde va

Cómo se dirige el trineo

El trineo **se hace girar basculando el centro de gravedad del cuerpo hacia un lado u otro**. Estos movimientos han de ser **lo más sutiles posible para evitar la pérdida de aerodinámica**

A la izquierda
La pierna izquierda se separa del eje central del cuerpo y se ejerce presión con el hombro izquierdo hacia abajo

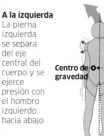

Centro de gravedad

EJE CENTRAL

A la derecha
La pierna derecha se separa ligeramente del eje central y se presiona con el hombro del mismo lado hacia abajo

Centro de gravedad

EJE CENTRAL

La importancia del peso

A la hora de competir, **el peso es una ventaja**, por lo que el conjunto deslizador-trineo debe tener unos **pesos mínimos**. Si no se llega a ese peso, **pueden adjuntarse lastres al deportista**, no al trineo.

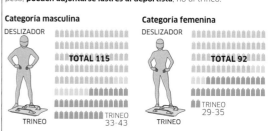

Categoría masculina
DESLIZADOR
TOTAL 115
TRINEO
TRINEO
33-43

Categoría femenina
DESLIZADOR
TOTAL 92
TRINEO
29-35

El trineo

Existen unos parámetros de **medidas máximas y mínimas**. Dentro de estas medidas, **se construyen de acuerdo a las preferencias del piloto**

CUNA
Estructura donde se recuesta el piloto. Se fabrica en fibra de carbono

MANILLARES
Sirven de agarradero en la salida y sujetan el cuerpo en las curvas

AMORTIGUADORES
Absorven los golpes contra los laterales del circuito

CHASIS
De acero, mantiene unido el conjunto

PATINES
Dos tubos de acero. Tienen la flexibilidad suficiente para cambiar la dirección

De 800 a
1200 mm

De 80 a 200 mm

FUENTE: VANCOUVER2010.COM Y AFP   GRÁFICO Y DOCUMENTACIÓN: MIRIAM BAÑA

243

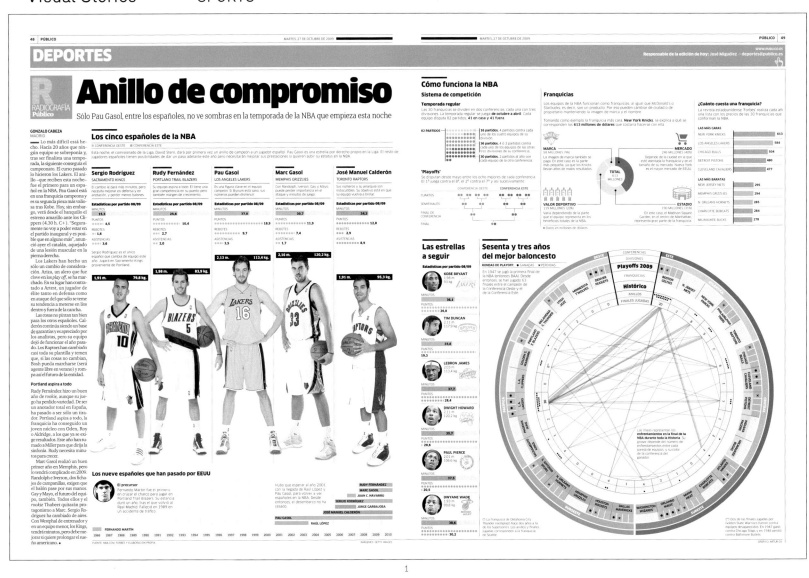

1

2

I INFOGRAFIA

o Artur Galocha
1 NBA New Season
As the 2009–2010 NBA season took off, Spanish players and their statistics from the previous season were examined. Here the way the league and the franchise system run, as well as a listing of teams that fought it out in the 63 playoffs since 1947, are explained.
Year: 2009—Client: *Público*—Photos: Getty Images

o Artur Galocha, Samuel Granados, Álvaro Valiño
2 Bolt Breaks His Own World Record Just One Year Later
A two photo finish illustrates a detailed analysis of the 200-meter record obtained by the Jamaican Usain Bolt at the 2009 World Championship in Track and Field in Berlin.
Year: 2009—Client: *Público*

Goles y pelotas
Promedio de gol por partido en cada Mundial

3,9	4,1	4,7	4	5,4	3,6	2,8	2,8	3	2,6	2,7	2,8	2,5	2,2	2,7	2,7	2,5	2,3
Modelo "T"	Federale 102	Allen	Super Duplo T	Swiss World	Top Star	Crack	Slazenger	Telstar	Telstar	Tango	Tango	Azteca	Etrusco	Questra	Tricolor	Fevernova	Teamgeist
1930	1934	1938	1950	1954	1958	1962	1966	1970	1974	1978	1982	1986	1990	1994	1998	2002	2006

La pelota oficial

Su nombre es Jabulani que significa "celebrar" en Zulu. Fue fabricada con la última tecnología pero igual los arqueros se quejan, dicen que zigzaguea.

Ficha técnica

Peso
440 g (+/-2 g)

Circunferencia
Debe estar dentro de los estándares de la FIFA.

Jabulani
69,0 cm (+-0,2)

FIFA
68,5 a 69,5 cm

Esfericidad
Se mide el diámetro en 16 puntos. La diferencia entre el diámetro mayor y el menor debe estar dentro de lo que exige la FIFA.

Jabulani
1,0 %

FIFA
1,5 %

Rebote
Se verifica la elasticidad del balón. Se deja caer la pelota 10 veces a desde una altura de 2 m.

10 cm

La diferencia entre el rebote más alto y el más bajo no debe ser mayor a 10 cm.

Color
La pelota tiene 11 colores que representan a los 11 jugadores de un equipo, los 11 lenguajes oficiales de Sudáfrica y sus 11 tribus.

Desde adentro hacia afuera

1 Cámara
Es la base de la pelota. Está fabricada en látex y su calidad depende de la estabilidad y la presion constante a lo largo de un partido.

Los gajos internos junto con la cámara garantizan la estabilidad estructural y el rebote de la pelota.

2 Gajos internos
Una estructura formada por 12 gajos cocidos de poliester y algodón recubre la cámara.

Diámetro
21,9 cm

Imagen de la pelota a tamaño real

3 Gajos 3D
Son 8. Están sellados al calor y premoldeados para garantizar una esfericidad uniforme en todos los puntos de la pelota.

Panel triangular
De los 8 gajos, 4 tienen forma de triángulo...

Panel trípode
...y 4 tienen forma de trípode.

4 Gráfica
Sobre un film transparente se imprime la gráfica. Para el último partido, se diseñó una versión dorada, que alude a Johannesburgo, llamada la "Ciudad de Oro".

Jabulani   Jo'bulani

Comportamiento en juego
Esta pelota incorporó la tecnología Grip'n Groove que consiste en una textura superficial que optimiza el agarre y la estabilidad.

Mejor agarre
La pelota tiene una micro textura llamada **Goose Bump** que mejora el control del balón bajo distintas condiciones climáticas.

El agua se aloja en el interior de la textura y mantiene seca la superficie de contacto.

Agua
Superficie seca

En el momento del disparo el agua se dispersa.

Más estable
Para que la pelota se mantenga estable durante el vuelo después de haber sido pateada se agregaron unas ranuras en la superficie de los gajos 3D.

La estabilidad depende de la cantidad de "costuras" entre gajos. Las ranuras actúan como costuras adicionales para mejorar la estabilidad.

Ranuras

Fuente: ADIDAS - EMLAY - FIFA | Infografía: VANINA SANCHEZ - PABLO LOSCRI | Investigación: GUILLERMO MILLA | Ilustraciones: ARIEL ROLDAN - JORGE PORTAZ

3

PABLO LOSCRI

3 The Ball of the World Cup

The special coverage on the World Cup South Africa 2010 included this infographic devoted to the official ball of the games. The ball received many criticisms and comments after it was presented; many players said that it was unpredictable and hard to control. The illustration aims to explain the ball's dynamic behavior as a whole by breaking down the technical features of each of its parts.

Year: 2010—Client: *Clarín*—Co-designer: Vanina Sanchez—Ilustrations: Ariel Roldan, Jorge Portaz—Researcher: Guillermo Milla

THE NEW YORK TIMES

○ Shan Carter, Ben Koski, and Kevin Quealy | Send Feedback

4 Top World Cup Players on Facebook, Day by Day

Using cutout action photos, the *New York Times* created an interactive infographic to demonstrate the fluctuating popularity of players during the 2010 World Cup. Readers can see how popular a player was on any given day; his photo increases or decreases in size depending on the number of mentions he received on Facebook each day.

Year: 2010—Client: The *New York Times*—Sources: Lars Backstrom and Cameron Marlow, Facebook

Top World Cup Players on Facebook, Day by Day
Millions of people around the world have been actively supporting – or complaining about – their favorite teams and players. Below, players are sized according to the number of mentions on Facebook during each day of the World Cup.

June 11

South Africa's Siphiwe Tshabalala was the first person to score in the 2010 World Cup, in South Africa's 1-1 draw with Mexico in the opening match.

Top World Cup Players on Facebook, Day by Day

June 26

Landon Donovan scored on a penalty kick for the United States in an overtime loss to Ghana.

Top World Cup Players on Facebook, Day by Day

June 11

Top World Cup Players on Facebook, Day by Day

June 11

South Africa's Siphiwe Tshabalala was the first person to score in the 2010 World Cup, in South Africa's 1-1 draw with Mexico in the opening match.

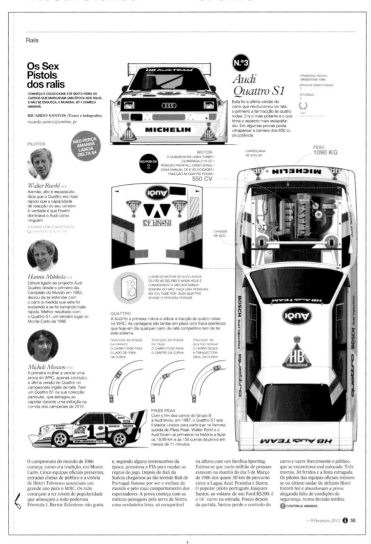

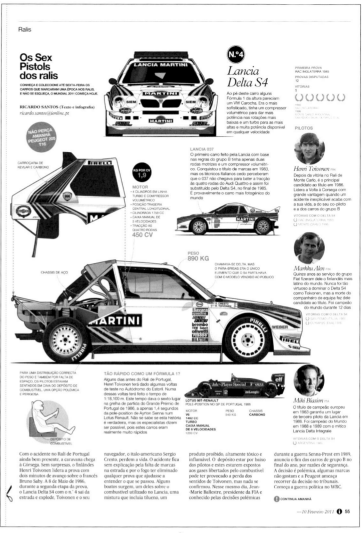

1

2

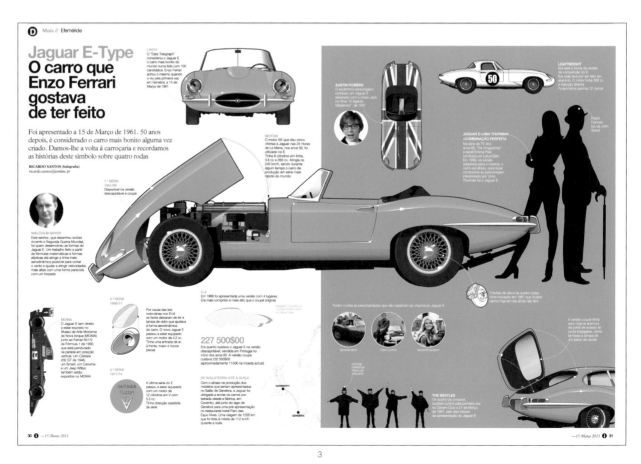

3

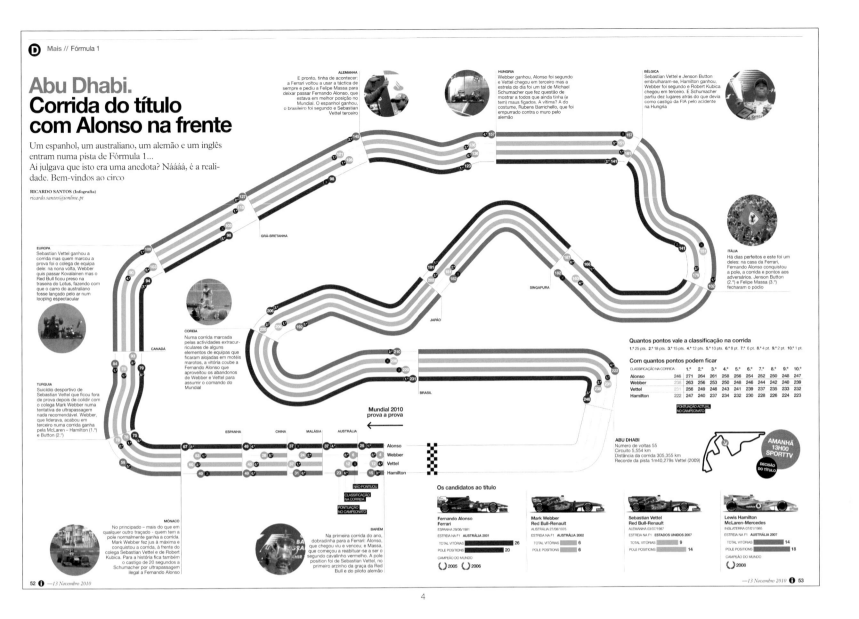

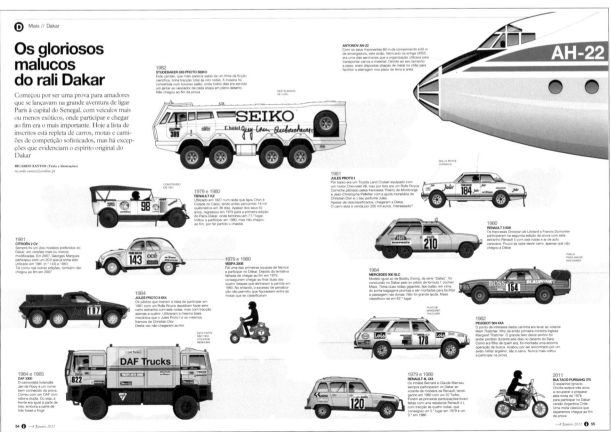

4　Abu Dhabi. Alonso Leads Before The Final Race
Standings and points for every race of the top four drivers in the F1 championship.
Year: 2010—Client: *JORNAL i*

5　The Glorious Crazy People of Dakar
The strangest cars that ever ran in the Dakar rally.
Year: 2011—Client: *JORNAL i*

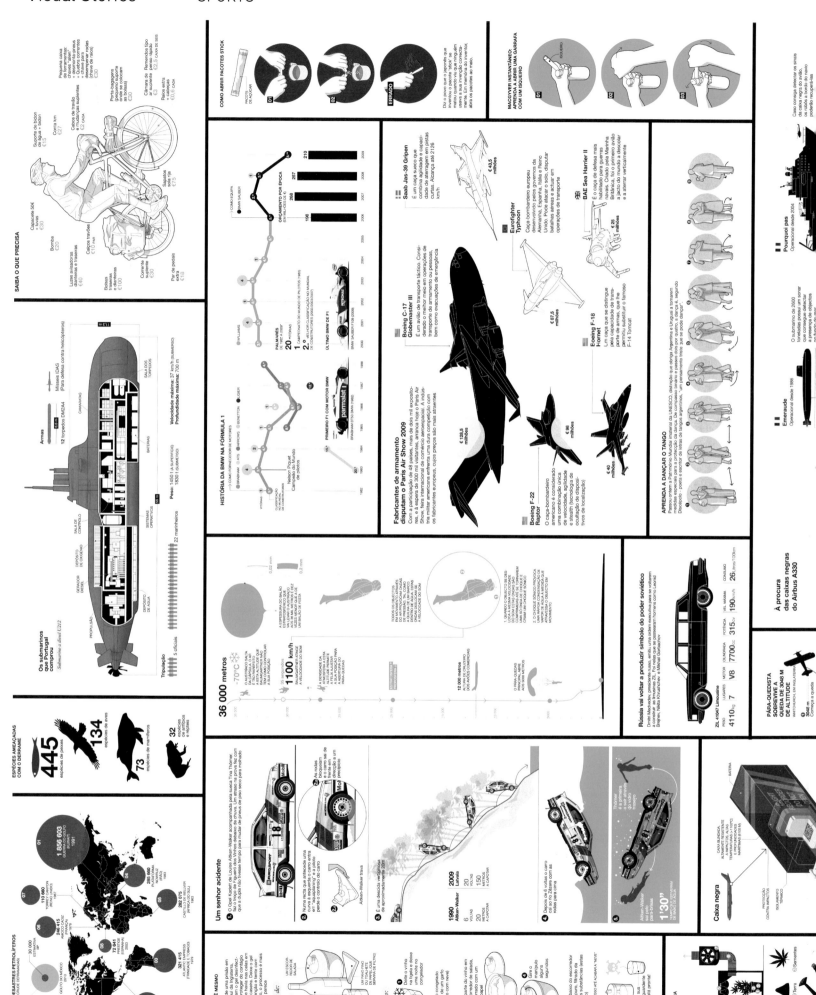

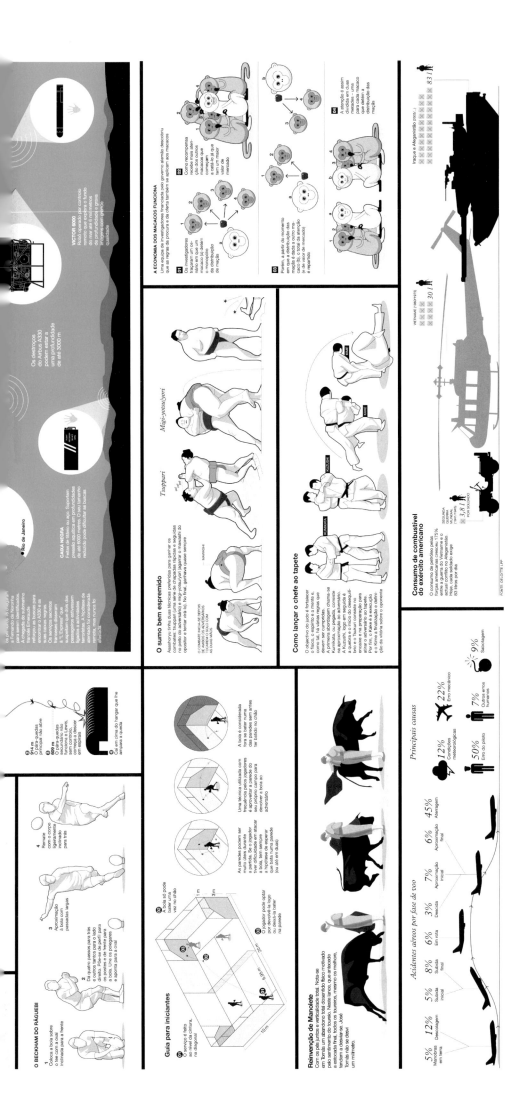

I INFOGRAFIA
o Carlos Monteiro and
Ricardo Santos
Collection—2
Poster-size collection of various
smaller graphics printed in *i*. Only two
prints of each were made.
Year: 2009/2010—Client: *JORNAL i*

INFOMEN
P.250 America's Cup
These graphics were developed
with an emphasis on the boats to show
a general overview of the crew of an
America's Cup sailing boat, as well as
the sport and its tactics. The information was presented as a bird's eye view
within a double page spread.
Year: 2006—Client: *El Mundo*

Las regatas de 'match race'

Las regatas de Copa América se disputan en formato 'match race', es decir un barco contra otro. Antes de salir al campo de regatas cada equipo analiza las condiciones meteorológicas con las que se disputará la regata para combinar a la mejor tripulación y la mejor forma del barco. Dentro de la regata la salida puede resultar fundamental para ganar la prueba. Entre un 50 y 60 % se ganan en este momento de la competición.

Los equipos:
Alinghi
BMW ORACLE Racing
+39 Challenge
Team Shosholoza
Emirates Team New Zealand
Luna Rossa Challenge
Areva Challenge
Victory Challenge
Desafío Español 2007
Mascalzone Latino - Capitalia Team
United Internet Team Germany
China Team

Valencia
ESPAÑA

Los elementos más importntes para el exito en esta regata son:

Velocidad
Tecnología
Diseño
Tripulación

Los **diecisiete** tripulantes activos de cada barco son los mejores en su especialidad, su función es hacer el mayor esfuerzo posible en ganar.

La persecusión

Salida

Barco de comité

La fase de pre-salida de un match-race es la primera oportunidad que tiene un equipo de conseguir ventaja sobre el adversario. **Los equipos se 'atacan' mutuamente, intentando que el otro barco cometa una infracción y sea penalizado,** esto para conseguir una posición de salida favorable.

1 Los barcos entran en la línea por barlovento. El rojo tiene derecho de paso desde el barco comité y puede forzar al barco azul a virar.

Que más transporta
Velas, algunas manivelas de polea de grinders, y los ordenadores de información meteorológica o móviles que se pueden utilizar hasta cuatro minutos antes de la regata.

1. Proa

La salida

Barlovento

sotavento

Barco de comité
Salida

Aproximación a la línea de salida

El barco azul tiene ahora dos posibilidades: virar a sotavento del barco rojo o navegar por detras y virar a barlovento.

Línea de salida

Salida

El retroceso

Retroceso

Barco de com

3

4

Es una situación muy peligrosa, es muy fácil perder el control del barco.

250

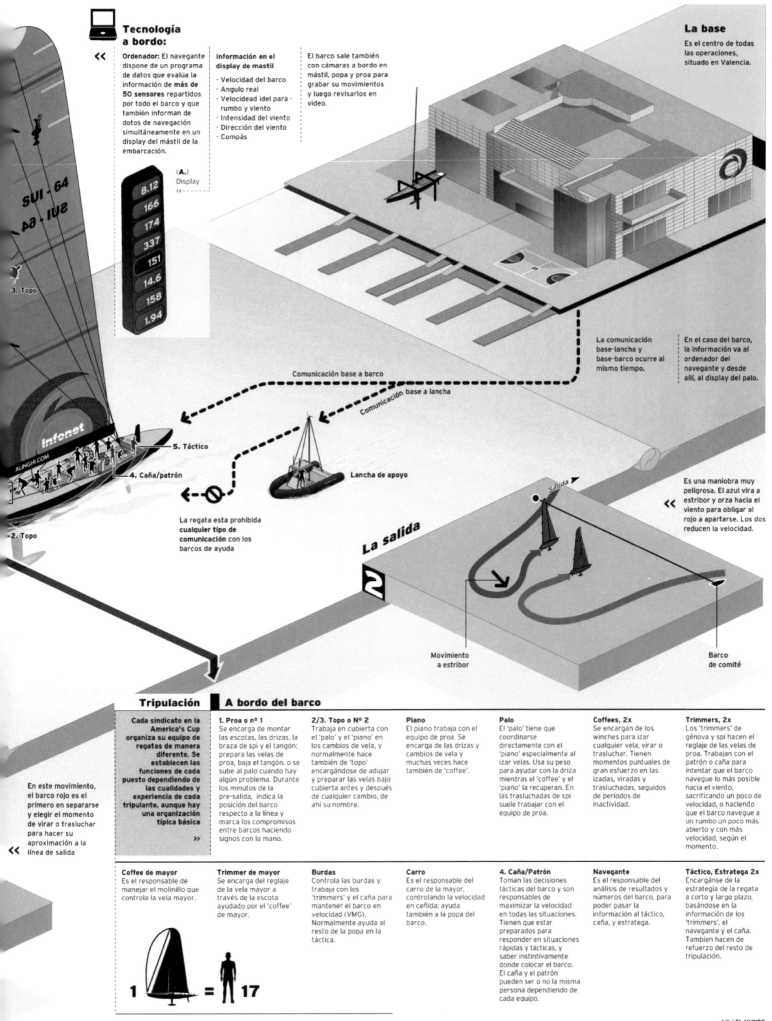

Tecnología a bordo:

Ordenador: El navegante dispone de un programa de datos que evalúa la información de **más de 50 sensores** repartidos por todo el barco y que también informan de dotos de navegación simultáneamente en un display del mástil de la embarcación.

Información en el display de mastil

- Velocidad del barco
- Angulo real
- Velocidead idel para rumbo y viento
- Intensidad del viento
- Dirección del viento
- Compás

El barco sale también con cámaras a bordo en mástil, popa y proa para grabar su movimientos y luego revisarlos en video.

(A.) Display

8.12
166
174
337
151
14.6
158
1.94

La base

Es el centro de todas las operaciones, situado en Valencia.

La comunicación base-lancha y base-barco ocurre al mismo tiempo.

En el caso del barco, la información va al ordenador del navegante y desde allí, al display del palo.

Comunicación base a barco

Comunicación base a lancha

3. Topo

SUI - 64

5. Táctico

4. Caña/patrón

Lancha de apoyo

La regata esta prohibida **cualquier tipo de comunicación** con los barcos de ayuda

2. Topo

Salida

La salida

2

Movimiento a estribor

Barco de comité

Es una maniobra muy peligrosa. El azul vira a estribor y orza hacia el viento para obligar al rojo a apartarse. Los dos reducen la velocidad.

En este movimiento, el barco rojo es el primero en separarse y elegir el momento de virar o trasluchar para hacer su aproximación a la línea de salida

Tripulación

Cada sindicato en la America's Cup organiza su equipo de regatas de manera diferente. Se establecen las funciones de cada puesto dependiendo de las cualidades y experiencia de cada tripulante, aunque hay una organización típica básica

A bordo del barco

1. Proa o nº 1
Se encarga de montar las escotas, las drizas, la braza de spi y el tangón; prepara las velas de proa, baja el tangón, o se sube al palo cuando hay algún problema. Durante los minutos de la pre-salida, indica la posición del barco respecto a la línea y marca los compromisos entre barcos haciendo signos con la mano.

2/3. Topo o Nº 2
Trabaja en cubierta con el 'palo' y el 'piano' en los cambios de vela, y normalmente hace también de 'topo' encargándose de adujar y preparar las velas bajo cubierta antes y después de cualquier cambio, de ahí su nombre.

Piano
El piano trabaja con el equipo de proa. Se encarga de las drizas y cambios de vela y muchas veces hace también de 'coffee'.

Palo
El 'palo' tiene que coordinarse directamente con el 'piano' especialmente al izar velas. Usa su peso para ayudar con la driza mientras el 'coffee' y el 'piano' la recuperan. En las trasluchadas de spi suele trabajar con el equipo de proa.

Coffees, 2x
Se encargan de los winches para izar cualquier vela, virar o trasluchar. Tienen momentos puntuales de gran esfuerzo en las izadas, viradas y trasluchadas, seguidos de períodos de inactividad.

Trimmers, 2x
Los 'trimmers' de génova y spi hacen el reglaje de las velas de proa. Trabajan con el patrón o caña para intentar que el barco navegue lo más posible hacia el viento, sacrificando un poco de velocidad, o haciendo que el barco navegue a un rumbo un poco más abierto y con más velocidad, según el momento.

Coffee de mayor
Es el responsable de manejar el molinillo que controla la vela mayor.

Trimmer de mayor
Se encarga del reglaje de la vela mayor a través de la escota ayudado por el 'coffee' de mayor.

Burdas
Controla las burdas y trabaja con los 'trimmers' y el caña para mantener el barco en velocidad (VMG). Normalmente ayuda al resto de la popa en la táctica.

Carro
Es el responsable del carro de la mayor, controlando la velocidad en ceñida; ayuda también a la popa del barco.

4. Caña/Patrón
Toman las decisiones tácticas del barco y son responsables de maximizar la velocidad en todas las situaciones. Tienen que estar preparados para responder en situaciones rápidas y tácticas, y saber instintivamente donde colocar el barco. El caña y el patrón pueden ser o no la misma persona dependiendo de cada equipo.

Navegante
Es el responsable del análisis de resultados y números del barco, para poder pasar la información al táctico, caña, y estratega.

Táctico, Estratega 2x
Encargánse de la estrategia de la regata a corto y largo plazo, basándose en la información de los 'trimmers', el navegante y el caña. Tambien hacen de refuerzo del resto de tripulación.

1 = 17

AID / EL MUNDO

...

—

INDEX

Index

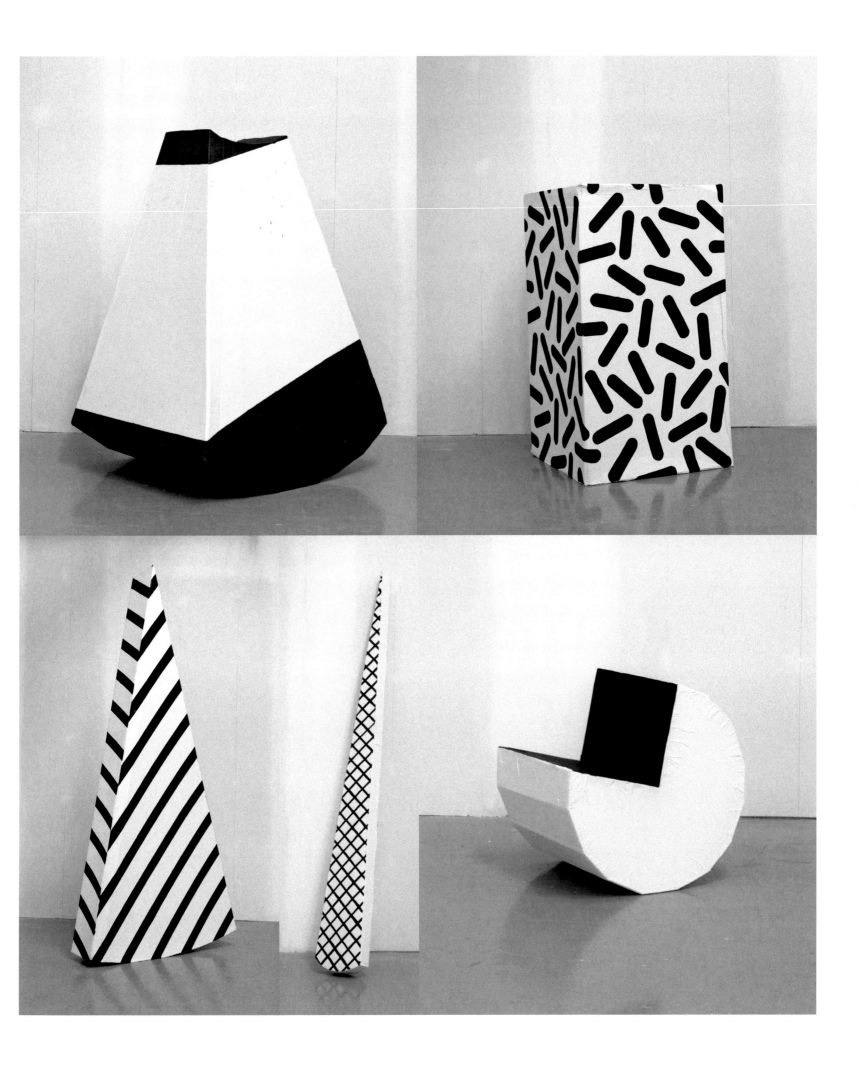

Château-vacant, *Memoz,* 2010

Imprint

VISUAL STORYTELLING

Inspiring a New Visual Language

Edited by Robert Klanten, Sven Ehmann, and Floyd Schulze
Text and preface by Andrew Losowsky
Project descriptions by Rebecca Silus

Cover and layout by Floyd Schulze for Gestalten
Typeface: Mercury by Radim Peško

Project management by Rebekka Wangler for Gestalten
Production management by Janine Milstrey for Gestalten
Proofreading by transparent Language Solutions
Printed by Offsetdruckerei Grammlich, Pliezhausen
Made in Germany

Published by Gestalten, Berlin 2011
ISBN 978-3-89955-375-8

For more information, please visit www.gestalten.com.

Bibliographic information published by the Deutsche
Nationalbibliothek.
The Deutsche Nationalbibliothek lists this publication in
the Deutsche Nationalbibliografie; detailed bibliographic
data are available online at http://dnb.d-nb.de.

None of the content in this book was published in exchange for payment by commercial parties or designers; Gestalten selected all included work based solely
on its artistic merit.

This book was printed on paper certified by the FSC®.

FSC — MIX
Paper from responsible sources
www.fsc.org   FSC® C011712

Gestalten is a climate-neutral company. We collaborate with the non-profit carbon offset provider myclimate (www.myclimate.org) to neutralize the company's carbon footprint produced through our worldwide
business activities by investing in projects that reduce
CO_2 emissions (www.gestalten.com/myclimate).

myclimate
Protect our planet